Why
I Left
Goldman
Sachs

Why I Left Goldman Sachs

A Wall Street Story

Greg Smith

GRAND CENTRAL
PUBLISHING

NEW YORK   BOSTON

Copyright © 2012 by Greg Smith
All rights reserved. In accordance with the US Copyright Act of 1976, the scanning, uploading, and electronic sharing of any part of this book without the permission of the publisher is unlawful piracy and theft of the author's intellectual property. If you would like to use material from the book (other than for review purposes), prior written permission must be obtained by contacting the publisher at permissions@hbgusa.com. Thank you for your support of the author's rights.

Portions of *Why I Left Goldman Sachs* first appeared as an op-ed in the *New York Times* on March 14, 2012.

Grand Central Publishing
Hachette Book Group
237 Park Avenue
New York, NY 10017

www.HachetteBookGroup.com

Printed in the United States of America

RRD-C

First Edition: October 2012
10 9 8 7 6 5 4 3 2 1

Grand Central Publishing is a division of Hachette Book Group, Inc. The Grand Central Publishing name and logo is a trademark of Hachette Book Group, Inc.

The publisher is not responsible for websites (or their content) that are not owned by the publisher.

LCCN: 2012945268

ISBN 978-1-4555-2747-2 (regular edition)

ISBN 978-1-4555-2825-7 (international edition)

To my mother

Contents

Why
I Left
Goldman
Sachs

CHAPTER 1

"I Don't Know, but I'll Find Out"

It was June 12, 2000, and I was sitting in a conference room at 125 Broad Street, thirty stories above Lower Manhattan. I was twenty-one years old, and it was the first day of my summer internship at Goldman Sachs. An intern named Josh was standing at the front of the room, red-faced, getting absolutely grilled. He was trying to explain risk arbitrage, but was floundering badly. What I didn't know at the time was that his dad was a billionaire and one of the most powerful financiers in the world. But this was Goldman Sachs, and it didn't matter who your dad was. You had to prove yourself like everyone else.

Welcome to Open Meeting: a form of boot camp for the seventy-five summer interns in the sales and trading program and a venerable tradition at the firm. A partner would stand at the front of the room with a list of names and call on people at will with questions on the firm's storied culture, its history, on the stock markets. Rapid fire. You had to be alive, awake, informed. Two people cried that summer under the interrogation. But there was no way around it: if you wanted a full time job at Goldman Sachs—less than 40 percent of the class would make it—this was a test you had to pass, over and over and over again.

An intern's performance in the Open Meeting was one of the three criteria the firm used to determine who would receive offers after graduation to come work at the world's most prestigious investment bank. During this ten-week internship, you also needed to find and cultivate a "rabbi" who would want to hire you. And you'd have to shine in the meetings and get your rabbi while walking the fine line between being competitive and being nice. Partners were always looking to see whether an intern had the makings of a "culture carrier," Goldman-speak for someone who is able to deal with clients and colleagues in a way that preserves the firm's reputation—one that has made it an incubator for senators, treasury secretaries, and central bank governors.

Interrogation and humiliation were not things this meticulously selected group had tasted very often. I was surrounded by the sort of superachievers that people whispered about and pointed at in Ivy League dining halls—the ones who got perfect scores on their SATs, graduated from high school at age fifteen, swam in the Olympics, played chess at the master level for relaxation, and, oh, yeah, Mark Mulroney, whose dad had been prime minister of Canada. But even for these superachievers, this was a tough room. Do well here, and you would be on the path to a career where even the average middle manager makes $250,000 a year and exerts some power and influence.

I was a pharmacist's son from Johannesburg, South Africa, and had never heard about investment banking until I got a scholarship to Stanford University and came to America for the first time.

Also flanking the whiteboard with Josh at the front of the room was another intern presenter named Adam, who would later become one of my best friends and go on to manage billions of dollars at a hedge fund. But at this moment, at the height of the Internet bubble on Wall Street, these two interns were under severe fire. Adam was flushed, too, but maybe it was just the thrill of the moment. An applied math major, he was crushing it; he knew his stuff cold. Josh, on the other hand, was an English major, and completely out of his depth.

There were two Open Meetings a week, held after the day's work on the trading floor was finished, usually on Tuesdays and Thursdays. The ninety-minute meetings were usually run by (in order of rank) a partner, a managing director, or a tribunal of three angry vice presidents, sitting imperiously at a table at the front of the room. Depending on the personal style of the people in charge, the meetings could be brutal. They were always intense.

Open Meetings started at 6:00 P.M. on the dot—not 6:01 or 6:02.

There were always three or four interns who got there at 6:03 or 6:05; they were almost always made to wait outside. If too many people arrived late, we would all have to come in at five the next morning for a makeup meeting; the partner would also show up at 5:00 A.M. Once again, if you arrived at 5:05, you were made to wait outside. This rule was strictly enforced. There were people who just couldn't get there on time, and it reflected poorly on them.

The interns sat behind long tables arranged in rows. On the tabletop in front of you, you'd place a pad of paper containing your preparatory notes. At the head of the room, the person in charge, armed with a list of all the interns' names, would kick off the meeting by cold-calling people—just picking names at random. Out at the rows of tables, every intern was praying, *Please, don't let it be me.*

I was nervous but ready. My strategy was to volunteer, very quickly, whenever I knew the answer to a question—then those running the meeting would be less likely to pick on me later, for an answer I didn't know. Some people seemed totally unfazed by being called on; but several, male and female, seemed undone by the experience:

VP (pointing): Okay, third row, second seat over. Stand up and state your name.

INTERN (standing slowly): Brynn Thomas, Brown University.

VP (firmly): Tell me about Microsoft stock. What is our house view? What does our research analyst think?

INTERN (caught off guard): Um, I think we like it. Uhhh...

VP (now angry): Come on, you should know these answers cold. Microsoft is one of the biggest and most important companies in the world. How can you not know this stuff?

INTERN (uncertain and scared): I'm sorry. I'm thinking...We have a buy rating?

VP (with voice raised): What is our price target? What are the catalysts coming up? How has the stock been trading? Come on.

[The Intern can't take the heat, and nothing comes out of her mouth. She starts to tear up and runs out of the room.]

The Open Meeting was an interrogation chamber where the meeting chairs tried to push you to the limit, to test your knowledge on a number of fronts. First and most basic was your market knowledge. You might be asked, "Where is the S&P 500 trading?" or "Why was crude oil down three percent today?" or "Why did Alan Greenspan lower interest rates?" There was no cut-and-dried way to prep for what they were going to ask.

The second category was Goldman Sachs history. I was relieved when they asked questions like "When was the firm founded? By whom? Who were all the senior partners from 1960 until today? Who is the current CFO of the firm?" I knew it all. I'd learned that Goldman had had some iconic leaders—such as Sidney Weinberg, the man who engineered the initial public offering of Ford Motors; and John Whitehead, who, after retiring as co–senior partner, served in the State Department and was the chairman of the New York Federal Reserve. I knew about its many admirable policies. For example, for many years, the firm never advised on hostile takeovers because it believed this to be bad business that would significantly detract from its clients' trust.

The third category of questions at the Open Meetings aimed to test our knowledge of current management and our understanding of the business. The meeting leaders would fire out the questions: "How does a trader quantify risk? What does a derivatives salesperson do? Who are the two managing directors who run the Credit Derivatives Trading group? What's the difference between market making on the NASDAQ and the NYSE? Which partner runs the Emerging Markets group globally?"

The point of the meetings, we gradually found out, was to teach us how to behave when we were on the phone being grilled by a tough client—and Goldman had a lot of very tough clients. The biggest mistake you could make in an Open Meeting was to fluff an answer and then try to wing it. The people who did that were often the people who ended up crying.

The most intimidating meeting leader was a senior VP named Valentino Carlotti. Val was a walking contradiction: very harsh in the Open Meetings—some of the moderators would joke around, but not

Val—yet, one on one, a terrific guy. At times during the summer, he even went out with groups of interns. One evening, he came to a night-club with us. What this showed me was that he wasn't being a dick just to be a dick. He was acting that way because management felt that by being tough on the interns, they could train us to be truthful, re-sourceful, collaborative—all the qualities they wanted in people who made the cut and became first-year analysts. These were also the qual-ities that clients appreciated—truthfulness being at the top of the list. Clients do not appreciate your making things up. They want to know the truth.

What Val hated most during the Open Meeting was any sort of fudg-ing. The best thing to say if you didn't have an answer was "I don't know, but I'll find out." The point was to teach us that when we were on the phone with an angry client, that person didn't want us to make up an answer—he wanted us to know how to get the answer and to call him back within five minutes. If you didn't have the answer in an Open Meeting, you had to bolt out of the room, take the elevator downstairs, run across Broad Street, race up to the trading floor, and hustle back with a response before the end of the meeting. Since the main part of the internship was trying out on different desks on the floor, this was where our skills in relationship building were tested. You needed allies, peo-ple you could run to in a pinch: the "rabbis" I mentioned earlier. You couldn't just ambush some senior VP who was in the middle of some-thing. "Get away from me!" might be the most polite thing you'd hear from him.

At the end of every Open Meeting, the moderator would assess how it had gone. Had he heard some good answers? Had he seen some good initiative from people who'd had to go find the answers? There were a few times that summer when the leaders thought a meeting had gone terribly, and it was the same as if too many of us had shown up late: they would bring us back the next morning at 5:00—or sometimes in the evening, making us cancel a social event—to teach us a lesson.

The meetings were hard, but there was something about them I en-joyed. I liked the fact that the firm took its culture so seriously; I liked that we were learning to be so serious about giving clients correct information. This is what the Open Meeting instilled in us: Don't make things up; don't exaggerate. Just be up-front. If you don't know something, be very skillful at finding it out, and that's good enough. And if you make a mistake, admit it—immediately. (This is something Goldman still tells its analysts: if you make an error, especially when you're trading, the worst thing you can do is not admit it. Failure to come clean will always turn the mistake into a much bigger monetary loss, and it will also ruin your credibility with clients.)

Two days before each Open Meeting, the whole intern class would get together to study. Each person would tackle a different area of the markets; then we'd prep one another and come up with various possible questions. Getting grilled like this, twice a week for ten weeks, brought us all together as a team. And teamwork was a value highly prized at Goldman Sachs.

I knew that we were being indoctrinated, handed a full cup of delicious Kool-Aid, but it was fine with me. I'd been a true believer before I ever set foot in the building. I might not have been dressed for the part, but I felt I had as much a right as anyone to compete for a job at Goldman Sachs.

During the summer of 2000, if you had asked me who the Brooks Brothers were, I would have answered, "The ugly kids who used to live down the street." The day before my junior year at Stanford had ended, I'd gone to Macy's in Palo Alto and bought a new wardrobe: eight shirts, three pairs of pants, and one blue blazer with gold buttons. I still had a couple of business suits from the previous summer, when I'd interned at the Chicago office of the brokerage house Paine Webber. My favorite was a light gray *Miami Vice*–style one with a shiny finish, almost like sharkskin. It had worked just fine for Chicago, but I had just enough sense to know that it wouldn't fly at Goldman Sachs.

Still, I cringe now at the memory of some of the dress shirts I bought that day: two were dark brown, one was black, and one was dark green; almost all had stripes in a different shade. Not exactly Goldman Sachs style. Wall Street, like so much of what I'd experienced since coming to

America, was literally a new world. I had arrived at Stanford in August of 1997 from Johannesburg with a great love for the United States, developed from American movies and TV shows. Tony Danza and *Who's the Boss* had found their way to South Africa in the 1980s, and had taught me much of what I needed to know.

I grew up in Edenvale, a middle-class suburb of Jo'burg, the eldest of three siblings: my brother, Mark, was a year and a half younger than me; my baby sister, Carly, nine years younger. My mom was a housewife, and my dad worked long hours to support us, but money was tight, especially with three kids attending private school—the King David School, an expensive Jewish day academy where all the students (many of them from wealthy families) wore uniforms: for the boys, khaki safari suits in the summer and blazers, blue ties, and gray flannels in the winter.

In eighth grade my best friend Lex Bayer and I made a pact to try to get in to college in America, a place we'd never been but had thought about a lot. Unfortunately, the rand-to-dollar exchange rate was five to one, and our parents—Lex's family was in much the same economic situation as mine—couldn't begin to afford to send us. Like Lex's brilliant older sister, Kelly, who'd gone to Stanford on a full scholarship four years earlier, we needed major financial aid—something that seemed almost unimaginable. We worked toward this goal for five years, borrowing Kelly's dog-eared SAT practice test books and prepping each other for both the American standardized tests and the statewide South African exams. Lex and I finished high school as co-valedictorians and were both amazingly lucky to be among the thirty-two people, out of the three thousand international students who applied, to receive full scholarships to Stanford.

My first idea was to be premed, but as happens with so many would-be doctors, I literally could not do Organic Chemistry. Still, in my first quarter, I took Economics 1 with a great professor, John Taylor, and loved the course. Taylor was an icon. He'd formulated the "Taylor rule," which prescribes how central banks should set interest rates; he'd written the book that became the standard Econ 101 text across all the universities in America; and at Stanford, he was legendary for a certain yearly lecture he gave.

The talk was on an economic concept called comparative advantage—the case in point was why California was better than Wisconsin at producing wine—and every year, when Taylor gave the lecture, in a huge hall that sat something like seven hundred people, he would teach the class dressed as a giant California grape. "I Heard It through the Grapevine" would be blasting over the sound system as you came into the hall. Then Taylor would begin the lecture. Comparative advantage, he explained, meant that, in contrast to Wisconsin, California had the weather conditions, it had the space, and perhaps it had the propensity to want to make wine. Comparative advantage showed that, all else being equal, not everyone was going to be able to succeed at the same thing, because success depended on climate and circumstances. Meanwhile, as he explained all this, you couldn't take your eyes off him in his grape costume.

I took in these concepts quickly, and they interested me. We weren't talking about, say, two molecules bonding, the way we were in Chemistry. Instead, we were talking about things such as "General Motors sells cars; Toyota sells cars. Why is there a discrepancy in how many cars they each sell, and who is being more efficient?"

On top of that, I aced the course; it came easy to me. It was my first quarter at Stanford, and this was a big confidence booster. Out of seven hundred students taking the class, I finished in something like the top five. It was a great feeling, but it was also the pinnacle of my academic career: I never again finished even near that high in a class. As you become more specialized, the kids around you become sharper and smarter, whereas this was an entry-level course; maybe that was the reason. In any case, I liked economics, and wound up majoring in it.

Eager to take my book learning for a road test, I tried to get a summer internship in finance as a sophomore, something that is seldom done. For these prized positions, banks typically want juniors, who are more mature and potentially hirable a year later. But I managed to land an internship by cold-calling some thirty or forty people at banks and brokerage houses. ("Hi, this is Greg Smith. I'm a sophomore at Stanford, and I'm looking to get some experience. Are you guys offering internships this summer?") When I finally reached Paine Webber, I told them I'd work for minimum wage—which did the trick. I worked in the Chicago office, in Private Wealth Management, under two brokers who managed the wealth of executives who worked at a major home-appliance company based in the Midwest. I thought highly of these two guys: they had long-term (three- to five-year) profit horizons for their clients. Theirs was a slow and steady business: they weren't frequently trading their customer accounts just to rack up fees. They were constantly in touch with their clients, offering advice; they would go visit them. They knew everything about them; they even knew their kids' and grandchildren's names. Even more important, they also knew their own business. They knew the stocks. This was the Old World model of "I've known you for fifteen years; you can trust me." And it was the classic fiduciary model: incentives were aligned. They did well if they did well for their clients. They were obligated to give clients the advice they thought was right for them.

The two brokers gave me some research projects that taught me how to value stocks and determine if something was a good investment. They'd say, "Here are twenty stocks; put together a presentation where you give us your one-page recommendation on each. What's the market cap? What are the catalysts coming up? What do you like about the company?" I loved the work. I'd be sitting there in my sharkskin *Miami Vice* suit, researching stocks, happy as Don Johnson. (I probably wouldn't have been sitting there at all if I hadn't cut off the shoulder-length ponytail I'd grown during sophomore year.) At the end of the summer, the brokers said I'd done a great job and they wanted me to come back after my junior year. With regret but also with anticipation, I decided to shoot for bigger game.

The selection process for any type of job at Goldman Sachs is extremely rigorous. On average, only one in forty-five people (2.2 percent) who apply for a summer internship, or a full-time job, get an offer. The firm asked you to send in a résumé, but so many people sent them that it was easy for yours to get lost in the shuffle. There was a way around the logjam, though: There was a little-known fact that two interview spots were open for the first people to apply online, beginning on a certain date. So I went to the Stanford computer center at midnight on that day in the spring of 2000, logged on to the website, and kept hitting the Refresh key, over and over, until the magic button appeared. I clicked it immediately, and got an interview. It would take place at the career center on campus.

The interview went very well, for two reasons. For one thing, I felt an immediate rapport with the woman who interviewed me. At that point in my life, I didn't know a lot about finance, but this was almost completely a personality interview; the interviewer wasn't grilling me; and she and I hit it off personally. The other thing was, I had prepared very carefully. I'd read *The Culture of Success*, a history of the firm by Lisa Endlich, a former Goldman VP; I'd also spoken to a few friends who'd interned at the firm the previous summer.

So I was very ready when the interviewer asked me the big question: Why did I want to work at Goldman Sachs? "Because it's the best, most prestigious firm in the world, and I have high goals for myself, and I love finance. I love the markets," I said. I told her about my internship at Paine Webber in Chicago, but said that I wanted a real experience working on Wall Street: if I was going to do that, Goldman Sachs was the best place to do it. Everything I was telling her was 100 percent genuine. Even so, I wasn't sure if I was going to make the next cut, because, of the fifteen people Goldman interviewed, only a few would be chosen to continue.

It turned out I was one of them. The next day I got a voice mail saying, "You made it through to the next round; you're going to have a Super Day in San Francisco"—meaning not that I was going to knock back a half-dozen Anchor Steams looking out from Fisherman's Wharf, but that I would next undergo a day of half a dozen back-to-back interviews, thirty minutes each, at Goldman Sachs's office there. "Super Day," as it happens, is what they call this trial by fire on Wall Street.

At the time, I didn't have a car, but I was an RA, or resident adviser, with sixty freshmen under my charge, and I had five co-RAs. We had all become extremely close, and one of them would often lend me his car, a beaten-up fifteen-year-old red Mazda with a stick shift, when I needed it.

Driving up to the city that day was a bit of a challenge. For one thing, in those pre-GPS days, I was using a road map, which kept blowing around in the breeze from the open windows (no AC). For another, I hadn't driven that much in my life, and I was a bit nervous—maybe more than a bit. I was in a navy suit, and I was sweating. It was March 10, 2000—the day the NASDAQ hit its all-time high of 5408.62, at the height of the Internet bubble.

Despite my nerves, I made it on time and in one piece to the Goldman Sachs offices at 555 California Street in downtown San Francisco. The building is the second tallest in the city, and Goldman's offices there, with floor-to-ceiling windows around the entire perimeter of the forty-fifth floor, have views of San Francisco and the Bay that are truly breathtaking; the place is simultaneously intimidating and impressive.

The first person I met with was thoroughly impressive but not intimidating: a terrific woman, a senior associate who was a Stanford alum; it turned out that her dad, a former Goldman Sachs partner, was on the board of trustees of my university. We had a friendly, easy conversation. She had just gone to South Africa on her honeymoon, and we spoke about that. I was really struck by how genuine and nice everybody I met with that day seemed. I'd interviewed with other banks—Deutsche Bank, Salomon Smith Barney—where the people seemed slick, much more concerned with trying to catch you out on tough finance questions than getting to know you. The Goldman Sachs people weren't like that at all.

The next person I met with was at his desk on the trading floor, and he was too busy trading to leave, so he said, "Take a seat on the stool next to me." Now, this was a tricky situation. First, a little stool is a demeaning perch. You're practically crouching next to the guy, all but asking, "May I please listen to your very important phone call?" Second, I wanted the guy's undivided attention, so he could make a fair judgment about me. But this guy's attention was very divided: he was eating a sandwich and trading at the same time, and his phone lines were ringing off the hook.

"All right," he said. "Pitch me a stock."

Luckily, I'd anticipated exactly such a request, and had even formulated a thesis. So I started pitching him NewsCorp; there was something going on with Rupert Murdoch at the time. (There's always something going on with Murdoch.)

Then the guy's phone rang again. He held up a just-a-moment finger and took the call. He schmoozed the client for a minute—basketball scores were discussed—then executed a trade. Finally he hung up.

"Sorry," he said. "Go on."

This happened several more times in the course of my pitch. I might have gotten flustered or annoyed, but I didn't. I knew the trader wasn't screwing around with me. This was just what the job was about. If I were lucky, someday I'd get to do it, too.

––––––––

Four other Stanford people besides me made it through the multiple Super Days and into the internship program. Since Stanford was on the quarter rather than the semester system, we all arrived in New York one week late. Most of the non-Stanford interns stayed in NYU housing for the summer, but because I was arriving when I was, I wasn't able to get a dorm room. Instead, I rented (online, sight unseen) a room from a family I'd never met, on the third floor of a brownstone on Ninety-Sixth between Columbus and Amsterdam. The rent was $1,000 a month, meals not included. My pay for the summer after tax was $5,000—a very nice salary for an internship, but as I was quickly to learn, money evaporates fast in New York City. A thousand dollars a month in rent seemed a little steep in 2000, but it was the best thing I could find given the time crunch. I wasn't sure about the idea of living with a family I had never met before. But, I thought, *How bad could this be?*

My flight from San Francisco was delayed—very delayed. I was supposed to land at JFK at 10:00 P.M., but I ended up getting in at 1:30 in the morning. And I was to start my internship the next day at 7:00 A.M. sharp. On top of that, it was hot. Summer had definitely begun in New York: it was ninety degrees and humid, even that late at night. I took a cab into Manhattan, got to the apartment, and rang the bell—no answer. Called the family on the phone—no answer. Rang the bell again—nothing. Not knowing what to do, I waited outside for half an hour. Finally—it was now close to 3:00 A.M.—I rang again, and the husband answered the intercom.

When he came down to let me in, he was wearing a robe and was kind of groggy—and he was a little bit annoyed that I'd arrived so late. We walked up to the apartment, he opened the door, and we went down the hall. It was very quiet. And hot. He opened a door and said, "This will be your room."

It was a tiny room, almost entirely filled by a green couch. I said, "Where's the bed?" He said, "The couch turns into a bed." When I started pulling out the folded mattress, the couch hit the back wall before the bed could fully extend. The husband and I had to angle it so it fit the room when opened. When he finally went off to sleep, I turned on the air conditioner. It looked like an antique, and it worked like one, too. It was so noisy that, finally, I decided to turn it off and just open the window.

The family had some strange rules. I had to log all my phone calls. They also said, "If you ever use the fridge, you need to note down if you have a glass of orange juice." I told them, "Don't worry. I'm not going to take any orange juice. In fact, you probably won't be seeing much of me this summer. I'm going to be working very hard."

———

The Goldman Sachs Equities trading floor, on the fiftieth floor of One New York Plaza, was a huge, open, football field–size space with towering, panoramic views of Lower Manhattan. Through floor-to-ceiling windows you could see New York Harbor, the Statue of Liberty, the twin towers of the World Trade Center, and the Hudson River. But the distant and spectacular views were upstaged by the urgent hum of activity in the giant room, which contained five to six hundred traders standing and shouting, wildly gesticulating, sitting tensely on the phone, running, walking, grinning, frowning, jumping up and making strange hand signals. Here everything was being traded, from the latest initial public offering of a red-hot Internet company to old-economy stocks such as General Motors and Citigroup. And these trades were not for individuals but for the biggest asset managers, pension funds, governments, and hedge funds in the world. When the traders weren't in motion, they were focused intently on their computer screens: in the summer of 2000, everybody on the floor had three or four screens plus a separate Bloomberg terminal for market data. (Today, "Bloomberg Market Data" is installed as software rather than hardware, and appears in a window on traders' screens.)

I stepped onto the floor for the first time with all of three hours' sleep under my belt. My eyes had felt as if they were lined with sandpaper as I walked from the subway to One New York Plaza, at the corner of Water and Broad streets, on the southern tip of Manhattan, just half a mile from the World Trade Center. Clutching my extra-large coffee, I had looked up at the formidable tower that housed Goldman Sachs's Equities trading headquarters. *Holy shit*, I thought. *I've made it to Wall Street, and it doesn't get any bigger or better than this.*

Along with the other interns who had arrived a week late, I was brought to a room for an introductory session by Human Resources. I remember walking in and seeing some of the other Stanford people I knew. There was real electricity in the room—this was everyone's first experience on Wall Street, and we were all talking excitedly and milling around. HR gave us a pile of forms to fill out, along with our Goldman Sachs e-mail addresses and our intern ID name tags. The name tags, laminated cards with a bright orange border, worn on a bright orange lanyard, showed our names and universities in big black letters. We were told in no uncertain terms that we were to wear the name tags around our necks every moment we were on the premises; failure to do so would lead to big trouble. The firm wanted there to be no doubt on the trading floor as to who the interns were.

Goldman ran a summer intern program in each of its divisions: one in Equities; one in Fixed Income, Currency and Commodities (FICC); one in Investment Management; one in Research, and so on. Back when I'd passed the interview process, I'd been offered two internships: one in Equities, in New York; and one in Investment Management, in Chicago. I had learned something about private wealth management the previous summer, at Paine Webber: it's a slower business, a smaller environment. You're dealing with individuals. For me, the exciting thing about Wall

Street was the big fish, the institutions. So I signed up for Equities. I wanted the real trading floor experience: standing up in a frenetic environment, shouting across the floor. In time, I would get my wish.

Walking onto that floor, for an intern, is thrilling and intimidating and bewildering all at once. The trading floor is not an environment for everybody, but I liked it immediately. Looking around, I found I loved the energy. I loved the chaos, the yelling, the tension. I loved the fact that it all added up to billions of dollars changing hands among the biggest and smartest investors in the world. I desperately wanted to understand it and be part of it. I wasn't intimidated by it. Maybe I should have been. Instead, I felt at home.

The day after the first Open Meeting, the speed dating began. There were some thirty groups, or "desks," on the trading floor, each one comprising about fifteen people: a partner, two or three managing directors, a half-dozen vice presidents, three associates, and three analysts. The seventy-five interns were grouped into pods of four or five people, and over the course of the summer, our little pods would rotate around to as many desks as possible, each of us carrying his or her little black folding stool. This was called shadowing. We'd spend two or three days shadowing each desk, trying to learn what its business was all about, trying to help out, trying to do more than just not get in the way.

The stool. Practically speaking, you carried it with you at all times because there were no extra chairs at the trading desks. But the folding stool, along with your big orange ID badge on its bright orange lanyard, was also a status marker: it showed that you were a plebe, a newbie, a punk kid. It was innately demeaning. When unfolded, the stool was all of eighteen inches high—so there you'd sit, next to and slightly beneath the exalted salesperson or trader or sales trader, looking like no more than a shoeshine boy while he or she performed some grand and mysterious task.

To spice up the situation, there was a perpetual shortage of stools. Whether this was purposeful on the part of management, a Darwinian musical chairs designed to separate the weak from the strong, it is impossible to know. But at the beginning of the day, the interns would grab for all the available folding stools, and invariably a few interns would get caught short. This could prove embarrassing, especially if, when you were stool-less, some trader said the magic words "Come sit with me." You'd excuse yourself and run madly to beg, borrow, or steal a stool. (There were a few hiding places around the floor, notably one storage closet, where a spare or two could sometimes be found.)

The internship was extremely demanding. You came to work at 5:45 or 6:00 or 6:30 in the morning, whenever your desk wanted you in. During the day, you'd do your best to be useful. How you spent your time—and whether you were actually of any use—depended on how inventive you were. Because we hadn't yet passed our Series 7 exam (the regulatory test required for everyone who works on Wall Street), we were not allowed to trade. We couldn't talk to clients. We couldn't answer the phones. And yet there we were, in a trading business, among extremely busy people in the middle of this giant trading floor. For a summer intern, there is a very fine line between being dead weight—just hanging around and annoying people—and trying to prove you can add some kind of value.

Even figuring out where you were supposed to go was challenging at first. The desks weren't marked; there were no signs reading, "Emerging Markets Sales Desk" or "Latin America Sales Trading Desk" or "U.S. Equity Trading Desk." You had to ask around to get directions; you needed to draw little maps for yourself to navigate the jungle.

You needed to be very entrepreneurial and creative. Adding value as an intern often began with getting coffee for the desk every day; frequently, interns also did breakfast and lunch runs. You would literally take a pen and pad and go around to the ten or fifteen people on the desk and take everyone's order. It's a strange concept, but Wall Street looks at attention to detail as an indicator of how people are going to do in their job. If a kid keeps messing up the lunch order, he's probably going to mess up something else down the line.

I remember one managing director—a few years after I'd started working at the firm—who was very sensitive about his lunch orders. He didn't eat onions or certain other things. One day he asked an intern for a cheddar cheese sandwich, and the kid came back with a cheddar cheese *salad*. The kid handed it to him so proudly: "Here's your cheddar cheese salad." I was sitting next to the MD, so I remember the incident well. He opened the container, looked at the salad, looked up at the kid, closed the container, and threw it in the trash. It was a bit harsh, but it was also a teaching moment. The managing director joked about it with the kid afterward; he didn't make a big deal about it. The lesson was learned.

There were all kinds of little ways an intern could add value: by getting the food orders right, by making photocopies, but especially by being creative at finding actual work to do. If an intern heard a salesperson or trader say, "My client is interested in biotech stocks," the intern, if he or she were entrepreneurially minded, could then say, "Why don't I go do some research on biotech stocks for you. Would that help?" Some Goldman employees responded enthusiastically to this kind of initiative, which could be a great thing for the intern—he could then show what good work he was capable of. Whereas if you spent the day just schmoozing with the people on your desk, there was a very real risk of your being seen as a mere tagalong, an annoyance. Yet there were some people who were geniuses at this. Some interns, like my friend Mark Mulroney, got jobs in part because of their innate ability to win people over.

There was a reason those stools folded: You were always picking them up and heading somewhere else. You weren't just sitting at some trader's feet the whole day. Every day throughout the summer, there were presentations and panel discussions that all the interns were expected to attend. A speaker might come in and talk about what derivatives were; another might discuss the various roles in Equities: What was the difference between a salesperson and a sales trader? How did you become skillful at each of these roles?

The point of the talks was to educate us, but also to help us narrow down in our minds which area we wanted to work in. Not everyone was suited to be a trader. Not everyone was suited to be a salesperson. Not everyone liked bonds. Some people liked stocks more than bonds. The math geeks usually became traders or "quants" (also known as "strats," for *strategists*). The jocks usually became aggressive traders or outgoing salespeople. The rest of us fell somewhere in between and had to decide. But everybody had to like hard work.

Invariably during the day, you'd be speed-dating on one of the desks, and one of the mandatory speaker events would come up. At this point, you'd have to get into a tricky negotiation with the managing director or VP you were sitting with. You had to say, "I'm sorry, but I have to leave for this event," at exactly the moment when you were working on a project that that person needed quickly, such as running a spreadsheet. And yet you *had* to attend these events. Roll call was taken; your questions and answers were assessed. This was another set of rapids to navigate, and there was no set of rules for getting through, but you were always being judged.

In addition to our very full slate of daytime activity, we were frequently given huge projects to do after hours—say, a twenty-page presentation on the pros and cons of the Glass-Steagall Act. There was no time during the day to work on something like this; you couldn't exactly sneak off for five hours and crank it out. That left the time after everyone went home—usually around 7:00 P.M.—and the weekends. Working till midnight on a weekday was not unusual; nor was coming in to the office on a Saturday or Sunday, or both. (We worked hard that summer, but we played hard, too. In our precious leisure time, we interns explored the city, sometimes en masse, sometimes in subgroups. On weekends, many of us would go clubbing together; on the Fourth of July, a big group walked over to the East River to watch the fireworks. And romance ensued. Two couples who met in the summer program ended up marrying a few years later.)

Every week, you had to list five people you had speed-dated with; those people would then review your performance. These weekly reviews were collected and catalogued, and at the halfway mark in the summer, you would sit down with the person running the intern program for a performance assessment. (In the summer of 2006, when I ran the program, I became that person.) The intern manager would say, "These are the things people think you're doing well; this is what you need to do better; this is how you need to change your attitude; these are your weaknesses." My midsummer critique was very generic. (I later learned that's exactly what you want.) I was told something along the lines of "You're very smart, but you've got to be more aggressive in getting the job"—meaning, I needed to be more forceful, needed to go up to people and introduce myself, shadow more traders and salespeople.

An opposite comment might be directed at an intern who was too aggressive and who alienated all the people on a desk, making them say, "Who does this guy think he is?" There's a famous story about a Harvard Business School summer associate who went up to a partner, the head of Government Bond Trading at the time—a small Chinese American woman who was renowned as the most vicious trader on the floor—and said, "Would you mind if I shadowed you?" The intern must not have known about the partner's reputation—you wouldn't have known it to look at her, but everyone was scared of her. What he certainly didn't know was that the moment he had chosen to make his request, 8:30 A.M., on a specific Friday in July, was the exact moment when the nonfarm payrolls number (economic data) was coming out, which was effectively the biggest day of the month for this trader. She absolutely flipped out on him. "Who the fuck do you think you are? Don't you know that the economic data are coming out? Get away from me!" The guy eventually got reprimanded. The way they do the math on Wall Street is to think, *Well, this guy has bad judgment. He should've known about the market data.* On the other hand, maybe he learned a lesson, and maybe his judgment was just fine. In any case, he didn't receive a full-time job at Goldman Sachs.

What I learned was that success at Goldman, in the internship program and afterward, depended much more on judgment than on knowledge. You'd see the smartest kids in the world—they might have gotten a 1600 on the SAT, they might have graduated number one at Harvard—go to Goldman Sachs and be absolute disasters, get fired within the first year. It happened all the time. This was because simple matters of judgment cannot be taught.

Several people got voted off the island that summer. Five or six weeks in, one Princeton guy got dismissed for being insubordinate: muttering sarcastic comments to managers on multiple occasions. And then there was another intern—a Harvard guy who wound up becoming a professional online poker player—who showed a truly memorable lack of judgment.

It happened toward the end of the summer, at a team-building outing at Bear Mountain State Park, about fifty miles north of the city. It was a Friday in late July; everybody was in a festive mood. At the beginning of the summer, each of us had been issued a Goldman Sachs gym bag loaded with GS-branded paraphernalia: wallet, T-shirt, sunscreen, sunglasses, flip-flops. Today was the day to bring that bag along, to fly the Goldman colors.

At the outing, we were divided into a dozen groups of six people, and we had to compete against one another in all kinds of events: rowing a boat together, three-legged races, brain teasers, and so on. The final event of the day was to come up with a song—it sounds cheesy; it *was* cheesy—whose lyrics would reflect what we felt we'd learned over the summer. Anyway, Mr. Harvard somehow persuaded his group to come up with an Eminem-style rap.

Bad idea.

There were two offending passages in the song. One was about Val Carlotti, the fearsome VP who ran a number of the Open Meetings, and who effectively helped decide our destiny. The lyric went something like "Dotty, dotty, I want to shoot Val Carlotti with my shotty." People's mouths fell open.

Then, to put a cherry on top, the Harvard guy and his crew rapped a verse about wanting to sleep with all the chicks in HR, singling out by name the two most attractive ones.

Everyone was truly thunderstruck. Number one, why on earth would the Harvard guy do this? And number two, how had he persuaded the other people in his group to go along with it?

The job prospects of MC Harvard's group took a sudden and dramatic turn for the worse.

Josh, the son of the Wall Street billionaire, also committed a series of spectacular lapses in judgment. The interns had a room on the forty-first floor nicknamed the Swamp. You had to go down to the ground floor and take a separate elevator bank to get there; it was our special intern preserve. The Swamp had about ten rows of computers that we could use to do some work or check e-mail or surf the Internet, as there were usually no desks available on the trading floor. One afternoon, Josh made a kind of bed out of three of the chairs, lay down on it, and went to sleep, right in the middle of the day. By a stroke of extremely bad luck for him, a VP chose exactly that moment to stop by the Swamp...

Then Josh managed to top himself. He committed a gaffe that resulted in a rule that to this day is laid down to all Goldman summer interns: When you're in an elevator, do not say anything. It doesn't matter what—a joke or even a remark about the weather—just keep your mouth zipped. You simply never know who might be in the elevator with you. Josh learned this the hard way. He was riding up in a full elevator on a day when the head of the Chicago office was coming to speak to all the interns, and when someone mentioned the event, Josh chimed in, "The head of the Chicago office? Who the fuck cares about the head of the Chicago office?" You guessed it: the head of the Chicago office was standing at the front of the crowded elevator.

Josh was a great guy, really well liked by everyone in the program, and he never once tried to use his status as the son of a powerful financier to his advantage. He would not end up at Goldman. Instead, he went on to a successful career as a lawyer.

At the beginning of the summer, we'd been told that only half of us would make it through the intern program and be offered a job; in reality, it would turn out to be more like 40 percent. Most desks would hire only one person—two, in a couple of cases. What this meant was that, by the end of the summer, out of the seventy-five of us, around thirty-five would receive an offer.

Everyone was aware of this. Management was very careful not to cite exact statistics, but they definitely gave the impression that fewer than half of us would be getting jobs. They wanted to keep the pressure on without creating such a sense of backstabbing competition that people would act maliciously toward one another: management was constantly talking up teamwork.

At the same time, all the interns were smart. We all knew that not everyone was going to get an offer. So you needed to walk the line: be a team player but not a bad person, but also advance your interests and try to nab a job, because it *was* a race. Oddly enough, *Survivor*, the reality show, had just premiered that spring, and it often felt as though we were locked in a real-life version of it.

Everybody knew this, but nobody came right out and said it: you were in competition with the rest of your pod. As the summer passed, you got a sense for what everyone else was interested in, which desks everyone was going after, and then you did the math. Say there were twenty people who liked this one desk, but the desk was hiring only one person—what were your odds there? Should you go on to a less desirable desk, where you had greater odds of getting a job? I remember the way one Stanford woman lost out: she was going after a group where nine people were vying for two spots. Statistically, it wasn't a good thing to try for, even though she was confident she was going to get it. Ultimately, it comes down to personality, and they liked two other people more. There's luck involved as well. Maybe the day this intern met the managing director he hadn't had his coffee yet.

What improved your chances of getting a coveted spot, though, was finding a rabbi—someone who liked you, thought highly of you, wanted to work with you, mentor you. Nobody came right out and said it, but that was what the whole internship program was about. This was confusing at first. You didn't quite know whether you were in a marathon—ten weeks is a long time—or a sprint. What was the long-term goal? To get hired. How? Short-term, you had to impress people. You never knew who was going to be the person who would put up his hand and say, "We need to hire Greg Smith." You needed someone to go to bat for you.

Many interns labored under the misconception that if they did a good job over the summer, they'd be hired. You got hired because you found someone who wanted to hire you: it was as simple and as cruel as that. You could have been the most exceptional person, you could have impressed everyone at the Open Meetings, you could have done great things, but if by week ten there wasn't a managing director who was willing to persuade a partner to hire you, you were out of luck. Some interns didn't get this concept until the end of the summer, by which point it was too late.

———

Yet, at the same time as the firm was putting us through the wringer, it was wooing us. Because Wall Street was competing with Silicon Valley for talent in 2000, Goldman needed to entertain the candidates. So while we were spending two or three nights a week preparing for the Open Meetings or whatever desk we'd be rotated to next, on the other couple of nights, we were going out to company social events. Attendance was expected. Some of the events were for networking: you'd get together in a big room and meet all the people on the various desks in an informal setting, over a beer. The point was to put yourself forward to people in an area that interested you.

And then there were events that were just for fun, to impress the interns. We went to a couple of Yankees games. They took us to Broadway shows; we saw either *River Dance* or *Lord of the Dance*—I can't quite remember which. And oh, did we eat that summer. Whenever we went to one of our meetings during the day, even if it was held at three in the afternoon, there would be a full spread of food outside the room—and not just cookies and tea, but sandwiches, giant platters of them, plus beverages and dessert. I put on about fifteen pounds that summer. There was a lot of muttering about overkill. We had just eaten lunch at noon, and now here were all these sandwiches. It seemed like a colossal waste of money.

As did the fruit. In those days, Goldman had fresh fruit, big plates of it, everywhere on the trading floor. There was so much of it that it couldn't possibly all be eaten—I remember seeing piles of rotting fruit with clouds of tiny flies swarming around them. It was said that Goldman was spending tens of thousands of dollars a month just on fruit. When the technology bubble burst, the fruit was the first thing to go.

———

But in the summer of 2000, the bubble hadn't burst yet: Tech was still booming. Dot-coms were all the rage. All a company had to do then was put that magic suffix *.com* after its name, or the prefix *e-* in front of it, and its value would instantly soar, to absurd, stratospheric levels. That summer on the Goldman trading floor, you saw a lot of "deal toys" (Lucite blocks commemorating tech deals) on people's desks; you saw a lot of celebratory baseball caps bearing tech company names; you saw a lot of high-fiving.

And amid this irrational exuberance, I found an island of solidity: I found my rabbi.

Early in the summer there was a lot of talk, in meetings and among the interns, about the roles we aspired to within the company. I gave the question a lot of thought. I had already decided that sales and trading, the last bastion of true, unadulterated capitalism, interested me more than asset management (a slower business, investing money for large institutions and wealthy individuals) or investment banking (helping companies raise capital or reconfigure themselves). Sales and trading itself contained three roles: salesperson, trader, and quant (aka strat). The last was immediately out, as far as I (and most everybody else in the program) was concerned: I was good at math, but I was no genius; I didn't have a PhD. The choice then became salesperson or trader. It was a decision you needed to make in the first two or three weeks of the summer, and the answer wasn't instantly apparent. When you walked onto the trading floor, you couldn't tell who was who. There were just rows and rows of people. Over the first few weeks, I began to understand who chose one specialty and who chose the other, and why.

The salesperson, of course, dealt with clients. And whether the client was a mutual fund in Boston, a macro hedge fund in New York, or a sovereign wealth fund in the Middle East, these clients managed hundreds of billions of dollars in assets, executed trades with the firm frequently, and paid Goldman commissions ranging from thousands of dollars per year to the double-digit millions. Salespeople called their client contacts every day, gave them advice, listened to their problems, tried to think of investment ideas for them. It was important to build a relationship of trust with the client, because that was what you were going to be measured on: how much business the client did with the firm. A typical salesperson was friendly, outgoing, a little bit schmoozy; able to keep calm in tight situations, to juggle a lot of balls at the same time. A salesperson had to be someone who was happy talking to people the whole day.

Traders were much more introverted. They sat at their desks managing risk. Was the market going up or down? Did they need to sell stock or buy? They were trying to protect the firm's money, make sure that nothing irresponsible happened, that we didn't lose $10 million doing a stupid trade. Trading was also a more quantitative role: you had to be quick, decisive, aggressive.

I quickly realized that I would not have been happy sitting at a desk, never talking to clients. I was very attracted to the idea of building relationships with some of the smartest investors in the world. What I also learned that summer was where the tension came between salespeople and traders. Traders were trying to protect the firm's capital; salespeople were trying to protect their relationships with their clients. These were contradictory things. It wasn't always obvious that helping the client was going to help the firm; in fact, a lot of the time, this wasn't the case. A lot of the time, protecting a client meant steering it away from risky trades—giving up what might be a short-term advantage to the firm in favor of the long-term relationship with the client. This was what Goldman's longtime leader Sidney Weinberg meant by "long-term greedy."

With regard to becoming a salesperson or a trader, usually the intern class splits about fifty-fifty: in the first few weeks of the summer, roughly half the class starts homing in on the trading desks; the rest gravitate to the sales desks.

Early in the summer, I became friends with an Israeli intern who told me about a small, slightly obscure subgroup of the Emerging Markets Sales group called New Markets Sales. Emerging Markets Sales sold stocks from the developing world (Latin America, Southeast Asia, and, in the group that interested me, Israel, South Africa, Russia, Poland, and Turkey) to U.S. institutional investors (hedge funds, mutual funds, pension funds). New Markets Sales felt like a natural fit for me: I was excited by the idea of emerging markets, and I was from South Africa; I also spoke pretty good Hebrew.

Then, in week five, some good luck came my way: my little pod and I spent three days on the Emerging Markets Sales desk.

What smart interns do—for "smart," read "determined"—is keep returning to the area they like. So whenever I had a coffee break, I'd come back and see the New Markets Sales team. I tried to get some work from them, to show them I could do things. I ran spreadsheets, did stock reports. I met the senior VP who was running the desk: a cool and correct woman. And I met her second in command, an associate named Rudy Glocker.

Rudy was a big guy, six-five. He'd played tight end and linebacker for Joe Paterno at Penn State. His nickname was the Beast. Some senior guy had given him the name not only because of his size but because Rudy was just so hungry: he made more calls to clients before 6:00 A.M. than anyone else on the floor. He was in his early thirties, a little old for an associate, but he'd been around the block: he'd taken some time off after college, sold sporting goods in the former Soviet Union, coached football, gone to Harvard Business School.

Rudy was old-school. By this, I mean that he came from rural Pennsylvania, and his values, politically and financially, were conservative. He was serious and straitlaced. He played basketball every Thursday night. He liked routine. With Rudy, the client came first.

Still, Rudy ruffled feathers. He could be acerbic, and he didn't care whom he was talking to. There's a story about Rudy and a research analyst, a partner, who was coming through the Boston office, where Rudy later transferred from New York. Rudy was to take the partner to see all his clients to discuss Goldman's research views. The partner, who had arrived with a big briefcase filled with heavy books, plopped it down and said, "Rudy, you wouldn't mind carrying this around for the rest of the day, would you?" "No problem," Rudy said, then added: "And leave your shoes; I'll shine them, too." Rudy's boss, who was standing right there, said, "Rudy, in my office right now."

One of Rudy's main jobs was selling IPOs, initial public offerings. IPOs occur when a formerly private company sells shares to the public for the first time, and these shares start trading on an exchange such as the New York Stock Exchange (NYSE). IPOs can contain an innate conflict of interest for a firm like Goldman. When a private company is going public, the bank that's doing the deal for them puts together a memo listing all the reasons their clients should love this deal. The problem is that the bank is on both sides of the deal: privy to what may not be so great about the company going public, but also trying to market shares in the soon-to-be-public company to its clients, all the while purporting to be objective.

Rudy would do the analysis for himself and say, "Yes, there are these three great things about this company, but there are also these three bad things, and we should be telling the clients about them as well." Often the client would call and say, "What do you think of this deal?" and Rudy would say, "Let me take you out for coffee this afternoon." Then, over coffee, he'd say, "Let me be honest with you: this is not a great deal; I don't think you should invest in this company." Rudy's bluntness, which made him very popular with clients, would eventually prove to be his undoing at the firm. And not just Rudy's undoing: this type of fiduciary minded salesperson would one day become an endangered species at Goldman Sachs.

By the end of the summer, there were three or four interns going after that one spot in New Markets Sales, and everybody was highly qualified. During the time I spent with Rudy's group and afterward, there was an odd dance going on. It's a little like a mating ritual, a tactical game that's integral to the internship. Both you and the group you want to work for have to show interest in each other—but not too much interest. They don't want to tell you (because they can't) that they're definitely going to hire you. And you don't want to tell them you're definitely going to accept their offer if they make one, because you're always encouraged to have a Plan B. Unfortunately, I was so drawn to New Markets Sales that I'm not even sure I had a Plan B.

The dance continued. I kept finding ways to spend time around, and to do things for, Rudy and his little crew. Finally, by week eight, the VP running the New Markets desk told Rudy, "Take Greg out for dinner"—a request that I think was a mixture of "Give him the final vetting" and "Give him the sense that we're interested in having him come work for us."

The dance heated up. I knew what was going on, and I was excited. This was what I wanted. It was South Africa, it was Israel. The desk seemed like a great starting point for my career: With just five people, it felt manageable. I knew I would get on well with the group; they got on well with one another. Plus, Rudy and I had clicked right away. The more I learned about business, the more I realized that everything was about personalities, and Rudy's and mine just meshed.

On the evening he and I went out for dinner, I was a little surprised at how casual the whole occasion was. I'm not sure what I was expecting. First, we stopped to pick up Rudy's dry cleaning. He dropped it off at his walkup at Sixty-Second and Lex. Then he said, "Why don't we get some sushi."

Today, twelve years later, sushi is my favorite food. At the time, though, I had never summoned up the guts to eat raw fish. I was a little hesitant. "Try it," Rudy said. "You're going to like it." A few pieces of yellowtail sashimi later, I started warming up to it.

I was a little bit nervous, but it was a good kind of nervousness. Rudy asked me about myself and my background—this was clearly the vetting part—but mainly it just felt like casual dinner conversation over sushi and Sapporo beer. We talked about the other members of Rudy's team, and then I could tell it was my move. Another intricacy of the dance: the interns had been warned early in the summer never to assume somebody you wanted to work for knew you wanted it. If you really want something, we were counseled, say so, in no uncertain terms. *When* to say so was the whole question. Now was the time. I decided not to hold back. I said that I really wanted to work with New Markets. Rudy smiled.

———

The last night of the summer program, about fifteen interns, a few women included, went on an extracurricular outing to Scores, the New York strip club that Howard Stern made famous on his radio show. We were all having fun drinking and enjoying the scenery, until I saw an intern I knew, an Asian guy named Jon, waving at me from the club's VIP section. (Jon, a man of refined tastes, had boasted throughout the summer how many times he'd eaten at Le Bernardin and Daniel, two of

New York's finest restaurants; like Adam, he would also later go on to manage billions of dollars at a hedge fund.) Another intern, a Persian pal of mine, and I walked up to the rope blocking the entrance to the VIP lounge, and Jon waved the two of us past the bouncer. This was exciting stuff. After what seemed like about five minutes of dances from a few blond bombshells, my Persian buddy and I were informed that we each owed $750. Seven hundred and fifty dollars! I certainly didn't have that kind of money to throw around—it would have been a significant portion of my total net worth. With dark looks and muttered threats, the bouncer escorted my friend and me out the back door. I remember thinking that we were very lucky not to have been beaten up on the pavement behind the club.

————

Minor misadventures notwithstanding, the summer had ended well. I knew that I wanted to work for Goldman Sachs, but did Goldman Sachs want me? When you leave for the summer, there's a protocol: the firm does not guarantee you anything. You have to wait a few weeks to find out your fate. I felt I had about an 85 percent chance of getting an offer. I went in to work on the last day and said goodbye and thanked everyone I had met. I made sure to say goodbye to my intern manager, a VP named Mike—he would probably be the guy who would call to say whether I'd gotten a job.

"Thanks for everything, Mike," I said.

"You did a great job, Greg. We'll let you know," he told me.

I turned around, feeling hopeful.

"Oh, one more thing," Mike added. "Next time you go out for a big night on the town, make sure you bring enough cash." He had a wry smile on his face.

News travels fast on Wall Street.

CHAPTER 2

Fall and Rise

At Goldman Sachs, passing the Series 7 exam the first time you take it is not optional; it is expected. The Series 7 is your first big test on Wall Street, a rite of passage that allows you to start calling clients and being useful. The exam is six hours long, and the material is about the thickness of two large encyclopedias, a daunting volume of information to master. Early on a Tuesday morning in September, I got in a cab outside my apartment on Chambers Street and headed uptown to take my shot at glory. It was a beautiful morning: bright, crisp, cloudless. But the beauty around me was in stark contrast to how I felt: very nervous and not at all ready.

My stomach was churning as I sat in the back of the Yellow Cab taking me to the testing center, at One Penn Plaza in Midtown. The early-morning sun was too bright, beaming like a giant searchlight down each Manhattan block we crossed. I couldn't help listening to a story on the taxi's radio about Michael Jordan's possible return to basketball, to play with the Washington Wizards. *Why?* I thought. *He had retired from the Bulls at the top of his game. At the top of THE game. There's nowhere to go but down.*

My path was just beginning. I'd gotten the magic call from Goldman Sachs about two weeks after my summer internship ended, in late August of 2000. I had gone home to South Africa to visit my family for two weeks before I started my senior year. Goldman Sachs generously paid for your ticket home, no matter where in the world that was: a nice perk of the internship. Because of the six-hour time difference between

New York and Johannesburg, I was anxiously awaiting Goldman's call at all hours of the night and day. But the frustrating part was I had no idea when the call was going to come. And if I didn't hear from them, did that mean I wouldn't be getting a job offer?

Then, at around 5:00 P.M. Johannesburg time one Thursday evening, the phone rang—and the news was all good. "We are very excited to offer you a full-time job at Goldman Sachs," the woman in HR said warmly. She apologized that Mike, the program manager who had found out about my Scores episode, was not able to jump on the call but said that he was very excited for me. He couldn't have been nearly as excited as I was. This was the golden ticket, a dream job for anyone who wanted to start a career on Wall Street. Goldman Sachs was the best of the best—the "Rolls-Royce of investment banks," as one of my Johannesburg friends had put it. I humbly played it down when he said that, but I knew it to be true. I felt incredibly proud that I had competed with some of the toughest, smartest people in the world, on one of the biggest stages in the world, and had succeeded.

"Will you be accepting your analyst offer in New Markets Sales on the wire?" the HR woman inquired. In Wall Street terminology, "on the wire" means "immediately." But I'm not an on-the-wire guy: I've always been cautious and deliberate. In school, if I finished a test twenty minutes early, I'd spend the extra time checking and rechecking my answers. And now I decided that I wanted to take the three to four weeks the firm had offered me to consider my decision fully, even though I was virtually certain I would ultimately accept. I later learned that this rubbed a lot of people the wrong way. Wall Street likes instant gratification and gratitude. They want to know *now*, and they want a big thank-you.

It was great to know so early what I'd be doing after graduation, at a point when many of my peers were still agonizing over where they were going to work. That was a big benefit of the Goldman internship. It gave you a taste of whether you actually liked Wall Street, and liked the firm. It gave you the opportunity to show your merit over a ten-week period, as opposed to relying on a thirty-minute interview to persuade someone to hire you.

Graduating from college was bittersweet. I'd loved my four years at Stanford, felt privileged to have attended on scholarship, and was sad to be leaving. My mind had been opened to things I would never have thought of in Johannesburg. I had made close, lifelong friends, and now we were being dispersed all around the country.

I had studied hard enough, but had managed to have fun, too. In my senior year, I was the social manager of Casa Italiana—in theory, a place for Italian majors or minors to immerse themselves in Italian language and culture; in actuality, thanks to its location smack in the middle of campus, a great place for parties, with the best chef at Stanford. I had a $2,000-per-quarter budget to throw parties for the whole school, and I threw them. We had a Jazz Night, a Sake Night, a Karaoke Night...

I didn't have any classes before noon my whole senior year. I would often think, *This is so funny—in just a few months my alarm is going to be going off every morning at 5:00 A.M. How the hell am I going to wake up?* I was on that college schedule of staying up till all hours and sometimes sleeping through lunch. It was great while it lasted.

Graduation weekend was a special time. My mom flew over from Johannesburg; my cousins came in from Chicago, as did my aunt from Florida. The day my mother arrived, we were attending a small graduation barbecue when, suddenly, a motorcade of three black SUVs pulled up and Chelsea Clinton, whom I'd known in passing from my freshman dorm, stepped out along with her dad (out of office just a few months) and Hillary. We all got to chat with the Clintons and shake their hands, and they posed for an endless series of pictures with overeager moms and dads, who seemed to have forgotten that the Clintons were proud parents, too. Bill and Hillary were beaming with happiness for Chelsea. I was always impressed by how nice and composed Chelsea was—even during the soap opera going on at the White House during our freshman year.

The graduation speaker for the Class of 2001 was Carly Fiorina, a Stanford grad and the CEO of Hewlett-Packard. The first woman to lead a Fortune 20 company, she had been named "The Most Powerful Woman in Business" by *Fortune* magazine a few years earlier. That day, she gave a very poignant speech, comparing her life to a novel that she had edited down, page by page, until she had distilled it into a one-page essence. She recommended that we all go through a similar process in the course of our lives. Her speech had a powerful impact on me, and I have reread it many times over the years. A few of my friends and I snagged front-row seats at the commencement address and were captured in a candid photograph that ended up featured prominently in our Class of 2001 yearbook. All five of us keep a framed copy of that picture somewhere, wherever we happen to live in the world. In it, I am looking optimistically into the distance. That is really how I felt. I was still in my opening pages, sad about closing that early chapter, but excited to move on to the next one. The idea of living in New York, being independent, and earning a living appealed to me enormously. When I graduated from Stanford, I had less than $3,000 in my bank account.

Goldman Sachs underwrites a house-hunting trip for new hires—it even pays for a real estate broker—so, in May, I flew to New York to look around for a place with my friend Adam and a friend of his. I struck out. I was trying hard to persuade the two of them to live on the Upper West Side, because of the great Jewish scene there: I thought it would be a good place to meet Jewish girls, plus there were dozens of synagogues, and of course Barney Greengrass ("The Sturgeon King"), on Amsterdam at Eighty-Sixth Street, had the best smoked salmon and potato latkes in New York.

But Adam and his friend wanted to live in Union Square, because of the trendy downtown feel. We kept going back and forth, and we couldn't find anything. I returned to Palo Alto with nothing in hand, having wasted my Goldman-financed house-hunting trip. Adam would end up finding an apartment by himself, in Murray Hill. When I came back to New York for the Goldman training program in late June, a Bangladeshi friend who'd been an intern with me the previous summer (but who ended up at Morgan Stanley) kindly agreed to let me sleep on a blow-up mattress in his apartment at Sixty-Second Street and First Avenue until I found a place.

On the first day of the training program, I met JF, a French Canadian guy who was a former national-level water polo player from Montreal and a ladies' man—and who spoke barely a word of English. Goldman had taken a leap of faith and hired him despite the language barrier, impressed by his determination and his ability to learn quickly. Their gamble would pay off: he proved to be an absolute killer at picking stocks (so good, in fact, that some of the senior VPs started using his ideas for their own clients when JF was only a few weeks into the job). JF loved nothing more than analyzing balance sheets and income statements and coming up with the best possible recommendations for his clients. While most of us were trying to figure out how to take the plastic wrapping off our Series 7 study manuals, JF was doing bottom-up analysis and looking at candlestick charts to determine whether his stock picks were going to break out of their range. His two weaknesses were extreme impatience and a short temper, which he sometimes didn't control properly at work. JF had a buddy from Montreal who was working as an accountant at KPMG, and the three of us decided to get a place together.

And not just any place. A real estate broker told us about Tribeca Pointe—a very new building at the time, and one of the tallest apartment buildings in the Financial District. It stood forty-three stories high at the corner of Chambers Street and the West Side Highway, right by the Hudson River, and it had amazing views of the water and Manhattan, especially from the upper stories. A two-bedroom apartment was available on the fortieth floor, the broker told us. The rent was $3,750 a month, very pricey for two beginning Goldman analysts—we were earning a base salary of $55,000 a year to start (about $750 a week after taxes)—but it might just work if we split it three ways.

But there were only two bedrooms.

The more we thought about it, though, the more hypnotic the idea of living on the fortieth floor of this magnificent building seemed. We thought it would be hugely impressive to friends and visitors; we hoped the spectacular views would mesmerize girls as well. When the broker told us that for a mere $1,000, a Russian contractor the broker used could build a temporary wall between the apartment's open-plan kitchen and living/dining room, creating another small bedroom (a practice we would later learn was very common among young Wall

Streeters setting up shop in pricey Manhattan), the three of us decided to take the plunge and open our checkbooks. So, on August 1, 2001, we moved into 41 River Terrace, Apartment 4004. That Sunday, my room-mates and I took drinks and cigars up to the roof-deck on the forty-third floor and toasted ourselves as we soaked in the glorious panorama of the harbor and the nearby twin towers of the World Trade Center. We'd paid a ton, but it felt worth every penny. (And we had plenty of com-pany: we would soon find out that the River Terrace buildings were practically high-rise dorms for Wall Street foot soldiers.)

Meanwhile, the hard work of preparing to work at Goldman Sachs had begun.

Yet, this was a very different Goldman Sachs from the firm I had left at the end of my internship. No more fruit platters; no more GS-branded T-shirts, flip-flops, and other paraphernalia. The tech bubble that had been pumping nitrous oxide onto the trading floor the previous sum-mer had popped in early 2001: companies that had been valued in the billions were now trading for pennies on the dollar. The economy was entering its first recession of the twenty-first century. Three people from the New Markets Sales desk, 60 percent of its staff, had been let go.

Only one person was left besides Rudy: an aggressive Slovakian who was a junior analyst like me, except a year older. Her English was only so-so, and she spoke very fast and very loud, perhaps thinking it would make her better understood. The Beast hadn't hired her, but he was stuck with her for the time being. She had already passed her Series 7 exam. In some ways she tried to coach me on a few things, but in other ways she tried to leave me in her dust—if I showed up for work at 5:30 A.M., she showed up at 5:29—but since I wasn't allowed to answer the phone yet, she didn't have much to worry about.

Rudy needed me to hit the ground running. However, to be legally allowed even to speak to clients, not to mention execute trades, I had to pass my Series 7—and the Series 63, a deceptively shorter but actually harder regulatory test. There was a lot of studying to do, and the tests were all memorization.

While my team wanted me chained to my desk, the firm wanted me in class learning about municipal bond regulations for the Series 7. And then there was the expectation that you would nail the exam the first time. Your test results become very public knowledge at the firm the moment they come in. There's even some semi-serious betting action on the floor on how various trainees are going to do. To fail either of the exams is extremely humiliating. This is an insane amount of pressure for a new kid on Wall Street.

The prep course for the Series 7 exam was a solid week of sitting in a conference room from 9:00 to 5:00 and being lectured on the most mind-numbing material: What are the laws around selling corporate bonds to a pension fund? What are the requirements for opening a new trading account for a mutual fund? The Investment Company Act of 1940—what was it? When was the SEC created? There were a few practical aspects to the material, such as methods for calculating hedging costs, but the joke on Wall Street was that this was information that, for the most part, you'd never again use, or even think about, for the rest of your career. You had to pass that exam so you could check that regulatory box that said you'd studied it. It was brutal; you had to drink gallons of coffee just to stay awake. As I sit here writing about it twelve years later, I can remember almost none of the specific material the exam covered.

After work and on weekends, I used to take my Sony CD Walkman up to the forty-third-floor roof-deck of my apartment building and, for five and six hours at a time, sit at a table in the small clubhouse listening to *Sinatra Reprise: The Very Good Years* while I studied securities regulation. I would put the CD on repeat and listen to it over and over again—I've always found this to be a helpful technique for getting a studying rhythm. I must have listened to "Summer Wind" and "It Was a Very Good Year" a thousand times. I still love those songs. I'll always associate them with the Series 7 and my early days in New York.

It was a hard slog. From time to time, I'd take the Series 7 practice test but not do particularly well, which was scary. When you do take the test, you want your score to be as close as possible to the lowest possible passing score, 70. It's a matter of pride. If you score too high, it means you studied too hard. In the low 70s is good. On the other hand, to get a 69, the highest possible failing grade, is a supreme embarrassment.

In the meantime, on the trading floor throughout July and August, the betting began.

The trading floor was a betting culture. Traders would wager on anything: Wimbledon, the Masters, how many White Castle burgers a first-year analyst could eat. Even the tech-bubble bust didn't put a dent in the action. I remember one trader, a very scrawny guy named Tommy, whom everyone used to make fun of. At one point, traders started betting on how much Tommy could bench-press. It turned into such a big deal that people started announcing their wagers over the Hoot, the floor-wide intercom system usually used for business announcements, originally known as the Hoot-and-Holler. Everyone had a view. The sentimental stance was that while Tommy *looked* scrawny—he was around five-ten, and 145 pounds, tops—he could probably bench more than people thought. There were also a lot of anti-sentimentalists. It became this huge market; everyone was going back and forth—maybe to compensate for some of the flatness in the real-life markets. Then, one day, during a late-morning trading lull, one of the managing directors said, "All right, we're settling this right now. Tommy is going down to the gym." A big argument ensued about how many witnesses were necessary. Finally three witnesses were sent down, and of course Tommy benched way more than anyone had thought possible. A lot of money changed hands that day. Years later, Tommy, too, would become an MD.

Now, in the summer of 2001, the betting action on the floor centered on how the new analysts would perform on the Series 7.

The betting worked just like trading. Sometime during a lull in trading, usually around 11:00 to 11:30 A.M., somebody would stand up at his desk and call to someone in the next row: "So the exam is coming up—what do you think? What are your Series 7 markets?" Full voice, loud enough for all to hear. "How do you think Greg is going to do? How about Mulroney? What about JF?"

Then, just as in trading, one guy would say, "Well, my market on Greg is 72 at 77." His "market" meant his spread: his bid and his offer.

Meaning he would buy a 72 (he thought Greg was going to do better than that) but he would sell a 77 (which meant he thought I was going to do worse than that).

Then the person he was betting with could either buy or sell his market. Let's say that person thought I was going to get less than 72. He'd say, "I hit your bid at 72." Meaning, 72 was now the bogey. So if I got higher than 72, the guy who'd bought it won. If I scored lower than 72, the guy who'd sold it won.

How much? Usually house minimum bets were a hundred bucks (or a "hundo," as they say on Wall Street). But money wasn't the real point. The point was to intimidate and provoke the analysts taking the test. To put them under pressure. To say, "You don't want to screw this one up."

I felt as if I was on the verge of doing just that. The night before the Series 7, I took a break from studying at the massive and ominous-looking Bobst Library at NYU in the Village—my old Stanford student ID card got me access—to phone a friend and fellow analyst, a Swedish guy named Kris Ekelund: "Dude, I'm only getting seventies and seventy-twos on these practice tests—what's going to happen here?" It was too close for comfort for me.

"Don't worry about it," Kris said. "We're going to be okay. That's all we need."

———

When my cab pulled up to One Penn Plaza, I saw the whole analyst class outside the building, milling around nervously. A few kids were sitting on the concrete benches trying to do some last-minute cramming. I went into Starbucks and bought a bottled water—I was too wired to drink coffee. *Don't fail. Don't blow this...*

Yet it was too late to do any cramming, so I just stood around chatting with people I knew, trying to steady my nerves a bit. I felt a little sick to my stomach. Finally, we began to head, in groups, up to the seventeenth floor.

It was 7:45 A.M. Outside the windows of the Prometric Testing Center waiting room, the office towers stretching from Thirty-Fourth Street to Lower Manhattan gleamed in the early light. People at tables were checking IDs. The test givers were very strict about identification; you had to have two forms of it with you—I had my South African passport and my California driver's license—and had to sign an affidavit swearing that you were who you said you were. Once you'd signed in, they gave you a numbered lock and key. You were then required to empty your pockets and put everything in your assigned locker. You couldn't wear a watch into the testing room; you weren't even allowed to take in a pen. None of this calmed my nerves.

A testing center escort then took each candidate to a computer in the windowless testing room. The Series 7 was a six-hour, 250-question multiple-choice exam, administered in two three-hour sessions with a short lunch break in between. It was given on a computer instead of in a test booklet—the upside/downside of this being that, at the end of the test, you got your result almost instantaneously. (The computer takes an excruciating five seconds to calculate your score.) We were given earplugs to wear if we wanted (I didn't), two number-two pencils, and scratch paper for calculations. We were told we were not allowed to speak to anyone; if we had to go to the rest room, we would have to sign out and sign back in when we returned...

And then, with a couple clicks of the mouse, the General Securities Representative Qualification Examination (Series 7) began.

About an hour later, knee-deep in multiple-choice questions, we heard an announcement come over the exam room's PA system: it was a man, saying in a calm voice, "Please, everyone, remain where you are. We will not be evacuating the building."

What was this—a fire drill? But there was no further word. *Strange*, I thought to myself. I went back to the test.

Then, ten minutes later, the man came back on the PA system, this time with a slightly more detailed announcement: "Please do not leave the building. We are waiting for word from the Mayor's Office." I wondered again whether some sort of drill was in progress, but once again, nothing more was said.

Ten minutes later the same voice came over the PA system: "We're waiting for word from the NYPD and the Mayor's Office. Please remain calm." Everyone looked at one another, baffled. Then, quite startlingly, a woman burst into the room, crying. She screamed at the top of her voice, "Everyone needs to get out, get out, get out! Right now!"

It was the moderator who'd been sitting outside the room, the one who signed us in and out when we went to the rest room. Everyone was shocked; no one knew what was going on. We were still in six-hour-exam mind-set: *What's going to happen to the exam? Are they going to stop the clock?* In addition to confusion, my other immediate reaction was slight relief. I had felt that the exam was going terribly for me.

We all walked out into the seventeenth-floor waiting area, where the testing staff were waving people toward the elevator to leave. *What the hell is going on?* Then I saw people crowded around the floor-to-ceiling window, muttering and pointing. I walked over and took a look.

In the sunlight far to the south, under a clear morning sky, the right-hand tower of the World Trade Center, the North Tower, was billowing smoke. Nobody had any idea what was going on. It was a bewildering, inconceivable sight.

A group of us crowded into an elevator and went downstairs.

Out on Thirty-Third Street it felt warm; the sun was still shining brightly. The traffic flowed across town—the city seemed to be functioning—but something was wrong. People had paused in groups on the sidewalk, talking to one another. One group stood by a parked car with the windows open and the radio turned way up. An announcer was saying something about a plane crashing into the World Trade Center. Nobody seemed to know anything; people were voicing theories. Was it an accident? Terrorism?

The one thing I knew was that I probably shouldn't go back to my apartment, which was just a couple of blocks from the towers. So Kris Ekelund and I, and a couple of the other Goldman analysts, huddled there on the sidewalk. If it was terrorism, we thought, we might be safest not staying in Midtown, among all the tall buildings, but instead heading down to Greenwich Village, where Kris lived.

We turned right on Seventh Avenue and started to head south. It was impossible to find a cab of course. At Twenty-Third Street we headed east to Sixth Avenue, then turned right toward the Village. Sixth is one of those avenues that gives you a straight sight line down to Lower Manhattan. So we could now clearly see huge clouds of smoke rising from both towers. Every block along the way, people were standing in groups staring down the avenue at the unimaginable sight. We just kept walking toward it, to get to the safety of the low-rise buildings in the Village. In retrospect, we should have been walking north, not south. But it was hard for us to think clearly about what was going on. For block after block we walked, alternately speculating to one another what had happened and staring, transfixed, at the burning towers.

Just before 10:00 A.M., the four of us saw something that did not seem real as it was happening: the incomprehensible sight of the South Tower coming down in a colossal, slow-motion roar of gray dust.

Time seemed to freeze for a few seconds. Then people started screaming and running. No one in the world had ever seen anything like this happen. No one knew how to react. I certainly didn't. I stood still for a second and tried to keep calm. It was a surreal few minutes that will always be etched into my brain with great clarity. Two big African American guys who were standing next to us stared at the falling tower, tears streaming down their cheeks. My friend Kris was crying, too. I had never seen so many grown men—so many people in general—all crying at the same time. Not knowing what to say or do next, I felt utterly sick. Thoughts were rushing through my head: thousands of lives were being lost; I was furious that America was being attacked, yet thankful to be alive.

"Let's get to my place as quickly as possible," Kris said. "It'll be tight, but you can stay as long as necessary." Everyone in the city was in this together.

I tried to call my family to let them know I was okay. They were a million miles away, in South Africa. I had no idea how much they did or didn't know; I hoped they weren't following the disaster in real time. But the cell phone circuits were out, and would stay out for hours. When we finally got to Kris's place, I used the landline to try to reach my mom in Johannesburg, but she wasn't at home and she didn't have a cell phone at the time. The first person I reached was my brother, Mark, who was then at the University of Cape Town. I remember this moment very clearly. My brother is not an emotional guy, but as soon as he heard my voice, he started crying. Then I did, too. He later told me that he thought I may have worked in the World Trade Center.

I finally got hold of my mother in the evening, her time: it turned out she hadn't known about the attacks until very late in the day, so she didn't have to worry for very long until she heard from my brother, who confirmed my safety. She has always said to me that she's very thankful she didn't have the whole day to worry about it.

As afternoon turned to night, a few of us sat around Kris's place watching Aaron Brown and Paula Zahn on CNN, in a trance. I finally collapsed, exhausted, on the couch. In the morning, surreally enough, I walked over to the 2nd Ave Deli—my favorite kosher deli in New York during good times, at Second Avenue and Tenth Street—and found it open. I hadn't eaten dinner the night before, and suddenly I was starving. I ordered a corned beef sandwich. While I waited, an African American man and an elderly Jewish guy argued at the top of their voices about why this had happened to America. Even more surreal was the scene on the streets of the East Village: they were as empty as something out of a postapocalyptic sci-fi movie. New York felt like a ghost town, the wind totally knocked out of it.

That same morning, I got a surprising but very welcome call from an HR person in the London office of Goldman Sachs. The guy said, "We know your apartment is a few blocks from the World Trade Center; we've got a full system in place to set you up. Number one, we're going to give you two thousand dollars to buy clothes and anything you need. Number two, the firm has already booked hotels all over the city, which we're going to be ready to provide to you, but we need a couple of days on that. And number three, we're going to be in touch to let you know when the markets are opening."

The call was a huge relief. Because I couldn't get back into my apartment, I was running low on cash, I didn't know how I was going to get clothes for work. I didn't have any shirts or underwear; I didn't even have a toothbrush. Now I could start to feel human again. A small, good thing.

I hung up shaking my head in amazement and gratitude. Within hours of the attacks, the London office had taken over the reins, found out where I was living, tracked me down, and extended a hand. This was Goldman Sachs at its best. I remember thinking that when it came to efficiency, execution, and generally having its act together, Goldman Sachs was the gold standard. It had the smartest, most resourceful people; no other bank on Wall Street came close.

It was hard to think about something as mechanical as the markets reopening when all anybody was thinking about was life and death. But it was important. Mayor Rudy Giuliani realized this. Osama Bin Laden had attacked America's financial center, only blocks from the New York Stock Exchange, the greatest symbol of capitalism in the world. Opening the markets quickly, efficiently, and in an orderly fashion would be a strong way to fight back, to get New York and America back on their feet, and to show our collective resilience.

I remember saying to my friend Kris, "The world has changed for good now. I wish we could go back to the way it was before yesterday morning." It was as though we'd been in the midst of a sweet dream and now we'd woken up in a nightmare, and there was nothing we could do to change it. I remember thinking, *I wish time would just pass*, and *When is the world going to seem normal again?*

It would take a long time.

———

My first day back at work was Monday, September 17, 2001. Because I still hadn't managed to get back into my apartment, I had crashed at Kris's for a couple days, stayed at the hotel Goldman provided (the Beekman, on First Avenue, at Forty-Ninth Street) for a night, then moved to another friend's place, across the Hudson River, in Jersey City. I could have stayed at the Beekman longer, but Goldman had offered a further cash stipend in lieu of my using the hotel, and I had less than $7,500 in my bank account. I knew times ahead were going to be tough, so I decided to take the money.

I got on the PATH train from Jersey City very early that morning, before 5:30. I had used Goldman Sachs's money to buy a new wardrobe at Banana Republic, but I was unshaven and groggy. After all that had

been going on in the world, it felt strange to be going to work. Once I
got to the building, I called my friend Mark Mulroney to see if he could
meet me on a different floor from ours with the electric razor I kept in
my desk drawer. (At the time, I preferred an electric over a razor blade.)
For my first day back, I wanted to look respectable.

On September 17 the markets had one of their worst days on
record—the S&P 500 (the benchmark most commonly used by investors on Wall Street) was down 5 percent, and the Dow was off 7
percent. Strangely, though, this day didn't feel like a panic or a crash. Investors were actually very satisfied with how orderly the markets were.
The NYSE and the NASDAQ opened efficiently, the bond markets were
operating, and commodities were being traded in the pits of the Chicago
and New York Mercantile Exchanges. It was a good day. People had
predicted far worse chaos and panic, and America showed that it was
open for business. I was proud.

I was also proud of how Goldman Sachs had worked round the clock
to make sure that our technology and operations were working and that
our clients could trade smoothly. Goldman also played an instrumental
role in ensuring that the NYSE was able to open as quickly as it did: less
than a week after the worst terrorist attack ever to take place on American soil.

When my roommates and I finally moved back into our apartment,
two weeks after the attacks, the rubble of the World Trade Center, just
four blocks south of us, was still smoking. The air was filled with a
burning smell that wouldn't go away. It was a smell I had never experienced before—a combination of burned steel, burned plastic, burned
bodies—and it was terrible. Crews with cranes and earthmovers were
working day and night to clear the site, trucking the debris to barges
docked nearby on the Hudson, practically at the foot of our building.
They worked for months, around the clock; the noise never stopped.

It was hard to live down there. We thought about moving out. I still
ask myself why we didn't just get the hell out of there immediately. But
our world was upside down, we were just starting our careers on Wall
Street, and we were trying to move forward as best we could.

The first weeks back at work were challenging on a number of levels.

For one thing, people were clearly in shock and not themselves. For another, whatever had been bad about the economy during the post-tech bubble and pre-9/11 was much worse afterward. The markets started tanking; clients were worried. Emerging markets (the group I was in) were turbulent. The markets were punishing us. We were the area everyone feared would go into a recession.

All this, plus we newbies were going to have to retake the Series 7, one month later.

September 11 had put into perspective what was important and what wasn't, and part of me wanted to think, *It's just a stupid test.* In reality, though, passing it was vital to my getting my career started on the right foot—to getting it started, period. There's only so long you can take coffee orders and make photocopies. At the same time, it was extremely challenging to go back and hit the books. Paranoia in the city, and at the firm, was high in the wake of the attacks. Would the other shoe drop? We prayed not. One colleague never came back to work after 9/11. She never even set foot in the office. We were just too close to the burning rubble and the trauma. It had been too much for her.

People at work were freaked out, but I was moved by how everybody pulled together and supported one another—and our clients. The overriding message was "Now is the time we differentiate ourselves. This is where Goldman Sachs becomes Goldman Sachs. Let's be ultra-attentive to our clients; let's help them get back on their feet, even if it doesn't benefit us immediately. Because that's what the clients are going to remember."

The message was classic Goldman Sachs, and the reason it could be proclaimed so strongly is because the old guard was still there. Many of the pre-IPO partners were still in place. This was early in Hank Paulson's tenure as sole CEO; he had recently forced out Jon Corzine. (Corzine, who had been a vocal advocate in the decision of the firm to go public, would go on to become governor of New Jersey, a U.S. senator, and then the CEO of MF Global, a futures brokerage that went bankrupt after using client funds to cover trading losses.) Paulson's letter to shareholders in the 2001 Annual Report, released soon after 9/11, reemphasized the firm's core values of integrity and commitment to

clients. The company also established a relief fund for people and organizations affected by the attacks; Goldman employees contributed $5.5
million, which the firm matched.

That was the macro. In the trenches, I was trying to learn my job
during that crazy period. Every morning at 5:30, we first-year analysts
would crowd into the copy room, our first interaction of the day, all
of us competing to use the photocopying machine first because we had
to make big stacks of copies to hand out to the senior people on our
team by the time they arrived at 6:00. We were copying research reports
on the stocks that Goldman analysts covered; we were summarizing the
stories in the *Wall Street Journal* and on Bloomberg that would be relevant to the day's trading. The idea behind aggregating and curating
these data into summary form was to make the senior people's jobs a
bit easier, to save them from having to wade through the material themselves.

My little claim to fame as a junior analyst sprang from an obser-
vation I'd made soon after arriving at the firm. Anytime a company
reported earnings, everyone on the trading desk wanted to have the
numbers at his fingertips—was this earnings figure a good number or
a bad number? When I got to Goldman, I noticed that everybody was
scrambling to find the research reports, to see what the numbers were.
So I came up with the idea of writing a simple five-line e-mail before the
earnings came out, and I sent it to all the sales traders and traders on the
forty-ninth floor. It read something like "This morning, Apple is releas-
ing its earnings. This is what we expect; this is what it did last quarter;
this is how many iMacs it sold; this is how many we predict it will sell."
It was like a little cheat sheet that all the traders had in front of them
ahead of time.

This was the kind of thing a junior analyst could do before passing
the Series 7. It may seem silly and small, but when people saw you doing
it, they thought, *This guy is resourceful. He's trying to think of ways to
help us.*

Another part of my day consisted of learning how to leave good voice
mails for clients. This was my apprenticeship, the way I learned how to
talk about stocks. Every day, I would practice getting the form down:

the voice mail had to be no longer than ninety seconds, and it had to hit four or five key points for the day. What were the big market-moving events? What did the client need to know? What was our view? I learned by listening to a master of the art: Rudy. The reason my rabbi was called the Beast was because he could bang these calls out to more clients than anyone else, always with enthusiasm and thorough market knowledge.

The Beast had a reason for delivering these mini-reports by voice mail instead of e-mail: he felt that the tone of his voice could convey exactly the right emphasis on any given point. Later on in my career, frankly, I started thinking voice mails were stupid. When a client receives a hundred of them in a morning, what are the odds he's going to listen to yours? And in any case, once I started getting to know my clients well, my relationship with them became good enough that they would pick up my call when they saw my number on their Caller ID.

The wagering action on how we first-years would do on the Series 7 definitely ratcheted down a few notches after September 11. Nobody on the trading floor was in an especially feisty mood. Nor was I. Having gotten a glimpse of how hard the test was, I buckled down even more in my studying, to the point where I was scoring 82 and 83 on the practice exams. But it was very difficult finding the motivation to study during this period.

A month after the attacks, the Series 7 test takers went back to One Penn Plaza. Same elevator. Same seventeenth-floor waiting room. Same staff monitoring the test. Same floor-to-ceiling window I'd looked through to see the North Tower on fire. It was a surreal experience. But I was far more prepared for the exam than I'd been the previous time. In a way, I thought then and still think now, it didn't seem very compassionate of Goldman to make us take the test again just a month later. But realistically, there was nothing to be done about it. Our passing it was a practical necessity.

And when I hit the key for my results after I'd clicked on my final answer, there was good news: I'd scored an 86. I was ready to be a sales trader.

Now all I needed were clients.

Gradually, as Rudy developed more faith in me, he started to give me a few of my own. On Wall Street they call them "practice clients"—there isn't much upside for the firm in any interaction with them, but there's not much downside, either. The ideal scenario is when there are junior people on both sides of the call, both trying to learn their way.

In the meantime, my Slovak counterpart seemed to be trying to raise her game. Whenever the phones rang—it was typically the first-year analyst's job to answer phones—she would always try to hit the line first. If I left ten voice mails for clients, she'd leave twelve. It all felt very strange to me: we were both on the same track, and again, I was not a threat to her in any respect.

Or maybe I was.

The previous summer, the firm had taken a Turkish telecommunications company public, and Rudy had needed someone to shepherd the CEO on a visit to some of the big hedge funds and mutual funds that were our clients. He looked me up and down and said, "Springbok, you're going to do this trip." Nicknames were important at Goldman Sachs, and the Beast had honored me with a good one: the springbok is the swift gazelle that's a kind of national mascot in South Africa, the symbol for the country's rugby team.

So there I was, just out of college, and there was this head of a billion-dollar corporation, and it was just the two of us, traveling in California and Texas, with me carrying his bag. He was a slick guy, with slicked-back hair, and you could tell that in his native Turkey he was a big shot. He could have kicked up a fuss about having some junior analyst assigned to him. But I think he felt a bit intimidated by being in America. For one thing, he barely spoke any English. (I spoke even less Turkish.) He had never been to San Francisco or San Diego or San Antonio, the three cities on our itinerary. Oddly enough for someone who'd been in the United States for only four years, I knew a lot more about what was going on than he did.

At first I wasn't sure how much I should speak in the client meetings. Should I keep quiet? Should I kick off each meeting with a few words about the Turkish company? But I soon discovered that the Turkish CEO was grateful for all the help I could give him. And I was learning more every day.

That trip brought a small triumph of another kind: after a day of meetings in San Francisco, I got to return to Stanford and see old friends—not just as an alum but as a Goldman Sachs employee. I was proud to tell people that I was in town on business. Amazingly, it was also the weekend of the Big Game, and we defeated Cal Berkeley, our football archrival, for the seventh consecutive time, 35 to 28. (This winning streak would be reversed horribly in the years to come.) Rudy knew he had done me a solid by sending me on that trip, and I appreciated it.

I went on a couple of other business trips that fall. Rudy used to joke that he was sending me to all these less-than-exotic places such as San Antonio and Dallas because he didn't want to go himself. But I was thrilled to go. When he said, "Springbok, you're off to Columbus, Ohio," I didn't roll my eyes. It was a chance to learn more about my adopted homeland. (Did you know that both Wendy's and Victoria's Secret are based in Columbus? I got a kick out of going to visit the very first Wendy's.) On every business trip, even after I was stationed in London and the firm sent me to Dubai or Frankfurt or Paris, I would try to take a few hours in the evening to find a nice restaurant and sample some of the local culture, even if it made me more tired the next day.

I loved traveling on business and representing Goldman Sachs. It was one of the big benefits of being on such a small team. My French Canadian roommate was on the Canadian Equity Sales team, which had fifteen people. He was not getting sent on business trips at such an early stage. I felt very lucky. The road miles I logged were putting me ahead of the curve for beginning analysts and giving me exposure to lots of clients. The extra experience got me that much closer to an important milestone.

———

Your first trade on Wall Street is a big deal, and mine was a proud moment for me, even though it netted the firm a grand total of $600—probably less than Goldman Sachs spent on soap dispenser refills on any given day. A mutual fund client whom I had been calling daily for about six weeks finally decided to pay me for my efforts and pulled the trigger on buying 500 *little* shares of South African Breweries (SAB). (When you use the term *little* next to a quantity of shares, it indicates that you actually mean only 500, not 500,000, as a trader would assume without such clarification.) But to Rudy's credit, he recognized the significance of the moment, and decided to make a big deal of it.

Rudy was a culture carrier. And he was sufficiently impressed with the gravity of the occasion to want to commemorate it in classic Wall Street fashion: by cutting the trader's tie in two and hanging the snipped-off piece from the ceiling.

The only problem was I wasn't wearing a tie that day.

A bit of background: Salespeople and traders at Goldman Sachs had worn suits and ties up until the late 1990s, but during the tech bubble, Goldman started to compete with Silicon Valley for the best and brightest recruits, and some of the new economy's customs had rubbed off on old Wall Street. (Goldman was ahead of the curve on this: some banks, such as Lehman Brothers, kept their suit-and-tie policy much longer.)

By the time my summer internship started, the firm had changed its dress code from business formal to business casual, and a number of eager interns had gone a bit overboard, with the women wearing short skirts and the guys black disco shirts on the trading floor. It got to the point where Human Resources was forced to send an e-mail around to the entire intern class, reading, "This is Goldman Sachs; this is not Club Goldman."

The following summer, when I joined the firm full-time, a second-year analyst took a few of us new analysts aside for an entrance briefing. "Let me give you guys a little useful advice," he said. "Two words: Brooks Brothers. That's the Wall Street uniform." So, with minor variations, we all paid attention. You went out and bought five pairs of Brooks Brothers khaki dress pants—maybe, if you were daring, you got a pair or two from Banana Republic; maybe a pair or two would be brown instead of khaki—and ten dress shirts in different shades of blue. To this day, some combination thereof is the standard attire among 90 percent of the males on Wall Street trading floors.

Almost all the partners and managing directors, however, wore expensive but understated suits that came from stores such as Brioni, or that had been custom-tailored on Savile Row or in Hong Kong. Hermès or Ferragamo were the standard when it came to ties, scarves, and accessories for men and women. The unwritten rule about how Goldman Sachs partners and MDs were expected to dress: make sure it was understated, in neutral colors, and not too flashy, but also make sure people could tell it was expensive.

A single one of these suits would have cost me more than three months' rent, so I stuck to the two baggy-ish Brooks Brothers suits I had invested in when I joined the firm full time. I would wear these whenever I met with clients—usually about once a week.

But as fate would have it, on the historic day I executed my first trade, the day my severed necktie was supposed to be ceremonially hung from the ceiling, I was dressed in business casual.

Like a good manager, Rudy improvised. From his seat next to mine at the head of a long row of salespeople, he stood up and announced to the few who were watching, "In honor of the occasion, I'm now going to cut your button off." He motioned to me. "Come over," he said. He took my shirt (incidentally, one of the dark blue ones I'd bought for my summer internship) by the collar, cut off the top button, and, to the applause of the onlookers, placed it on top of my computer screen. I shook Rudy's hand firmly.

Rudy then did something I hadn't expected. He took the liberty of sending an e-mail to about twenty-five people on the International Equities trading floor, all the most senior people included. It read, "Today is a big day, and a significant milestone in the career of Springbok. He did his first trade, in South African Breweries. This trade made the firm $600. Please join me in congratulating him and wishing him a long and successful career on Wall Street. In recognition of this special day, instead of cutting his tie, I have cut a button off his shirt." Soon after the e-mail went out, a stream of people, a number of them managing directors, started coming up to my desk, in complete seriousness, to shake my hand. I was being welcomed to the club. It was a proud and happy moment.

Still, there was nothing soft about Rudy Glocker. During my first weeks on the desk, he gave me a copy of Chris Matthews's *Hardball*, with its practical advice on how to succeed in a cutthroat political environment. Rudy was hard-core and liked things punctual, perfect. He hated vulgarity, and kept a curse jar on his desk: you had to put a quarter in every time you swore. Most of all, he detested lateness. Early on, I got into a few situations where I took our research analysts to see clients and, because the clients had extra questions, the meetings ran late, throwing the whole schedule off. Rudy was irate—and was able to make his feelings very plain without a single profanity. I learned to make sure meetings ran on schedule.

This is what made his congratulatory e-mail unexpected and all the more meaningful. He could have just cut my button and put it on the screen and said, "Well done," instead of publicizing my success to the whole trading floor. The traditionalist in him took pleasure in the ceremony, but some part of him enjoyed making an untried kid feel good.

CHAPTER 3

The Springbok Has Landed

One morning in early 2002 Rudy said to me, "Today is going to be a scary day. Some people are going to get their marching orders."

The year 2002 was a tough one at Goldman. The markets were in a state of severe contraction post-9/11, and people were being let go. There was also a worry that Goldman Sachs was just not big enough to compete with banks such as JPMorgan Chase, Citigroup, and Bank of America, which had massive balance sheets and could extend huge loans to corporations in order to win business. Morale in the office was low, and tensions ran high. You could see that your bosses were fearing for their jobs. Many fears were well founded.

Marching orders, I thought. *What a funny expression.* I'd never heard it before. But I knew right away what it meant.

"But don't worry," Rudy said. "Everything will be okay." I took this to mean that our three-person team would remain safe. Then I saw people starting to get called in to the partner's office.

All the offices and conference rooms on the forty-ninth floor had glass walls—you could see exactly what was going on inside, in good times and in bad. In fact, it's true across the board at Goldman Sachs: it's company policy for all offices on Goldman's trading floors around the world to have transparent glass walls.

So I could see right into the office where the partner in charge of the forty-ninth floor sat facing the person about to get the axe. The partner has to do the dirty work himself—has to look the person in the eye and say, "I'm sorry, we're letting you go." Thankfully, I've never heard

53

those words said to me, but they were something that everyone feared those first couple of years after September 11.

Even the partners themselves weren't immune. It was at this point in 2002 that the firm started flushing out a number of the old guard—the pre-IPO partners, some of whom had been at the firm for decades—to make way for the new breed. The newer partners and MDs seemed to carry themselves with a swagger: less understated, more flashy. Less plastic Casio watch, more gold Rolex. It was hard to feel sorry for people worth tens of millions of dollars who were getting the axe, but the traditionalist in me thought that it was sad to be losing people with such long institutional memory. Another thing I noticed: in early 2002 Goldman hired a very senior guy from another firm to run sales. In the pre-IPO, pre-1999 world of Goldman Sachs, a high-level lateral hire would have been considered sacrilege. You were supposed to build your talent from within.

One firing during the bear market stands out in my memory. It was of a guy just out of business school and considered an up-and-comer—he had just been given a whole batch of new clients to start covering. Everyone was surprised he was let go. But on his desk, he was the low man on the totem pole, and therefore expendable. (Wall Street follows a last-in, first-out policy, and Goldman Sachs was no exception.) I clearly remember that when this guy left, he stormed out, his face bright red. Then he stopped by one managing director's desk and made a kind of odd backhanded gesture at him—a flick of the fingers from the forehead. It was a hand signal I had never seen before, but I knew one thing: it was not a friendly goodbye.

We did everything we could to hold on to clients in 2002. Once, I was called on to make a special contribution of my own to the cause.

As I settled into my role as a salesperson on our desk, I began covering some of my own clients—one of whom, to my good fortune, turned out to be a former Stanford classmate and buddy of mine, an Indian guy named Prakash. Small world. Prakash worked in the Boston headquarters of a mutual fund behemoth with hundreds of billions of dollars under management, as a sector specialist in the technology space: his job, as a research analyst, was to tell the rest of his firm what he thought of the stocks in that sector so the company could form an objective opinion—i.e., one not clouded by the advice of Wall Street (in the form of Goldman Sachs, Morgan Stanley, etc.)—on how it should invest its assets.

(Clients such as Prakash's employer liked doing their own stock research because of an inherent conflict of interest within investment banks, one that would ultimately result in a $1.4 billion settlement between the ten biggest banks and the government in 2003. Eliot Spitzer, then the New York Attorney General, led the charge in bringing light to this conflict and sought to install strict separations between investment research and investment banking. Research analysts—who were supposed to be objective in their recommendations to clients—started putting huge valuations on Internet companies that had no apparent earnings, in order to win lucrative investment banking business from the same Internet companies they were writing about in their reports. The result? A massive Internet bubble that ultimately burst.)

Prakash reported to a number of portfolio managers (PMs), who would use his research and opinions to determine whether to buy for their specific funds any of the tech stocks he covered.

At the time, a number of popular and forward-thinking technology companies were Israel-based, and Israel was one of the territories our sales team covered. My job was to advise Prakash on Israeli tech stocks. In the course of business, I'd call him almost every day: it felt quite surreal to be on the phone with a buddy I used to get hammered and go to Stanford Cardinal hoops games with, discussing hot tech stocks such as Check Point Software and Comverse Technology.

Prakash was a hard sell. The technology bubble was still bubbling in Israel, but he took an extremely skeptical view of stocks for which many investors were willing to pay huge sums. It made him (and still makes him) extremely good at what he did.

Eliot Spitzer wasn't alone in his suspicion of investment banks. Prakash used to give me a hard time about the role Goldman had played in the Internet bubble, which had burst while we were seniors in college and before our respective careers in finance began in 2001. I had gotten used to Prakash's inquiring, sometimes cynical, worldview: not just on markets, but on questions like whether Tyrone Willingham was doing a good enough job as Stanford football coach. Prakash could almost have been called a "perma-bear," Wall Street's term for an investor who always sees the glass half empty. Still, some of Prakash's points had given me pause.

In underwriting companies like Webvan and eToys, had the firm been giving them its golden stamp of approval, telling the investing public that it was safe to go into the water? Did the firm's research analysts really believe that these companies were worth billions of dollars, even though they were losing money at the time of their IPOs? Was Goldman doing something highly irresponsible by inflating a bubble: luring investors into subpar companies so that the firm could collect 7 percent in investment banking fees and a big payday when taking the companies public? Prakash was a research analyst himself, and liked cold, hard objectivity. He didn't think Goldman was being objective, or fair to the investing public.

I used to see Rudy ask hard questions of our bankers before pitching deals to clients, but I can't say many other people were doing this. *Even if Prakash has a point*, I thought, *weren't investors also to blame for buying into the hype?* And besides, Merrill Lynch, Salomon Smith Barney, and Credit Suisse were far more egregious about making conflicted recommendations. *This is Goldman Sachs*, I thought. *We may have made some missteps, but we hold ourselves to a higher standard than the other guys.*

Prakash's shop was one of the eight-hundred-pound gorillas of the asset management world—a massive client for all of Wall Street, arguably one of the biggest and most important due to its sheer size and market-moving influence and its ability to pay millions of dollars annually in commissions. So the fact that I had a contact there who was also a buddy—one who was often able to give me a quick scoop on whether his company was bullish or bearish on certain stocks—was a lucky and valuable thing for me. Rudy certainly valued the connection. Once, he and I flew to Boston to play basketball with Prakash and his colleagues in a Goldman Sachs–versus-client matchup—although, Rudy, at six foot five, and Prakash, at about six-two, made me feel as if I were playing a different sport. Every time Prakash came to New York, Rudy encouraged me to take him out for a fancy dinner, on Goldman Sachs's tab, of course. Usually Prakash humored me and let me choose the restaurant; often we went to SushiSamba in the West Village.

One day Rudy happened to let drop that Ted Simpson, one of Goldman's Boston salesmen, had been running an annual Ping-Pong tournament for years for all its clients there. "Oh," I said. "I used to play very seriously growing up."

"How seriously?" Rudy asked, seriously.

"I played on the South African team at the Maccabiah Games," I said. "We won a bronze medal."

Rudy's eyes lit up.

I realize that having been a table tennis phenom may not command the same respect as, say, beating Tiger Woods on the PGA Junior Series or outgunning Roger Federer at Junior Wimbledon, but it seemed to impress Rudy. I started playing at age ten in Johannesburg, with my father, on a fold-up table we had in the garage. We began by just hitting the ball around now and then, but it soon got to a point where we were playing every day after he got home from work. My dad considered himself quite a good player. Within three months, though, I started beating him consistently.

I loved the game and improved quickly. I had also been a serious tennis player for a while, and this helped. I liked hitting the ball hard, and I had an even temperament. There was a table tennis team at the King David School, and I joined it. I ended up winning the school tournament in fifth grade, beating a seventh-grader in the final in a heart-stopping best-of-three-setter, where I came back to win from five match points down with fifty students and teachers watching and cheering. Then my teacher sent me to a club to play league table tennis, and I started getting lessons. I was selected to represent the state team in the national championships when I was thirteen, and I went to the Maccabiah Games in 1993, when I was fourteen.

The Maccabiah Games (sort of a Jewish Olympics) are one of the five largest sports gatherings in the world, bringing five thousand Jewish athletes from more than fifty countries to Israel every four years. Nineteen ninety-three was the first year that South Africa, which had previously been boycotted by international sports federations because of apartheid, was allowed to attend. We took a big contingent to Tel Aviv that year: a couple hundred athletes. It was the experience of a lifetime for me, just past bar mitzvah age and never overseas before.

Playing in the junior-age class, our three-boy team—I was number one in singles—outlasted teams from Argentina, Brazil, Canada, Denmark, Germany, Great Britain, Mexico, and the United States. Israel crushed everybody, and took the gold medal; Australia won silver. My best friend, Lex, had also attended the Maccabiah Games, as goal keeper on the soccer team, and when we got back to King David, we both got special blazers to wear: blue with gold trim.

After hearing of my past sports success, Rudy immediately fired off an e-mail to Ted Simpson, saying, "Springbok will be representing the New York desk at the Ping-Pong tournament."

Simpson wrote back: "Who's Springbok?"

In response, Rudy e-mailed him a photograph of a springbok, the actual animal. You had to be there, but I thought it was hilarious.

So I flew to Boston on Goldman's tab—the justification being that, while there, I could meet with Prakash and talk Israeli tech stocks—and met Ted Simpson.

Ted was a VP in his mid-thirties, a salesman in the mold of Rudy, whom he physically resembled, right down to the bald dome, though he wasn't as tall. Like Rudy, Ted was hardworking and thoughtful; he did what was right for his clients. He had nurtured deep client relationships in the Boston investing community, where the biggest players were (and are) Fidelity, Putnam Investments, Wellington Management, State Street, and The Boston Company. These mutual fund giants are some of the caretakers of Main Street's retirement savings. The culture of Boston was much more geared toward long-term-oriented mutual funds (which managed retail money), as opposed to the high-flying hedge fund world. Simpson's laid-back personality and dry sense of humor were a good fit for the environment in Boston and the type of clients he covered.

The backstory of the annual Goldman Sachs Ping-Pong Tournament, Ted told me, was that the same guy, an Indian portfolio manager from Putnam, had won it five years in a row, and that winning the tournament was the highlight of the guy's year. But from the moment I walked into Jillian's—a pleasure palace replete with free-flowing alcohol, spicy chicken wings, bowling alleys, plasma TVs, and dozens of Foosball, pool, and table tennis tables—and saw my alleged competition practicing, I knew he didn't have a chance against me.

I'm not trying to brag. But competitive table tennis, like every sport, has its levels. Any number of internationally ranked players could have (and had) made mincemeat of me, yet simply put, the Putnam portfolio manager (let's call him PPM) and I were not in the same league. I was confident he wouldn't be able to return my serve, and if it came to a rally, he wouldn't be prepared for the kind of severe spins I could put on the ball. I could see that he was a very good basement player, nothing more. I could have beaten the guy in my sleep.

The tournament draw was posted. Thirty-two people, and PPM was seeded number one. Since the organizers knew I was good, I was the number two seed. Play began.

I was rusty—I'd been working such long hours since joining Goldman that I'd barely picked up a paddle—but I soon remembered my form. And nobody gave me a serious challenge. PPM and I plowed through our halves of the draw, heading toward an inevitable confrontation. I watched a couple of his matches. PPM's opponents were easy pickings: recreational players dressed in jeans and polo shirts. And PPM, looking very professional in his special sneakers and running shorts, T-shirt, and headband, was mopping them up. Of course he'd brought his own paddle—a serious player would never show up without his own stick. And of course I'd brought along my trusty Donic Appelgren blade with Vario rubbers—red on one side, black on the other.

Ted Simpson and I were looking on as PPM took down another pigeon. "So what are we thinking here?" I asked Ted. "I'm going to meet this guy in the final, and if I play properly, I'm going to beat him twenty-one to two. What's the right course of action?"

Ted looked thoughtful. "Well," he said after a moment, "this guy is one of our biggest clients; he takes this stuff really seriously." At that moment, PPM whaled away at a forehand that just clipped the table edge and skipped off, unreturnable; he raised his arms in victory. "We need to make it a close game," Ted said. "Get some good rallies going."

I told Ted I had been thinking along the same lines. That I should beat PPM, because it was obvious I could beat him, but that I should keep it close. Not embarrass him. I knew how to do that, I said. You just make a few unforced errors here and there.

"Hmm," Ted said.

"You have a different idea?" I asked.

"Well, the guy *is* one of our biggest clients," he repeated, giving me a significant look.

"You're suggesting—?"

"Maybe," he said. And then: "Watch for my signal."

I gave Ted a look—he was smiling—and took my Donic out of its case.

The match began. A crowd had gathered to watch us play. Everybody was having fun—except for my opponent, who was taking the match very seriously. When I won a few points in the early going, I could see him getting upset.

So I eased up. I could have really turned on the heat, hit some crazy shots past him that would have whizzed by his ear—but I didn't. My whole plan was to keep the ball in play. To give the crowd a good show, instead of slicing the ball back when PPM smashed it at me, I would lob it up for him so he could smash it again. Smash, lob. Smash, lob. Oohs and ahs from the onlookers. After three or four exchanges like this, I'd either hit it into the net or give PPM such an easy pop-up that he could make a legitimate put-away on me. I was letting him show off for his fellow clients a little bit. He loved it.

He won the first game 21 to 17.

The matches were best two out of three, and my plan was to squeak out a win in the second game, then maybe win by just a little more in the third. But when I was ahead 15 to 12 in the second, Ted Simpson caught my eye. He gave a little shake of the head, and then, using his left hand as a shield, gave a quick thumbs-down with his right. I'm quite sure nobody but Ted and I knew what was going on. I nodded. After all, wasn't putting the client first number one of John Whitehead's 14 Business Principles?

The Putnam portfolio manager was very magnanimous in victory—as was I in defeat.

———

The Ping-Pong tournament was a bright spot in a dark summer. The worldwide recession continued, and emerging markets, a niche area in the best of times, started falling apart. That summer, the sharp-elbowed Slovak analyst on my desk was moved to Goldman's London office to become a European shares sales trader. Now it was just Rudy and me, and the management buzz saw seemed to be headed straight in our direction: the writing was on the wall for Emerging Markets Sales. I knew I needed to find a lifeline—a new job—in order to survive at the firm.

Apparently Rudy had the same feeling about himself. As the summer wound down, he became uncharacteristically secretive, constantly leaving the desk for "private internal" meetings, talking extra softly on the phone. Even though we were partners in crime and sat right next to each other, he wasn't acting much like a partner anymore. I had a pretty good hunch what was going on, a hunch that was confirmed when Rudy turned to me one day and said, "Springbok, I'm moving up to the fiftieth floor, to U.S. Equity Sales, on Monday. I know this is scary, but you're going to be fine. I'll do what I can to help you."

Another colleague on the floor pulled me aside that day and gave me some unsolicited advice that stuck with me for a long time. "Change is scary," he said. "But often change is good. It can lead to new and interesting experiences. Keep your head up and keep an open mind."

In retrospect, I realized what Rudy had been up to: tapping his contacts in the U.S. Equity Sales group with a view to moving there. It was a more stable, less volatile area than Emerging Markets Sales, focused on selling larger and more liquid U.S.-based stocks to U.S. investors. But it was also a bigger playing field, with dozens of salespeople: Rudy was becoming a small fish in a big pond.

But stability was what he was after. All along, he'd been effectively interviewing for a new position, without saying anything about it to me. Part of me thought he should have tried to save the two of us together, by negotiating a "package deal" with the U.S. Equity Sales desk—it wasn't completely uncommon for a VP to change teams along with a "trusted analyst," a sidekick. Maybe it was unfair of me to expect this of him; it's even possible that Rudy tried to negotiate such a deal. I don't know for sure that he didn't. But with all the firings, times were so tough that it isn't surprising that he negotiated his own move first.

Rudy moved up to the fiftieth floor in September 2002. The international group was being decimated. For several years, it had occupied the entire forty-ninth floor; now there simply weren't enough of us left to justify the space. Soon we all went upstairs to fifty, where all Goldman's Equities trading operations were now consolidated. I was the last man standing in my group, which I kept running by myself—calling clients with market ideas and information, setting up meetings. But the buzz saw was still closing in.

I also couldn't stop thinking about the fact that the clock was ticking on my two-year contract. I'd passed my one-year anniversary in July, and I knew that Goldman promoted only about half its analysts to a third year—maybe, in this market, it would be even fewer.

Yet I felt strangely optimistic that I could hustle hard enough to find a new place in the firm before time ran out. Goldman has an annual 360-degree review system in which you pick ten of your colleagues (both senior and junior) to score you from 1 to 5 in a host of categories such as technical skills, teamwork, commercial ability, compliance, and recruiting. HR then tabulates the scores and your manager gives you your numbers and quartile ranking, plus some qualitative feedback. Both my comments and my numbers had been good. I was in the top 25 percent, the top quartile, of analysts.

I felt I had a fighting chance to stay on. It was much the same feeling I'd had as a sophomore at Stanford, when the odds of getting a summer internship in finance were minuscule, but I knew that if I knocked on enough doors, someone would give me an opportunity.

I followed many leads. A lot of them were dead ends—the climate was so bad that people just wouldn't commit to hiring anyone. Then I got an e-mail from a woman I knew in HR, saying, "Corey Stevens is looking for an analyst on the Futures Execution desk. You should go interview with that group."

Futures—I had studied them a little bit in college, but my practical knowledge of the subject was virtually zero.

It was right around this time that I decided to apply for a Rhodes Scholarship. An odd decision, you might think, for someone who had made a commitment to investment banking—and, more to the point, to an investment bank. I still believed in Goldman Sachs, and even in my ability to find a new job in the firm. It was the markets I was worried about. Further deterioration would cause the firings to move up the echelons: no one would be safe.

But more to the point, I was only twenty-three years old. My whole life was still ahead of me, and lives can take many paths. I thought getting a Rhodes would be a great achievement, and could be a terrific experience. I might even be able to go to Oxford for two years and then return to Goldman as an associate, the graduate-level position. A few years earlier I had read David Maraniss's biography of Bill Clinton: I'd been impressed at how Clinton had handled the tough Rhodes Scholarship interview process, and enthralled to learn about his experience at Oxford, where he'd made enduring friendships with Strobe Talbott, who would go on to cover U.S.–Soviet relations for *Time* and then become Clinton's deputy secretary of state; and with Robert Reich, the economist who would serve as Clinton's secretary of labor.

In the meantime, I met with Corey Stevens.

Stevens was an associate who carried himself like someone much more senior: that is to say, with great style and a certain air of mystery that fell just on the cordial side of aloofness. He was an intensely private guy. Well groomed and suavely dressed at all times, he favored custom-made suits and shirts; business casual held no allure for him.

There were seven candidates for the job as Stevens's right-hand man on the Futures Execution desk in Goldman Sachs's Derivatives Sales group. Little did I know that Corey would consult a special, and very famous, adviser the night before the interviews were to take place: an NFL superstar happened to be Corey's half-brother and closest confidant.

Corey would later tell me that his brother got a good feeling from my resume, and for some reason he picked it from the pile of seven. He also apparently got a kick out of the fact that I spoke Zulu.

Well, a little bit, anyway. In the space for "Languages" on my résumé, I'd written: "English, Afrikaans, Hebrew, Zulu (three years)." Which was exactly true. I'd studied Zulu for three years at the King David School in Johannesburg. I could say things such as "Hello," "How are you?" and "The giraffe is running fast."

"What do you know about derivatives?" Corey asked, beginning my interview.

Derivatives are securities that derive their value from an underlying asset. They can be complex, and they have a long and controversial history of creating havoc. But if understood correctly, derivatives can help investors hedge against (or speculate on) very specific risks. The term *derivatives* can be used as a catchall to include products such as options, swaps, and futures. And you can get derivatives on all asset classes: equities, foreign exchange, commodities, fixed income. At Goldman Sachs, derivatives teams were divided by asset class. Corey's Futures Execution desk was a subsector of the broader Derivatives Sales team.

I took a deep breath and told Corey the whole truth. "I did a little bit of it in college," I said. At Stanford I'd taken a course called Economics 140, which dealt with the basics of options, futures, and other derivatives. After my summer internship, I'd taken another course on the subject, in the business school. But it was all theoretical stuff. Once I'd joined Goldman full time, I never interacted with a derivative. The theory of derivatives was kind of rattling around in the back of my head, but I suspected that the practice of trading them was a very different matter indeed. I said as much to Corey.

He smiled a little. He was stocky, on the short side, but powerful-looking. His hair was trimmed closely, as was his goatee. He was wearing what looked like a Hermès tie, knotted under a heavily starched spread collar. "Look," he said. "I didn't know a lot about derivatives either when I started on this desk. If you're smart, you can learn this stuff."

It was a short conversation, but it felt promising. The next morning, the HR person e-mailed me: "Three people made the cut—you're one of them. Corey would like to meet with you again, and have you meet a couple of the people on the desk."

That day, I went by Corey's desk. He had lined up a series of interviews for me with six different derivatives salespeople—mostly VPs and associates. None of the really big guns yet. But less than two years after my summer internship Super Day in San Francisco, it now felt as if I was having another one. Fortunately, I brought a good game. I was honest about my limitations but expressed strong excitement about the product, and a desire to learn. I liked the derivatives salespeople. None of them grilled me: the meetings were mostly about personality, and we got on well.

Afterward, the HR woman e-mailed me again: "You made the cut. One more hurdle—Corey's boss."

CHAPTER 4

The End of Something

Corey's boss was Michael Daffey.

Daffey, still in his mid-thirties, was a rapidly rising star at Goldman Sachs. An Aussie, he was a lateral hire from another bank who began working in Asia for Goldman in the late 1990s. By the time I was a summer intern in 2000, he had come to New York as a vice president; by the end of that year, he'd made managing director. He then became a partner in 2002—an almost unheard-of jump in two years' time.

Daffey was about six foot two and lightly balding, with an athletic build and a friendly, open face. A friend of mine called him the Curiously Tall Guy, for his tendency to slouch in his desk chair and then surprise you with his height when he stood up. He was probably the most charismatic guy on the whole trading floor, universally liked and respected.

A Daffey story: Once Gary Cohn—then the global cohead of the Securities division, later the president of Goldman Sachs—walked onto the trading floor while Daffey was at his terminal, in conference with a genius strategist named Venky, a twenty-five-year-old who'd graduated from the legendary Indian Institute of Technology (IIT). The subject of his and Venky's discussion was a crazy spreadsheet Venky had created: the spreadsheet tracked, in real time, every possible statistic of every player at that year's Masters Golf Tournament. Daffey, who loved to bet on the Masters, was in golf nirvana. "Gary, come over here!" he yelled to Cohn.

The floor went dead quiet. It was like one of those moments in a Western when someone calls out the big gun in the middle of a saloon.

Few people would have had the familiarity or the guts to yell an order at Gary Cohn. But Gary went over.

"Gary, meet Venky. Venky, meet Gary," Daffey said. Towering over the diminutive strategist, Gary shook Venky's hand. "Venky is smarter than you and me combined," Daffey told Gary.

Venky lit up. Daffey had just made his year. Venky then demonstrated to Gary how the algorithm on his spreadsheet worked. Gary was also impressed. "Send me a copy," he said. (Venky would go on, a couple of years later, to be the main brain behind the reinvented VIX volatility index on the Chicago Board Options Exchange. The VIX is widely followed and traded as a gauge of fear in the marketplace.)

A lot of Daffey's popularity stemmed from senior management's sheer awe at his client base, which consisted of the biggest, smartest macro hedge funds in the world. Hedge funds are investment funds that can undertake a wide range of strategies, both going long (buying an asset with the view that it will rise in value) and getting short (selling an asset without actually owning it, betting it will go down in value). Because these funds are not highly regulated, they are open only to very large investors such as pension funds, university endowments, and high-net-worth individuals.

Macro hedge funds—named for their tendency to bet on big-picture events such as movements in interest rates and currencies, as opposed to stock prices—command exceptional respect. Daffey's client portfolio was almost like the Cowboys, the Giants, the 49ers, and the Patriots. He knew all the big guns:

Tudor Investment Corporation, run by southern investing legend Paul Tudor Jones, manages more than $10 billion. Tudor Jones, a billionaire in his own right and usually ranked in the top few hundred wealthiest people in the world, first made his name with his prowess for commodity trading, then developed a stellar track record of generating returns for his investors year in and year out. He founded a charity, the Robin Hood Foundation, which has become one of the foremost innovators in fighting poverty in New York City; it has distributed more than a billion dollars over the last two decades and raises millions of dollars at its annual star-studded benefit.

Moore Capital, founded by Louis Bacon, also a billionaire, and a significant donor to environmental causes, manages assets in the double-digit billions. Bacon got his start by betting correctly both on the 1987 crash and the subsequent recovery. Moore has offices all over the world: in New York, London, Geneva, and Hong Kong, among other locations.

Duquesne Capital was founded by Stanley Druckenmiller of Pittsburgh. Druckenmiller worked for George Soros as the lead portfolio manager at the Quantum Fund, where the two of them famously made $1 billion in 1992 by shorting (betting against) the British pound sterling. Druckenmiller later started Duquesne Capital, where he became one of the most successful hedge fund managers of all time, generating average annual returns of 30 percent and never having a losing year until he voluntarily shut down the fund in 2010. He once tried to buy the Pittsburgh Steelers and has been a major philanthropist, giving hundreds of millions of dollars to foundations that support medical research and education and fight poverty—among them, Harlem Children's Zone and NYU School of Medicine.

Fortress Investment Group is a hybrid investment management firm with both a private equity arm and hedge funds. Michael Novogratz, a former Princeton University wrestler and U.S. Army helicopter pilot, was Daffey's guy here. Novogratz (or "Novo," as he was called) was a pre-IPO Goldman partner. Fortress eventually went public in 2007, and at the time, managed $30 billion in assets.

Daffey developed a strong rapport with these four clients, becoming not only their buddy—he had a high-stakes fantasy football league with all of them for a long time; the proceeds went to charity—but also, in effect, a common link among men who were essentially competitors.

Because these clients knew how smart Daffey was, and understood that he was in the center of this high-powered information flow, it wasn't hard for him to persuade any one of them to do a trade he liked—in massive size. It sometimes took him less than two minutes. He had turned it into an art.

Daffey: "Dude, implied correlation is too high. The markets are normalizing. You need to get short correlation."

Because of his reputation, this was about as detailed as a Daffey sales pitch needed to get. The essence of this hypothetical trade was that stock prices were all moving in unison because of macro fears in the world. Daffey was betting that this correlation would break down and the individual stocks would start dispersing. There is a complicated way you can place this bet using derivatives. But Daffey didn't even need to go that far to explain it.

Client (with a thick southern drawl): "You think so, Michael?"

Daffey: "I know so. Everyone is putting this trade on. It's our highest-conviction idea right now."

Client: "Fine. I'll do half a billion dollars of this trade."

Just like that. I saw it happen any number of times, with any number of trades. When you are talking to a billionaire who runs a multibillion-dollar hedge fund, he can make decisions quickly. Daffey didn't need to go through five layers of portfolio managers. He just went straight to the big guy. This gave him an aura that Lloyd Blankfein (a rising star at the time, later to become CEO of Goldman Sachs) and Gary Cohn loved.

Clients and colleagues alike respected Daffey because he was a rare combination: a charismatic guy's guy with a deep understanding of people, who also happened to be the smartest guy on the floor. Typically at Goldman, people were either very smart and not so adept socially, or they were politicians and schmoozers. Daffey blended all these qualities perfectly, hence his rapid rise to power. I would learn more about his legend later on. At the time, all I knew was that he was an Aussie, a newly minted Class of 2002 partner, and the head of U.S. Derivatives Sales.

When I first met with Daffey, I expected to find a Very Important Person who'd be glancing at his watch as he asked me a few pointed but perfunctory questions. This was how I'd always found very senior Goldman people to be: at best, displaying short attention spans; at worst, inattentive. Instead, Daffey seemed to have all the time in the world for me; he chatted with me as if I were one of his buddies, shutting out the rest of the world—he never checked his BlackBerry or lost focus once. I later realized that he was a kind of social genius: he could be comfortable with absolutely anybody. He passed a test I would learn about years later, in a Goldman Sachs leadership program called Pine

Street: the Onstage/Offstage Authenticity test measures to what extent someone acts and talks the same with the CEO of a corporation as with the mailman or the security guard. Onstage/offstage authenticity is a trait that truly admired leaders display. I was ten levels below Michael Daffey, yet he didn't really seem to care.

He asked me how the Stanford basketball team was looking. He threw a few gibes at me about how much better Australia was than South Africa in rugby and cricket—the rivalry in both sports is ancient and intense. Warmed to the occasion and the company, I teased him right back. "You guys got lucky winning the last cricket World Cup," I said.

"It's not luck, buddy. It's skill," he told me. Then he said, "Dude, tell me—why do you want this job?"

I didn't feel I had to make anything up. I said, "It seems exciting. I like the idea of derivatives. I'm looking for something more quantitative and fast-paced." Emerging Markets Sales had been interesting to me, but often we could be talking about the same stock for days at a time. Derivatives changed by the minute.

"Well, then you've come to the right place," Daffey said, smiling.

———————

I did get the job with Corey, much to my relief. But then there was the pending matter of the Rhodes Scholarship.

I'd submitted my written application in September, not long before my interviews with Corey and Daffey. I then found out that I had made it through to the second round, also known as the state round, of the Rhodes. This involved flying to Johannesburg in November for a two-day evaluation—and to pay a springtime visit to my family. (I had been in the States so long now that I had to remind myself that November in South Africa equals spring.) Despite the interrogation-like atmosphere of my formal panel interview for the Rhodes, which was conducted at a big oval table with me at one end and the eight judges at the other, I felt calm, and afterward I was notified that I was one of three Johannesburg candidates to go on to the final round.

In early December 2002, I flew to Cape Town (on my own dime) for the final interviews, which were conducted by some very high luminaries from South African society: a justice of the Supreme Court and the CEOs of some of the biggest companies in the country. From the first moment, it seemed as though I couldn't say anything right—a palpable scent of disapproval hung in the air, and it centered on my association with the United States.

This was during the lead-up to the U.S. invasion of Iraq, and I could tell at once that all the Rhodes judges, and particularly the justice, were critical of the U.S. response to the 9/11 attacks. America, they all agreed, was rattling its sabers, and worse, it meant to take the sabers out and use them. It was an imperialist power on the order of ancient Rome, bent on a foreign policy of colonization. Someone at the table actually said this to me.

I disagreed—passionately. I had experienced 9/11 personally, I told the judges; I had keenly felt its terror and heartbreak. The United States had to hunt down the perpetrators and punish them. How could the judges extrapolate from an understandable wish for justice to imperial longings? I loved America, I said. It was far from perfect, but unlike so much of the rest of the world, it was a land of optimism and possibility. I had prospered there, academically and professionally, and I was grateful.

The judges looked sideways at one another, with narrowed eyes. In the end (my high school principal found out from some of the people on the judging panel), I had ruffled too many feathers. Four of ten South African candidates were selected as Rhodes Scholars; I was not one of them.

It was a big disappointment. At the same time—maybe it's my Jewish upbringing—I tend to think that things happen for a reason. I had an important new job to do, and I was ready to do it. On December 16, 2002, five days after I turned twenty-four, I went to work for Corey Stevens on the fiftieth floor of One New York Plaza.

———————

Moving up from the forty-ninth to the fiftieth floor was a little like being called up to the Major Leagues from Triple-A baseball. If forty-nine was like a camping trip to Yosemite, fifty was like being thrown into the middle of the Amazon jungle with just the clothes on your back and no survival guide. Back in Emerging Markets Sales on forty-nine, I'd mostly spent my days phoning institutional clients and talking stocks—the action moved steadily but fairly slowly, because the job wasn't particularly transaction-oriented. On the Emerging Markets Sales desk, I'd had two computer screens; in my new chair, right next to Corey's on the Futures desk, I had four screens. I had wanted something fast-paced, and I would get exactly what I wanted.

Multiple computer screens aside, the fiftieth floor at One New York Plaza was not the kind of gleaming, sterile environment you might see in the Hollywood version of a trading floor. In fact, Goldman's trading floor was, in the early 2000s, borderline shabby: people's desks were piled with crumpled paper, takeout containers, and empty soda bottles; the gray carpet was threadbare and stained. Sterility was not on the program. The five or six hundred people on the floor were packed in like sardines, cheek by jowl, desk by desk. You were right on top of other people's family photos, sports memorabilia, private phone conversations, and lunch smells. You had no privacy, so you had better get to like the person who sat next to you.

The Futures desk was smack in the middle of a rectilinear array of twenty-eight derivatives salespeople. Corey and I sat next to each other at the end of one row, positioned centrally to make it easy for the salespeople around us to yell out trades for us to execute. Two rows of seven salespeople extended lengthwise in front of us, and two additional rows of salespeople sat directly behind us, only positioned crosswise, so they were looking directly at the backs of our heads. The best thing about the chaotic layout was that the men's restroom was about ten steps from my desk. I loved having the easy access.

Each row contained a different derivatives sales pod, and the pods were classified according to the types of clients they covered. There were teams that covered macro hedge funds, long/short hedge funds, asset managers, mutual funds, pension funds, insurance companies, and Canadian-based clients. Every team had different intricacies and personalities, and Corey and I handled the futures business for all of them.

That first day, a Tuesday, the very first thing Corey did was call up Goldman's guys on the Chicago Mercantile Exchange, Patrick Hannigan and Bob Johnson, and say, "I want to introduce you guys to Greg Smith; he's going to be my right-hand man. Please treat him well as he gets up the curve."

Chicago, as a city, has a prominent place in Goldman Sachs lore. Some of the firm's most successful leaders—a disproportionate number—have come up through the Chicago office. Just to name a few: Hank Paulson, former Goldman CEO and U.S. treasury secretary; Bob Steel, former Goldman vice chairman and then CEO of Wachovia; and Byron Trott, who became known as "Warren Buffett's favorite banker." John Thain was born near Chicago, and Jon Corzine studied there. For info on these last two guys, Google "$68,000 antique credenza" and "MF Global debacle," respectively. My connection to Chicago? Most of my family now lives there, and I think it's a great town.

In the early 2000s, before electronic trading of futures became more mainstream, most of our client futures business was executed in the pits of the Merc (as the Chicago Mercantile Exchange was familiarly known), so we relied on Patrick and Bob's accuracy, knowledge of the markets, and ability to execute quickly and seamlessly, all of which made us look good in front of our clients. These two guys had the safest hands in the business.

Hannigan and Johnson, Corey told me, were lifers at Goldman, and I came to see them as the moral center of the Derivatives desk. Both were warm, humorous, solid: family men. Patrick—in his mid-forties then, with a shaved head—was brilliant, quirky, and exceptionally well read. Bob, known as "the Captain" because of his leadership of the desk, was a little older, gray-haired and charismatic, and a stickler for honesty and accuracy.

The Merc, as I would soon discover from direct experience—it was a tradition for junior analysts to be sent to Chicago to see one of the last relics of old-fashioned trading in the financial world—still operated exactly as trading pits had operated since time immemorial, on the open-outcry system: with eye contact and hand signals and shouting instead of computer keyboards and terminals.

It was a totally transparent kind of trading, and as the facilitators of the trades, Patrick and Bob were also totally transparent—they wanted nothing more than to make the clients happy. There was absolutely no trickery to the way their business worked. Their reputation was based on a simple claim: nobody could handle a client's order better, represent the client in the pit better, than Goldman Sachs. Patrick and Bob would fight hard for you, they'd get you the best price, and they'd represent you proudly and well.

Equally important, once Patrick and Bob took you under their wing, once they liked you, they would take significant steps to look out for you and make you look good. They were also inveterate coiners of nicknames for all the derivatives salespeople they dealt with in New York. I had once been Springbok, but Springbok got shot, stuffed, and mounted after Hannigan and Johnson had tested my mettle: with them, I became "Gregor MacGregor," spoken with a Scottish burr. Why? Besides the play on my first name, they probably just liked the way it sounded.

They bestowed other monikers with similar logic. An Indian salesperson named Nitin—six-two and kind of tough-looking, and a great favorite with the ladies—became Nitin the Kitten. Then there was a six-foot-three redhead who, for no apparent reason, Patrick and Bob dubbed Cocoa—because he'd traded some cocoa futures? Maybe, maybe not. In any case, that guy *hated* being called Cocoa. Another tall associate—six-five this time—became known as the Mullet because of his big mop of hair.

Sitting a few seats from me was a guy they called the Jewish John Kennedy; they were referring to JFK *Jr*. This guy, Bobby Schwartz, was a year older than me, clumsy, and prone to making occasional trading errors, but highly book-smart and gifted with a photographic memory. Bobby had an uncanny (and irritating) ability not to have to pick up girls—they would simply walk right up to him and introduce themselves. I didn't believe it until I saw it happen.

Worse, though, would have been to have no nickname at all. Not being christened by the guys at the Merc was a bad sign. Typically, the people who didn't get nicknames were junior analysts who Hannigan and Johnson could tell early on were not going to make it. People who made million-dollar errors right and left. Walking disasters. As I would quickly see, derivatives were highly leveraged products: you were borrowing money for your bet, so returns or losses were greatly multiplied. If you mistakenly said "Buy" instead of "Sell," or got the quantity wrong, you could rack up huge errors. First- and second-year analysts did this all the time, out of sheer carelessness. So before the Merc guys started joking around with you or bestowed a nickname on you, you had to prove you could be accurate. And accuracy meant survival.

My new education commenced. (I was also, at this time, studying for the Series 3 Derivatives exam—another regulatory requirement now that I would be trading derivatives.) Corey began our first lesson about three steps ahead of me, assuming that I understood trading terminology. "Please assume I know nothing," I told him. "Start from the very beginning."

So, at 7:00 A.M., before the trading day began, or at 6:00 P.M., after it ended, Corey and I would spend hours going over everything. The first priority, he told me, was to use the right terminology. Don't fudge. Don't say something that's 80 percent correct. Say it 100 percent correctly at all times. "No ambiguity, no errors" was his mantra. Over and over again he said, "This stuff needs to come to you cold."

One way I learned at first was to listen in on Corey's client phone calls.

This was common practice for apprentices. Everybody on the desk had what was called a trading turret, a big rectangular phone bank with several rows of buttons and a small screen on which you could make, receive, and prioritize calls to and from clients and to the exchanges. Some of the buttons gave you direct connections to major clients such as T. Rowe Price or Fidelity or Wellington; some were the salespeople's private lines; some connected to brokers such as Hannigan and Johnson at the Mercantile Exchange. (Theirs was a particularly popular line to listen in on. Not only could you hear the big trades that were going through, but you could also catch up on the latest gossip: who had gotten the most banged up at the holiday party, which management changes were coming, how bonuses were looking. A lot of this information seemed to flow through the guys in Chicago.)

Each salesperson had two phones: one was a handset and one was an earpiece or a headset. Anytime Corey was on with a client, he would point it out to me, and I would push the Mute button on my phone and pick up the line. I would listen in on his client conversations, and then, at the end of the day, I would ask about everything I hadn't understood. Wall Street lingo, I saw right away, was not intuitive. "Hit your bid"? "Lift your offer"? I asked Corey for a refresher course.

A bid, he reminded me, is how much someone is willing to pay for something. An offer is how much someone is willing to sell something at. The way the markets work, he said, is that every security has a bid and an offer. Say there's a stock I'd be willing to buy for $50 a share and willing to sell at $55. When a client asks, "What's your market?" the correct response is "My market is $50 bid at $55 offer"—or "50 at 55," for short. Then the client will think about it. Let's say he wants to sell. He'll say, "I hit your bid," which means he sells it to me at $50. Or let's say he decides he wants to buy it. He'll say, "I lift your offer," which means he buys it from me for $55.

And then there were the hand signals.

Even though the Goldman Sachs trading floor had become completely computerized by the time I arrived, salespeople and traders there (and on Wall Street generally) instinctively still used hand signals the same way the traders at the Chicago Mercantile Exchange used them: to indicate "I lift your offer" (the buyer's open hand moving toward himself, closing into a fist) or "I hit your bid" (the seller's open hand moving away from himself, then closing into a fist). When you first walk onto the floor of the Merc, Corey said, it'll look like chaos, but in fact it's a very orderly system. People will be buying and selling futures contracts through eye contact and hand signals.

Since I'd spent my first year and a half at Goldman Sachs dealing only with plain-vanilla stocks, Corey had a lot of work to do to get me up to speed on my newly adopted product. Futures, he contextualized for me, were the original form of derivatives, going back hundreds of years, to farmers who needed to protect their crops against droughts, rainstorms, and uncertainty of demand. In order to hedge themselves, the farmers would make deals with their buyers. Instead of taking the risk that their wheat could be worth $100 a bushel when they needed to sell it, or $200, or as little as $20—they would lock in a price of, say, $120 per bushel for future agreed-upon delivery. They were taking a gamble by setting a price now that might be too low, but hedging against the risk of being unable to sell all their crop in the future.

So futures contracts started out with the whole gamut of commodities—where you might have to take actual physical delivery of things such as wheat, milk, orange juice, pork bellies; gold, silver, iron ore. Then people started thinking, "Well, we can apply this to anything. Let's apply it to stocks." So there then arose stock index futures: you could implement your viewpoint on where the S&P 500—or the DAX, in Germany; or the FTSE (pronounced "footsie"), in the United Kingdom; or the CAC, in France—would be in the future. There were also interest rate futures and foreign-exchange futures. The introduction of futures on other asset classes led to more speculation, but also provided more avenues for investors to hedge their risk.

In any derivatives market (or almost any market, for that matter), investors are divided into two groups: hedgers (people who have a genuine use for the product, or who are looking to protect themselves) and speculators (in other words, bettors who are taking a view—looking to monetize their opinion). Who would take the other side of the hedgers' trades, Corey asked, if speculators didn't exist? The existence of both hedgers and speculators, he said, kept markets smooth, efficient, and liquid. It matched buyers up with sellers.

Corey explained that half the business on our desk was in equity index futures such as the S&P 500 or NASDAQ contracts. Of the other 50 percent, some was in commodity futures such as grains, orange juice, and pork bellies, and the rest was in currencies and interest rates: people betting on the future price of government bonds, or the dollar, the yen, or the euro.

As an early on-the-job training exercise, Corey had me start sending the rest of the derivatives desk informational e-mails about flows (the daily buying and selling done by clients) and trends we were seeing in the marketplace. It was a great training device, because it forced me to try to draw themes from the flow we were executing. It also gave me some early visibility to other people on the desk before I was allowed to trade. Sometimes just getting simple but reliable information in front of people can be quite powerful. A typical e-mail, on a day when we were seeing a lot of buying of technology, selling of crude oil, and two-way flow of German index futures, might read:

> *Today we have been active in tech—2:1 better buyers of NASDAQ March futures (ticker: NQH3); in commodities we are 5:1 better to sell in March crude futures. Over in Europe we are seeing heavy two-way flow in March DAX. We have seen a mix of activity from both fast money [hedge funds] and asset managers [institutional investors]. Please call the desk with any questions.*

Corey vetted the e-mails at first, but then he came to trust my attention to detail. Next up was learning to execute my own orders.

It was mid-January 2003, 6:30 A.M. The phones were already ringing: clients wanted to trade. The markets had been open in Europe for a few hours already; the Asian markets were closing. By now I had started speaking to clients, writing up order tickets, and executing client trades. At the beginning, Corey would stand behind me, watching and listening as I executed the orders in our trading system, which was called Spider. He checked my tickets to make sure I was writing them up correctly.

The tickets were triplicate forms about the size of a Starbucks napkin, with carbon paper between the sheets: the original was white; the middle copy, pink; the bottom copy, blue. Each ticket had a line down the center: the section on the left was marked "Buy"; the section on the right, "Sell." Whenever a client called in, you immediately pulled out a ticket and waited for the order. Once it was given, you wrote the name of the future (or option) on either the left or the right side of the ticket, depending on whether it was a purchase or a sale, along with the size of the trade. Then you quickly inserted the ticket into the time stamp, a machine similar to a time clock a factory worker might use.

Time-stamping the ticket immediately was important: you needed an exact record of when you took the order from the client. Then you time-stamped it again when the trade was executed. That way, if the market was volatile—if it moved significantly in or against the client's favor—you would have a paper trail to show that you had represented the client well and given the best possible execution. If a client gave you an order at 3:15 P.M. and you didn't execute it till 3:45, and the market had moved 100 ticks (one tick being the smallest increment a futures contract can move) in those thirty minutes, you could have a big error on your hands.

The tickets piled up throughout the trading day. At the end of every day, after you'd stamped all your tickets—when you got the price for the trade, you'd write that on the ticket as well—you pulled out the middle copy of each ticket to keep as a record, and sent the original and the back copy to the Compliance department, where they were kept in a vault for five years in case there was ever a client dispute or a regulatory investigation.

Then, very early the next morning, another trading day would begin. It was controlled chaos. The phones rang all day with client calls; meanwhile, my fellow derivatives salespeople on the fiftieth floor would stand and yell out orders to Corey and me, instinctively using the appropriate hand signal for "buy" or "sell." And not just traders: Michael Daffey—loving the theater of getting in the trenches with the rest of the troops (and gaining the respect of junior employees who saw that the boss was not above doing the actual work, and knew exactly how to do it)—might shout, "Greg Smith, buy me two thousand June S&P futures!" An order of two thousand contracts may not seem especially big, but it represents approximately half a billion dollars in equity market exposure, which shows how risky and leveraged futures can be. And everyone knew that if Daffey was doing the order himself, it must be for Tudor Jones, Druckenmiller, Soros, Novogratz, Bacon, or some other hedge fund icon. Daffey loved the showmanship of it all and yelled louder than everyone else.

When there was an order, I'd pick up the phone, call Patrick Hannigan or Bob Johnson in the Mercantile pit, and stay on the line with him. I'd say, "All right, where are the June S&P futures trading? I have two thousand, total, to buy, but I need to work these carefully." Then I would rely on Patrick or Bob's description of how the crowd in the pit was. Were they getting aggressive? Should we slow down or should we speed up? I'd give him instructions accordingly: "Buy me a hundred. Buy me another hundred with a nine-fifty top. Hold off." You wouldn't want to buy all two thousand at once, or else you'd reveal your hand to the crowd too quickly—an order of that magnitude could scare the market, create panic, or cause all the traders in the pit to start trading against you. Meanwhile, two other phone lines were ringing...

The protocol when you were on the phone with a client and another, more important client called on the other line was to give a hand signal to whoever had picked up the call. Say Fidelity was on the line and you wanted them to hold while you quickly finished up the call you were on: the correct signal was to hold up an index finger, as in "Just a moment." If you couldn't get off and wanted to call them back, the signal was to twirl the finger. One day early on, when I was on two lines at once and feeling a little overwhelmed, a third call came in and I gave the callback signal—except that I twirled my whole arm instead of just the one finger. To a couple of the more senior people who found this hilarious, particularly the Mullet, my exaggerated hand move became known as "the helicopter."

Then, one morning, I made a real mistake.

It was 6:30 A.M., I was busy drinking my coffee, but effectively still half asleep, when a pension fund client called with a tiny order: "Please buy seven front-month DAX futures," the client said. But, by mistake, I *sold* seven futures. It's a very easy error to make: you just click the Sell button instead of the Buy button. I knew right away what I had done, and I moved fast. A big thing that analysts are taught is that the quickest way you can blow yourself up is by not knowing when to ask for help. You need to be able to swallow your pride and say, "Look, I'm in trouble. I need help quickly."

So I turned to Corey, who was on the phone next to me, and signaled calmly but firmly that I needed him right away. He hung up. "I've sold these instead of bought them," I said. "What do I do now?"

Corey was as calm as he always was. One of the first things Corey and I had learned about each other was that, despite the big differences in our backgrounds, we shared an ability to be serene in high-stress situations. He got out of his chair, stood behind me, and put his arm on my shoulder. Then he pointed to the screen and said, very coolly, "All right, let's get out of this. Let's buy these back." We did it together. We triple-checked everything. We covered the error, traded out of it, and put the correct trade on. In all that time—it seemed like ten minutes but was probably one—the market had moved only one tick.

The error had cost Goldman Sachs $80.

Had the market moved one percent, it could've been $8,000. A few more percent, $80,000. But an error was an error. I apologized. I wanted Corey to be proud of me, and my apology was sincere. He was kind but firm. "It's all right," he said. "Everything is going to be fine. We've learned a lesson from this. Now you need to write the error memo."

"Do I need to tell Daffey?" I asked.

Corey nodded. "Go to his desk and tell him."

I did. Daffey listened carefully as I recounted, seriously and apologetically, the story of the eighty-dollar error. "Thanks for telling me, dude," he finally said. "Just don't do it again."

As I thanked him, I saw that he was barely suppressing a smile. "Don't worry about it," he said.

But I wasn't smiling. I was determined never to make the same mistake again.

There were analysts who had to have that conversation with Daffey under much less pleasant circumstances. I remember a specific situation where the error was $1 million. Much worse than $80.

It happened in a way that's any derivatives salesperson's worst nightmare: when you realize your error only the next day. Let's say a client—for example, a pension fund manager based in Kansas—tells you, "Overnight, when the French market opens, I want you to buy ten CAC futures." You execute the order, then you get in the next day and realize that instead of buying ten, you bought a thousand. On Wall Street this is known as a "fat finger." Instead of hitting the zero once, you hit it three times.

The analyst in question comes in the day after fat-fingering the buy by a factor of a hundred to find that, overnight, the European Central Bank raised interest rates and the market moved 5 percent. The client's position is now out $1 million. The client is never going to accept this, obviously, so Goldman Sachs has to write the client a check for $1 million. Because it wasn't the client's fault. It was Goldman's fault.

Now, the analyst to whom such a thing happened was not fired for making that mistake. In fact, almost every analyst makes some major error at some point in his first few months. If he does it two or three more times, it's a different story.

My eighty-dollar error turned out to be the last one I made—in my career.

I've always been finicky about detail; Corey taught me to be paranoid. "It's better to get something right, and take ten seconds longer, than to be quick," he told me. "If the client starts getting annoyed that you're taking too long, just tell them you're taking the time to get it right. Always triple-check—check it once, check it twice, get it right."

Corey taught me to think and act like a trader: quickly but carefully. It was critical, for example, to understand the multipliers that were used to calculate the notional value (total financial exposure) of a futures contract. Corey drilled it into my head: *always triple-check multipliers with clients*. Did they understand that what they were trying to buy or sell was worth $1 billion? Or had they multiplied their contract incorrectly? It had been known to happen.

Corey introduced me to all the brokers we used in the different futures pits—besides the Merc, there was the Chicago Board of Trade, the Chicago Board Options Exchange, the American Stock Exchange (AMEX), the Pacific Exchange on the West Coast—and to the various people I'd be interacting with on the Derivatives desk and across our own trading floor at One New York Plaza. It was a lot to learn.

After I'd been on the job a few weeks, the perimeter of one of my computer screens was almost completely covered with green Post-it notes listing all these facts and names—anything I would need to remember: the closing times for each market in Europe and in Asia; the multipliers for each futures and options contract; the phone number of our broker in the foreign exchange pit. Details were exceptionally important, and I needed to have them at my fingertips in order to do well at this job.

Soon my terminal was so covered with Post-its that I could barely see the screen anymore: I told myself I had to come up with some system to remember all these details. But ultimately there was no system; I learned by hearing and observing and remembering, day in, day out. One by one, the Post-its came off.

―――――

With the memory of the eighty-dollar error fresh in my mind, I began to pride myself on my reliability and accuracy. Corey, who had a reputation for not making mistakes, began to refer to me as his "franchise pick"—a football term I didn't understand at the time but grew to appreciate. The two of us became known around the floor as the guys who, if you needed to put the ball in someone's hands in the final stretch of the game, were not going to screw it up under pressure.

The athletic comparisons are apt. Corey had been a point guard on his college basketball team. He and I had so much volume coming in at all times that it was like constantly having a hundred balls in the air. You had to prioritize continuously. What was most important: to execute this trade, to give the client the price, or to reply to the e-mail from the Operations department to book the trade? The phone kept ringing, and it was just the two of us, stamping tickets all day long. By the end of each day, we'd have a stack a foot high.

The use of futures and options tickets was almost laughably archaic, like something you might've seen on Wall Street before World War I, but the equities industry demanded them for compliance purposes. We became masters at handling them. Some people struggled to tear out the middle copy; we prided ourselves on being able to rip it out flawlessly every time without even thinking about it. Some people made a mess of jamming the triplicate forms into the very thin slot of the time stamp; now and then, when things slowed down a little, Corey and I would try to top each other at the Zen of time-stamping, the goal being to insert a ticket then pull it out—zip!—in one swift and seamless motion.

Someone always has to rain on your parade, though. Lloyd Blankfein, who in early 2003 was a vice chairman who oversaw the FICC (Fixed Income, Currency and Commodities) and Equities divisions, used to like to cruise by Derivatives Sales to say hello to Daffey and hear the latest buzz about his pals Jones, Bacon, and Druckenmiller. Lloyd wanted to know, "What's the smart money doing?"

One day he stopped at my desk and raised an eyebrow. "What is it with these tickets you guys are using?" he asked. "In the FICC world we don't use tickets anymore."

It was true—Lloyd Blankfein's side of the world had gone electronic a few years before. Corey and I told him that was just the way it went in the old-fashioned world of Equities.

After I'd been on the desk for about a month and a half, Corey looked me in the eye and said, "You're doing very well—time to throw you in the fire."

What he meant was that he'd decided to take a day off and let me handle the whole trading book without him. He had taught me a lot, but he knew I would learn quickest by facing the chaos alone. I had passed that threshold where, even though things could still go horribly wrong, he thought I was ready. Going it alone would test my stamina and concentration and, if I made it through unscathed, give me a big shot of confidence.

I was both nervous and excited about this opportunity. Between the two of us, Corey and I had been executing about 150 trades a day. His taking a day off wasn't going to diminish the flow. But the competitor in me was ready for the challenge.

I really had no idea what I was in for.

I got in at 5:30 that morning, an hour early, to deal with orders from our Asian offices, where it was the end of the trading day. There were at least twenty e-mails in my in-box from my counterparts in Tokyo, Hong Kong, and Sydney, many with messages such as "For the Sydney Teachers Retirement Fund, I need you to buy 250 NASDAQ futures on the close."

I shook my head. Which close? The U.S. close? The Asian? The futures? The cash market? Corey and I had tried to train these guys to be very specific about what they meant, but they didn't always stick to the script. And he had taught me that if they could hold an error against you, they would, because they wanted to offload all their risk on you. I would wake these guys in the middle of the night if necessary to get them to clarify their instructions. Better to get it right than to be sorry later.

At 7:00 A.M., everyone in our whole section of the floor had a conference call to discuss the business for the day. What were the catalysts? What were the things we needed to focus on? What ideas could we be calling clients about? Each person took a quick turn, giving a little spiel on what he or she thought.

Then, when the bond market opened at 8:20 A.M., it was all hands on deck—except that I was the only hand on deck.

Within seconds, three phone lines were ringing at once. They didn't stop ringing all day. Between 8:20 A.M. and 4:30 P.M. on that day at the end of January 2003, I ate nothing; I drank nothing. I never had time for a bathroom break.

I barely noticed. I was operating at hyper-speed, all my senses engaged, 100 percent focused. It was what I imagined a Zen state might feel like: three phone lines ringing at the same time, and someone on the floor yelling at me, "I need to buy $200 million of Treasury Bond futures!" and another client waiting for his price back, and Patrick Hannigan calling me to try to give me the price...

Don't make a mistake, don't make a mistake, don't screw anything up.

I had to keep concentrating, making sure that I was writing everything down, that I wasn't forgetting anything. The worst thing you could do was to forget to execute an order. That could cause a million-dollar error as quickly as any fat finger.

I had to keep listening, hard, because everyone was in a hurry. Corey had drilled into me that when people were in a rush, you needed to slow them down, because if they gave you an incorrect instruction in haste, they would try to blame it on you. If someone said, "Buy me a thousand

Microsoft June 30 call options," I would say, "All right, you want to buy a thousand Microsoft June 30 call options, is that right?" Then they would have to say, "Yes, that's right," and then, and only then, would I execute the trade.

Between 8:20 A.M. and 4:30 P.M., time vanished. I had never in my life done anything that stretched me to that capacity.

And at the end of the day, I hadn't made a single mistake. I was as exhilarated as if I'd sprinted across the finish line at a marathon.

———

Just before 4:10 P.M. on Thursday, August 14, 2003, a ferociously hot day in New York City, the overhead lights on the Goldman Sachs trading floor flickered. A moment later, they flickered again—the only evidence that a massive power blackout had taken down much of the northeastern United States. At no point did our terminals go off; the Goldman backup generator had kicked in seamlessly. A minute or two later, we were able to see, on CNBC (which broadcast constantly on monitors around the trading floor) and on Bloomberg (on our terminals), what had happened. Both news outlets immediately interrupted their usual scrolling ticker of headlines with a frozen headline in red type reading, "POWER OUT IN VARIOUS PARTS OF THE NORTHEAST... AWAITING REPORTS FROM FEMA..."

It was a spooky moment. September 11, 2001, was less than two years in the past; the United States had just invaded Iraq that spring; and we were on the fiftieth floor of one of the tallest buildings in downtown Manhattan. Oddly, it was the end of the summer internship program: I was mentoring a number of the interns who were spending time at my desk. They looked scared. I told them to get out of there. People were rushing for the elevators. Some ended up taking the stairs because they were nervous about what was going on.

The timing of the event couldn't have been stranger. For one thing, it happened to be one of those relatively rare days when Corey was out of the office: I was the sole person on the entire six-hundred-person trading floor responsible for trading the futures contracts. For another, the futures markets were about to close temporarily, as they did every day between 4:15 and 4:30 P.M., for bookkeeping purposes on the Mercantile Exchange. When people want to react quickly in the markets, they don't trade individual stocks or bonds—they buy or sell futures contracts, because these are the most liquid, transparent things you can trade. Between 4:15 and 4:30, investors were going to be forced to take a time-out. The market was closed.

At this moment, people began reacting very quickly. Even between 4:10 and 4:15, I could see on my screen that futures were ticking down: investors were selling. On Wall Street, the way traders gauge how people are perceiving any major event is by looking at the futures. If the futures are tanking, it means that the market is really scared. This market was scared. The phones were starting to ring: clients calling. "Are you guys going to be there if we need to do something when the markets reopen at four thirty?" they were asking. "We really need you to stick around," they said.

An announcement began to blare, over and over, on the PA system: "Please evacuate the building in an orderly fashion..." But almost everybody had already left. There was blood in the water; it was important that someone stay. By 4:30, Michael Daffey and I were two of the few people remaining on the fiftieth floor; the trading floor had become a ghost town.

I had spoken to several clients during the futures closure, and they were talking about executing big trades—really big trades—when the markets reopened. Everybody was selling: shorting the markets, betting that the blackout was some sort of terrorist attack. One client in particular, a hedge fund, wanted to execute a significant-size trade: $2 billion in S&P futures. Yet he wanted to make the sale through a product that was not very liquid—what is called a "big futures contract" instead of an "E-mini." The big contracts were five times the size—worth $250,000 per contract versus an E-mini at $50,000—and they were clunkier. E-mini contracts were created to give investors the ability to be nimbler and to trade in smaller increments, and they were available to be traded around the clock electronically. It was as if the client were planning to make his escape by car and had a choice between an old, dilapidated Toyota and a brand-new Lexus. In effect, the client was say-

ing, "I want to drive this old Toyota because we're really used to it."
Yet we knew, as experts, that he'd be much better off driving the Lexus.
He'd be able to weave in and out of traffic more nimbly, he would get
to his destination quicker, and the safety mechanisms on the Lexus were
much better. That was the difference. The client wanted to trade a product that he was accustomed to but that was not very functional; and the
trade was going to wreak all sorts of havoc on the markets, which in the
end would be bad for him. I needed to get a partner involved.

I went to Daffey's desk, which was probably twenty yards from mine,
and said, "The market's about to open, this client wants to sell two
yards [billion] of S&P futures, but he wants to do the wrong contract.
I've been adamant with him—I've told him that it's not in their interest,
and that they're going to move the market much more doing it in the
big contract rather than the mini."

Daffey completely agreed with me. "Let's call this guy," he said.

Daffey didn't know the client, so we called him together. "Look,"
Daffey told him. "This is Michael Daffey; I'm the partner who runs
Derivatives, and it's not in your interest to trade the big futures—you're
going to crush the market. You're going to trade E-minis."

The guy was nervous, but he was hearing the voice of authority, so
he put up no fight. "Okay," he said.

But Daffey wanted the guy to formally acknowledge the trade. "Do
you understand you're selling two billion dollars of futures in the E-mini
contract?"

"I acknowledge," the client said.

———

Daffey and I could have left the building at 4:30 along with everyone
else. We could also have let the client execute the trade the way he
wanted to in the first place. As futures traders, we were acting as agents
(who work strictly on commission) rather than principals (who take the
other side of the client's trade using the firm's money), so we would
have made a similar (not very large) commission either way. The reason we stayed is because we wanted to prove to the clients that we'd be
there for them if they needed us. We thought it was the right thing to

do. And we'd convinced this particular client to change his contract because it benefited him, not us.

The market reopened at 4:30, down a couple percent from the close, and I executed the trade with little market impact. The client felt he had done the right thing, and so did we.

————

I did about ten trades in the next half hour, all with jittery clients looking to short the markets, all for smaller but still relevant amounts: between $50 million and $500 million in notional value. At around 5:00, the phones stopped ringing. Daffey stopped by my desk. "I'm going to get out of here," he said. "You really should, too." Nobody knew yet what had caused the blackout. But by now the air-conditioning on the fiftieth floor had gone off. It was starting to get hot.

Everything in my body was telling me to leave, but my mind was telling me to stay. Corey had drilled into me, with those 150 trades we were doing daily, that it was essential to take a full hour at the end of every day, even when you were exhausted (and you were always exhausted) to triple-check each trade, one by one, to make sure you weren't ambushed the next day with a problem you hadn't spotted. The worst thing that could happen would be to come in the next day to find you'd left off a zero, or put in one too many, and you had a million-dollar problem on your hands.

I finished up by 5:30. Before I left, I called my biggest two or three clients and said, "I'm leaving now; is there anything else you need?" They said, "No, we're out of here, too." I was the last person on the fiftieth floor; it was now very hot. *Time for me to get out of here as well*, I thought.

I sent Michael Daffey an e-mail confirming everything I'd done since 4:30. "Client sold $2 billion; it went smoothly; these are the other trades," I wrote, summarizing everything else. "I'm going to head out now."

He e-mailed me back: "Great job, dude; you went the extra mile," he said. "If you need a place to go, a few people are coming to my place in Tribeca."

But at that point, I had no desire to socialize with anybody from work. I just wanted to get the hell out of there and go home.

————

The elevators weren't working, so I walked down all fifty flights of stairs. The stairwell was sweltering, eerily lit by the emergency light. By the time I got to the ground floor, I had completely sweated through my khakis and a blue Brooks Brothers dress shirt.

The street was full of hot, exhausted people, some of them sitting on the steps outside the building. I immediately recognized two of the summer interns I'd been mentoring on our desk. It suddenly went through my mind that tomorrow was to be the final day of their ten-week program. They were on edge, waiting to find out if they'd get a job.

They looked at me expectantly. "Do you have any idea what's going on?" one of them said. I wasn't sure whether he was talking about the blackout or the firm's decision on his hiring.

All I could do was shake my head. "Wow, guys, crazy way to end the summer," I said.

As I walked off into the asphalt kiln that was Lower Manhattan, it occurred to me that while my own summer internship felt like five minutes ago, three years had gone by. I had just executed more than $2 billion in futures trades in the midst of a blackout. This felt like a seat at the grown-ups' table.

CHAPTER 5

Welcome to the Casino

I was sitting in a hot tub in Vegas with three Goldman VPs, a managing director, a pre-IPO partner, and a topless woman. No, this is not the setup for a joke. This really happened. The woman was, let us say, unnaturally buoyant. As was the general mood in the tub. My new boss, Tim Connors, once dubbed the Mullet, was one of the VPs, and we had all flown in for his bachelor party. He was wearing a baseball cap marked with the logo of a company called TrendWatch. TrendWatch was a stock-charting product that predicted which direction the market was going. By this point TrendWatch's job had become easy. The market was going only one way: up.

Welcome to high tide on Wall Street.

It was April 2006, and the deep recession that had struck the markets after September 11 had faded, as recessions inevitably do, and been replaced by a new bubble, thanks to easy mortgages and the Federal Reserve pumping cheap money into the financial system the way Vegas pumps oxygen onto unsuspecting gamblers.

The only trouble with bubbles is that it is hard to tell when you're in one until it bursts. The technology bubble by now seemed a distant, almost ancient, memory. Bankers on Wall Street were toasting one another's wisdom, just as homeowners were smiling as they watched their houses grow more valuable every week. The rising tide was making everyone feel smart.

I was allowing myself to feel a little bit smart, too. I had survived the brutal rounds of firings that had rocked Goldman from 2002 through

2004; I had gotten promoted from analyst to associate—a bump that was meaningless to the outside world but one that only about 40 percent of analysts make. It was important because, as an associate, I was now a full-time employee of the firm—I was no longer on a two- or three-year analyst contract that the firm could decide not to renew. The next rung up the promotion scale was vice president, a rank typically achieved after four years as an associate, yet one that most people in the sales and trading business attained. The next level was managing director, and the topmost was partner—a level very few people reached. (Most prized of all at Goldman was to have been a pre-IPO partner: many of them were said to have made in the tens or hundreds of millions of dollars when the firm went public in 1999.)

If you were new at the firm and couldn't quite tell who was a partner and who wasn't, there were a couple of easy tricks. One was listening for something called the Partner Laugh. This occurred when the trading floor was dead quiet and suddenly you heard some kiss-ass VP erupting into fits of laughter and slapping his knee in response to some joke the person by his desk was telling. The longevity and high pitch of his laugh would tell you that the person by his desk was a partner. (A close relative to the Partner Laugh was called the Custy Laugh: short for Customer Laugh. This sounded just as fake but was reserved for sucking up to your biggest clients and usually was louder and built up at a more gradual pace than the Partner Laugh—only a trained ear could tell the difference.) The other way to pick a partner out of a lineup: they were always tanned—even in the winter months.

————

So how did I find myself in this Vegas hot tub? The change had occurred for me back when the markets were slightly less carbonated. Corey and I had become a well-oiled machine and were executing billions of dollars in futures across equities, commodities, fixed income, and currencies. We had expanded our product offering to include options (another type of derivative, one that gives the buyer of the option the right, but not the obligation, to acquire or sell an underlying asset at a future date at a specified price). Everything we were trading was as an agent (on behalf of the client), and we were collecting flat commissions when clients decided to trade with us. We were talking to the trading desks of the biggest mutual funds, hedge funds, and pension funds in the world, who had come to trust our safe hands.

By mid-2004, with a horrendous bear market all around us, our business was thriving, partly because we had started from a low base, but also because futures were a macro instrument and investors relied on them during tough market environments. In a year and a half, we had doubled the commissions in our business, and growth had become so rapid that we were allowed to hire a new person to join our team.

But just like Rudy before him, Corey now found it was time to move on: Daffey wanted his help in covering the macro hedge funds. Corey would now become a pure derivatives salesman—he would spend more time discussing with clients investment ideas in options, futures, and swaps, and less time executing. When he needed to execute, he would call his old desk: me. His departure was bittersweet for me. He had been generous and kind, and always set a high standard of integrity for me to follow. But I knew the move would be good for him, and I had a feeling he would keep looking out for me.

I had been his right-hand man; with his departure, I became the main futures trader. This helped me build my profile on the fiftieth floor. When anyone, from partner down to analyst, needed to trade a future, they came to me and my associate. Seeing all this flow had another benefit: it helped me sharpen, and gain confidence in, my views on what the markets might do next.

When Corey moved, I was given more resources—we got to hire a couple of new people, whom I trained. Still, the times continued to be hairy at the firm and more broadly on Wall Street: the firings continued; desks got cut down and merged. The Equities division started merging with FICC to form what would eventually become one giant, all-powerful (and sometimes all-knowing) Securities division. Along with this, my mini Equity Futures desk merged with the FICC Futures desk.

One day in January 2005, Daffey sent me an e-mail: "Dude, I have an idea for you. Swing by my office." I headed down to forty-nine.

"I need your help," he said as I walked in.

He began his spiel by talking about Laura Mehta, a woman he had hired recently from Morgan Stanley to be an MD in Derivatives sales and his effective number two. A number of clients had urged Daffey to try to hire her—she was a brilliant Princeton grad, and highly regarded by some of the biggest sovereign wealth funds, hedge funds, and asset managers on the Street. My initial perception of her was that she was a class act. In addition, she exuded a quality that was rare on trading floors: she was genuinely pleasant. When she arrived, Daffey had needed to pair her with someone, and he had assigned Tim Connors as her counterpart VP.

I had known Connors—as with Daffey, no one ever called him by his first name—in passing since the summer of 2000, when we were interns together: I at the undergrad level, he at the MBA. Another former college athlete (crew), he stood six-five, had the luxuriant mane indicated by his onetime nickname (though, in reality, his hair looked nothing like a mullet), and could be quite charming when the situation demanded. He had the ability to stay out till all hours drinking and smoking, then make it through work the next day.

I'd also noticed, in my early days on the Futures desk, that he could be impatient, irritable, and acerbic when frustrated. As he learned the business and became more comfortable in his role, though, he mellowed. And over time, we'd built a strong rapport; we shared a similar dry sense of humor.

Connors had had a rocky start at Goldman, working for some really hard-nosed managers he didn't get along with. They were immune to his charms and alert to his occasional tendency to make detail-related errors: mixing up multipliers, buying instead of selling. The rap on Connors was that while he was a great salesman, he didn't entirely understand the theoretical principles of derivatives. (This is more common than you might imagine, even at high echelons in the financial world. Derivatives are complex beasts.)

I have a vivid memory of an incident that happened with Connors in December 2002, around the time I first joined Corey's team. He had made a client error, a quantity error, buying or selling the wrong amount of some futures contract. It was a large error, in the hundreds

of thousands of dollars, but he had compounded the error by not noti-
fying Daffey about it until hours later. Daffey, who didn't anger easily,
was irate. He stuck his head around his computer screen and shouted,
"Connors, pick me up on line one!"

The way the Hoot works is that everybody could now quickly hit line
one and listen in on mute. Corey quickly told me to pick up the line. He
knew the context of the error already, and thought it would be a good
teaching moment for me. But the Hoot was barely necessary. Daffey
was so incensed that he was screaming quite audibly, absolutely laying
into Connors as if he were a junior analyst—which he wasn't: having
started in the business a little bit later than some other people, he was
an associate at the time, and in his early thirties.

"This is unacceptable!" Daffey yelled. "You're old and mature
enough to know you need to admit these things immediately! We have
a lot of risk at stake, and if this happens again, there's going to be big
trouble!"

There was a time when it looked as if Connors could have been let go,
but he held on. Daffey saw something in him, and was giving him another shot now, with Laura Mehta joining the firm. Connors had been
"drifting in the wind," Daffey told me in our meeting, until Laura came
along. She had helped give him some focus and structure, Daffey said,
but his attention to detail and organizational skills were still not his
strong suit. To be fair, though, there are many people on Wall Street who
are good at the big picture but not good at the details. As far as Connors
was concerned, this was where I came in. Laura was too senior to get
into the weeds; she was often in management meetings. Daffey needed
someone by Connors's side to help build the business. Would I do it?

I was immediately excited. *When the partner in charge of Derivatives
Sales offers you an opportunity like this*, I thought, *you jump on it*. I
jumped on it. The new job was an opportunity to learn a broader set of
derivatives products and diversify my client base into sovereign wealth
funds, quantitative hedge funds, and state pension plans. Also, I thought
it would be fun.

And it worked out. The markets turned around in 2005, and our
little Derivatives Sales team—Laura, Connors, and me—began to fire

on all cylinders. The fanatical attention to detail that Corey had taught me helped our desk consolidate our gains. Connors and I made a great team. I did the heavy lifting, saw to the nuts and bolts, and did some schmoozing. He worked on strategy and did a lot of schmoozing.

Then Daffey himself was transferred.

It happened in the spring of 2005, a turning point on Wall Street. The recession was ending; the housing market was beginning to percolate. Moods around the financial markets were beginning to pick up. On the Goldman Sachs trading floor, Daffey's boss, Matt Ricci, a former Yale basketball player and a very gung-ho partner, was leading the charge. Every Friday morning, Ricci used to stand up at the podium on the edge of the trading floor and give these sometimes rousing, sometimes cheesy pep talks to the troops. There was a microphone on the podium that broadcast into the Hoot, so if you were somewhere on the outskirts of the huge trading floor and couldn't see Ricci, you still couldn't escape his voice. And he was very fond of catchy abbreviations: a favorite of his was one he'd borrowed from David Mamet's *Glengarry Glen Ross*—ABC, or "Always Be Closing." (I don't think he quite realized that Mamet's play was a dark satire of unethical business practices.) He also relished GTB, or "Get the Business." And then there were the sports analogies: "Let's give it the full-court press." "Let's bring this one across the line." "Let's all raise our game into the end of the quarter." "Let's play through the whistle."

He also coined some terms that became widely used around the franchise: one of them was *elephant trades*, trades that netted the firm over $1 million in revenue. An imposing figure, tall and always dressed in a suit, even on casual Fridays, Ricci used to love to stand at the podium and say, "Let's go out and find some elephants today! Let's go get the biggest trades to the tape!" People had mixed opinions on the guy. Some people found his stuff inspiring; others, not so much.

Ricci was also the guy who advanced the concept of gross credits, or GCs. For many years at Goldman, managers would judge an employee's performance by several measures—some objective, some subjective. Most important: Was he commercial and did he bring in the business? This made up about 50 percent of the equation, and was obviously crucial to any organization whose primary purpose was to book profits. But the other half of the equation—and this is what made Goldman Sachs different from other banks for a long time—was more subjective: Was he a leader who set a good example for junior employees? Was she a culture carrier who promoted collaboration and teamwork and the values of the company? Was the person someone who had the long-term interests of the organization at heart? Could he or she at times have the foresight to turn away bad business, knowing it would be detrimental to the firm's reputation in the long run?

Matt Ricci instituted a culture where the evaluation became far more scientific and specific: "What's the number next to his name?" Your cumulative annual GCs became known as your "attribution" for the year. Over the years, GCs and attribution became things that people started worrying, talking, and fighting about more than stock markets and clients. It is human nature: if you are going to be measured by a number, you are going to do what you can to make sure your number is as big as possible. It was a change that would ultimately prove highly detrimental to Goldman's culture and morale, even a decade later.

Matt Ricci was the guy who decided to transfer Michael Daffey, a morale-booster on the trading floor, to London.

It was a hugely disappointing move to everybody in the franchise, but it wasn't completely illogical. It is an axiom in the investment banking business that the farther an office is from company headquarters, the more diluted its culture. And Goldman Sachs London, as an American bank competing with European banks, needed a shot in the arm. Management's thinking was, if we move a major producer who embodies the culture, maybe he'll raise London's game. Successful people are often transferred out of the blue to Tokyo or to Hong Kong for similar reasons.

Ricci called us all into a room, the entire Equity Derivatives Sales force, and said, "I know a lot of you are upset. If you want to know who you should be upset at, it's me. I'm the one who made the decision." And he looked everyone in the eye. It was a strange moment, but I was impressed with his lack of bullshit. Yet it was also a sad moment—it's very rare to have a boss you like as much as everyone liked Daffey.

In June, the Derivatives group (both sales and trading) threw him a farewell party, at the Soho House in the Meatpacking District. In a strange turn of events, the room we were in, called The Library, had a huge stereo system but no music to be played. I was the only one there who had my iPod, so I stepped into the breach as amateur DJ for the night. I took song requests from some of the partners, but mostly I played the music I liked. Nelly's "Ride Wit' Me," Jay-Z and Linkin Park's "Numb/Encore," and U2's "Beautiful Day" were some of the tunes people enjoyed that night.

There were a lot of senior people there, and everyone, including me, drank a lot. A few words about drugs, smoking, and drinking at Goldman Sachs may be in order here. In my whole career, I never once saw a colleague take any kind of illegal drug at work or at a social event. Drugs were severely frowned upon at Goldman, even regarded with a certain horror. To indulge in them would have been looked upon as severely reckless—and reckless people didn't survive very long at Goldman Sachs. Disciplined people survived. Being caught using would have been grounds for immediate dismissal.

Smoking: in the New York office, there was a smoking crew who would take cigarette breaks outside the building every two or three hours. Usually the group consisted of either European expats or quants, or a combination of the two. The smoking crew in the London office consisted of: The Entire London Office.

Alcohol was a big part of the culture at the firm, as it is on Wall Street in general. Getting smashed with your clients was a regular occurrence. The key was knowing how far to go. At Daffey's party, one associate got very drunk and kept telling everyone how hot he found the new female analyst, who was standing a few feet away. Even though I was also pretty hammered at the time, I remember thinking, *Holy crap! This guy is embarrassing himself, perhaps irreparably.*

Drinking with colleagues was tricky, but there seemed to be a completely different standard for senior people when it came to alcohol. If you were a junior person, you didn't want to be perceived as a stick in the mud; you needed to show people you could hold your own. At the same time, it was important to strike a balance. Senior people simply had more license. I've seen some very senior people get ridiculously drunk, slur their speech, and then pretend the next day that nothing happened. They kind of get away with it—they're the bosses, after all.

Daffey was one of those Aussies for whom alcohol only heightened his natural exuberance and seemed to make him more charismatic. At his farewell party, he was calling people over one by one and giving us each a minute to say goodbye. When it was my turn, he made the usual crack about South African rugby, then turned serious. "Dude, keep at it," he said. "You're the kind of guy who I think could do any job at Goldman Sachs—I would put you in any seat, trading or sales." He then lost his train of thought and moved on to the next person. The next morning he called me and thanked me for being DJ.

Then he left for London.

————

After Connors made it through his rough early days at the firm, it was clear that he had some significant skills. He was about as good as anyone at getting to know clients, showing dedication to them, understanding their problems, and helping them work toward solutions. Clients loved him. Sometimes the solutions he found were very profitable for the firm, but Connors would have to work hard and long to get these trades to the tape. They were not quick wins. Hedge funds may be able to trade "on the wire" (immediately) in response to an idea you give them, but as a general rule, institutions such as pension plans (both corporate and state), sovereign wealth funds (governments such as Abu Dhabi, China, Hong Kong, Norway, Qatar, Saudi Arabia, and Singapore), insurance companies, and mutual funds (e.g., Fidelity, Wellington, T. Rowe, Vanguard) take much longer to work toward executing on a solution or investment idea. Sometimes this is because they are being thoughtful and have a long-run horizon. Other times their slowness could be a result of bureaucracy and the size of their organization; at worst, it could be because of lack of sophistication.

Connors had great success servicing clients that many people within the firm had thought were dead ends: particularly sleepy state pension plans all over the country, which no one ever thought could do any business with Wall Street. The managers of these funds really appreciated his patience and focus on them.

Connors was primarily a big-picture guy: his working habits when it came down to the nitty-gritty were idiosyncratic. He had a reputation for disappearing from the desk at odd hours. It was my job, as his backup, to cover for him—to help out whoever was looking for him so it wouldn't be a big deal that he wasn't there. I never asked where he'd been. The etiquette at Goldman was that you didn't inquire why someone more senior than you wasn't on the desk. If internal people or clients asked, I would just say, "Connors is off the desk. Can I help?"—even if it was 4:30 P.M. on a Friday and he had clearly left for the weekend.

I don't know for sure, but I think Connors liked to sleep in a little bit at times; maybe sometimes he liked to squeeze in a morning workout. He would come in late, but to be fair, he would often stay much later than everyone else—occasionally until 11:00 P.M.—working on projects for clients. He moved slowly, but always seemed to get where he needed to go eventually. This type of elongated day was acceptable when the revenues were coming in. A lot of things were acceptable while the tide was rising.

And it was rising fast: the first quarter of 2006 was the best quarter ever for our pod in Equity Derivatives Sales. We had brought in millions of dollars in revenues, almost doubling the previous year's total.

It was at this loaded moment that Tim Connors invited me to his bachelor party in Las Vegas.

———

It was nice of him to ask me. In effect, it was kind of a reward for all my hard work—plus, maybe a tacit acknowledgment that I'd done more than my fair share of the heavy lifting. Still, the invitation gave me pause. For one thing, a big weekend in Vegas was the kind of fun I wasn't sure I could afford, because when Goldman heavy hitters go to Vegas, the price point is very different from going with your college buddies.

Between airfare, hotel, gambling, and incidentals, I estimated that this bachelor bash could wind up setting me back two or three thousand bucks. That may have been a drop in the bucket for a VP or managing director, but for me it was real money. Was it worth it?

I was still an associate at this point, albeit a senior one, and though my total 2005 compensation (including bonus) had come to more than $200,000, after paying taxes, sending money to my family in South Africa, shelling out the $2,500-per-month rent on my 650-square-foot Upper West Side apartment—I'd moved from 41 River Terrace to my own place in 2004—and spending considerably on taxis and New York City restaurants, I just didn't feel that it would be responsible to blow three grand on a weekend.

I was also concerned about the experience itself. I knew at the outset that I would be the most junior person there. Did I really want to watch my boss and other higher-ups misbehaving in Vegas? Scenes from Daffey's farewell party kept replaying in my head. I already knew there was a double standard between management and underlings when it came to drinking and other pursuits. Did I want to have to rein myself in while trying to keep up? It is one thing to go one Cuervo over the line with your buddies; it is another to throw up on your boss's John Lobbs.

Also, I may have been overthinking it, but I wanted my work to speak for itself in the success that accrued to me. Cringe if you like, but I didn't want to have to impress the boss by showing him how many shots of tequila I could drink. I generally didn't socialize every weekend with my colleagues; I didn't try to ingratiate myself with senior people so I could go out with them on weekends. I didn't like to mix my private life and my work life, and this party threatened to do just that. At the same time, I liked Connors, and wanted to be there to celebrate with him. And if I could just lighten up a bit, this could be fun.

I consulted Phil. Phil, who is two years older than me, the son of a Mayflower WASP father and a Chilean mother, was (and continues to be) an important mentor of mine. We met on the first day I joined the firm and quickly became close friends; he'd worked in the Latin American pod of Emerging Markets Sales before Goldman made a decision to start pulling out of the Emerging Markets in 2003. (He became a successful wealth manager at a white shoe private partnership, handling ultra-high-net-worth Latin American clients: a perfect job for him.)

Phil not only knew which forks to use; he knew a lot about a lot of things. Because of his mother, he spoke fluent Spanish. He'd grown up on Park Avenue and spent summers at his parents' house in Southampton, where his doubles partner had been George Soros—Phil called him "Big George"—and his family belonged to Shinnecock Hills, a golf club so exclusive that Goldman partners such as Daffey and Ricci practically salivated at the sound of its name. (One time, I played Shinnecock when the whole Derivatives team was in the Hamptons for a team-building clambake, a real bull market event, and all the partners' jaws dropped when I mentioned this.) While Phil was at Goldman Sachs, all kinds of senior people used to cozy up to him despite his junior status, perhaps hoping for an invitation to Shinnecock, or maybe so that some of his style would rub off on them.

With a background like his, Phil could easily have been a lightweight. Instead, he was motivated—serious without taking himself too seriously; thoughtful, humorous, and focused. He seemed to understand the world for what it was, neither overestimating the big things nor underestimating the little things. So he became my go-to guy for counsel on matters large and small, both professional and personal: which Goldman MDs to invite to the rooftop bashes my roommates and I used to throw on the forty-third floor of 41 River Terrace; what to wear to a formal engagement party in Central Park; when Turnbull & Asser was holding a sale, and which sales guy to ask for.

On one of our first days at Goldman, Phil pulled me and a couple of other junior analysts aside and gave us some advice that I've never forgotten. "Everyone here is a salesman," he said. "It doesn't matter if they're a trader, if they're a quant, if they're a salesperson. Everyone is selling something." His point was: never assume that people are not trying to advance their own agendas. He opened my mind to being a little bit skeptical (as opposed to being cynical), to giving a hard (but not necessarily harsh) look at what might be behind requests and compliments.

He advised me to be alert to people, even people senior to me, trying to win my favor. You can never be sure where people are coming from, Phil said.

When I asked Phil if I ought to accept Connors's invitation, I watched with fascination as his tactical computer processed advanced algorithms. It didn't take long. "I think you should go," he told me.

"You do?"

He nodded. "You need to show these guys that you can have fun, that you're part of the gang," he said. "That even though you're a young guy, you're not too nervous to go hang out with them."

So I went to Vegas.

Unlike Connors and the other, more senior people—he had invited fifteen guys in all, including nine from Goldman—I didn't take any time off. I was too junior to do so. (Connors left after work on Wednesday and didn't return till the following Tuesday.) I flew out on a Friday evening, landed in Las Vegas close to midnight, dropped my bags off in my room at the (newly opened) Wynn Hotel, and, as instructed, proceeded to the Lure Ultra-Lounge on the outskirts of the main casino floor to meet Connors and crew, who'd been in town for two full days drinking steadily.

———

The light was purple; the music was pounding. To Connors's credit, despite the fact that he was swaying in his seat, the first question he asked me—he had to yell to be heard—was about a big total return swap derivatives trade we had done earlier in the day with a large pension plan. It had gone just fine, I told him. He smiled woozily.

Nine or ten of us, a half-dozen Goldman guys—including Bobby Schwartz, aka the Jewish John Kennedy—plus a few of Connors's old pals from college, business school, and elsewhere, were sitting around a table laughing loudly enough to compete with the music. People were slapping the bridegroom-to-be on the shoulder: he was the cool guy, the magnetic guy, the reason everyone was there. The waitress was a knockout, a ten; the drinks kept coming. A managing director from a regional office—everyone called him Bill-Jo; he was, by far, the senior

Goldman guy at the table—was buying: vodka soda was the drink of the night. I had two, and felt a nice buzz. Then I had a third. Then I had a fourth. By the time we all left the lounge, around 2:00 A.M., I was walking carefully, as if I were on the wet deck of a sailboat on the high seas. I slapped Bill-Jo on the back (a familiar gesture I wouldn't have tried without the vodka in me) and thanked him for buying me all those drinks.

"Let me tell you something," he said rather seriously, though he had had a number of drinks himself. "I never let anyone more junior than me pay for anything when they're with me. It's a policy I was once taught and have always followed." I've remembered this ever since.

We were all walking out of the Ultra-Lounge, past the blackjack tables, where the action was hot and loud. I watched with awe as a high roller in a bolo tie put down a pile of $500 chips on a single hand.

"I wonder what it'd be like to bet that kind of money on one hand," I said casually.

Bill-Jo looked at me with the intent focus of someone trying hard to marshal his faculties. He was two or three drinks ahead of me. "Come with me," he said. "I'll show you what it's like."

We walked up to a table that had a vacant chair; he took a $500 chip out of his pocket, put it on the table, and the dealer dealt him in. Bill-Jo showed me his down card: a Jack of diamonds. The dealer dealt him a four of spades.

"Hit me," Bill-Jo said.

He drew a seven of clubs. The dealer pushed back Bill-Jo's $500 chip with another one sitting on top. Bill-Jo took both chips and put them into my hand. "*That's* what it's like," he said. "Enjoy the weekend."

————————

Fast-forward to the next afternoon. There we were, seven brave men of Goldman savagely hungover and bobbing along with Ms. Silicone in the bubbling Mandalay Bay hot tub, under a sweltering Vegas sun.

Sipping an ice-cold Red Stripe took the edge off, but my brain was buzzing anyway, with social/corporate/ethical discomfort. It had nothing to do with the topless girl: that part I was loving. What was making me queasy (besides the hangover) was the awkwardness of being in this situation with people who pretty much controlled my destiny. There was my boss Connors in his tattered TrendWatch cap; and there, astonishingly, was the pre-IPO partner Dave Heller, who as one of the heads of trading, was two levels above Bill-Jo, three levels above Connors and the other two VPs in the tub, and in relation to me, somewhere to the left of Alpha Centauri.

Heller was, quite simply, a rock star at Goldman Sachs. He had credibility with traders because he was so damn good. People used to say that even though he was managing thousands of people around the world, he could sit down in any trader's seat, figure out the trader's risk by himself within seconds, and probably do that trader's job better than he or she could. That type of skill garners a lot of street cred.

He was aware of his status, yet carried himself with an air of quiet confidence and humor, never arrogance. In the early 1990s, as a young derivatives trader in Tokyo, he had done something that has become an urban legend within Goldman Sachs: he made tons of money in the aftermath of the rogue derivatives trades by Nick Leeson that brought down Barings Bank. Remember: for every loser on a trade, there are ultimately winners as well. No one ever confirmed this to me, but Heller's brilliance was said to have made the firm millions, and in gratitude and recognition of his skills, Goldman made him a partner at age twenty-eight, one of the youngest in the firm's history.

I had encountered Dave Heller a number of times before. When I was a young futures sales trader back in 2003, he would sometimes come by the desk or (more often) call Corey and me and ask us to execute trades for his proprietary account, or to hedge the firm's risk. The thing I noticed about Heller was he was always right. If he sold futures, the market would go down the next day. If he bought futures, the market would rise. However, my most recent encounter with Dave had had nothing to do with business, and had been semi-awkward: the morning after Daffey's farewell party bacchanal at Soho House, Heller had pulled up at the urinal next to mine in the fiftieth-floor men's room, glanced at me, and spoken these immortal words: "Good time last night."

Heller had just been making washroom chitchat then. But now, less than a year later, here was that same underling, and we were at a bachelor party together.

Heller had come because he liked Vegas, because Connors was a cool guy and it was fun to be friends with him, but most directly because Connors's twenty-six-year-old fiancée had befriended Heller's young wife. The friendship may have been completely natural, but as a political move, however unintentional, it didn't hurt Connors's prospects at Goldman a bit.

Here was I, however, a guy Heller knew to say hi to, but still a foot soldier and an underling—and one who would retain the memory of him sitting in a Vegas hot tub with a topless twenty-three-year-old. How would that affect *my* prospects at Goldman?

To add to my worries, there was the little matter of the $1,000 in chips a very drunk Bill-Jo had slapped into my hand the night before. Should I have handed the chips back to him at once, with a "Bill, I really can't accept this"? Probably. But I hadn't. Should I say something to him now?

I didn't. While my colleagues made small talk with the big-breasted girl, I sipped my beer and kept my mouth shut and wondered (also wondering if the other guys were wondering, too), *Will what happens in Vegas really stay in Vegas?*

When I got back to the office on Monday, I phoned Phil to ask his sage advice on the Bill-Jo situation. Did he think it was unethical of me not to have immediately given the chips back, or at least tried hard to? It felt too late now. Should I just assume that a thousand dollars was a mere rounding error for a managing director, that it simply didn't matter? Or (the paranoid view) could this be some kind of trap? If I didn't say anything, would Bill-Jo somehow pass judgment on me?

Phil said I should mention the thousand dollars later, in some casual way—maybe buy Bill-Jo a dozen golf balls or something at a later point—but for now say, "Thanks for treating me." I did exactly that: he seemed to have only the vaguest idea what I was talking about.

And oh yes, a day or two after I returned, Dave Heller once again pulled up to the urinal next to mine in the company washroom. He gave me a quick, sphinxlike smile. "That was a fun time this weekend," he said. The king of understatement.

The year 2006 was a big one for Goldman Sachs. The markets kept booming, and Derivatives Sales continued to rack up revenues. Clients were confident: they were trading; they were taking risk. I was executing well for them, which led to more business, because they knew I was looking after them. My clients included some of the biggest asset managers, quantitative hedge funds, and sovereign wealth funds in the world. The commission business—flat, transparent fees on agency orders in things such as futures, exchange-traded funds, and options—was flourishing. The cash register was ringing.

But change was in the air. At the end of May, our CEO, Hank Paulson, was appointed U.S. secretary of the treasury, and Lloyd Blankfein became CEO and chairman of Goldman Sachs. Many at the firm were shocked that Paulson had left when things were going so well. Remember: times were good. Hank could have stayed at Goldman and collected a few more years of multimillion-dollar pay packages. He was liked and well respected by both bankers and traders. But he accepted President George W. Bush's call, in the tradition of a long line of former Goldman leaders who went into government service at the top of their careers. I admired his decision.

In retrospect, I recognized that this was also the trade of the century for Hank Paulson. To avoid conflict of interest while at the government, he was obligated to sell all his Goldman stock ($500 million worth) at the top of the market, before the crash. Also, due to a tax loophole, for accepting government service he avoided paying capital gains tax.

But as hard as it might be to believe, I think Paulson's going to Treasury when he did would end up being an even better trade for the American people.

However, there was a group of people at the firm who thought that Paulson left because the writing was on the wall for him at Goldman. Paulson was a banker; Blankfein was a trader. Blankfein's trading divisions (FICC and Equities) were bringing in massive revenues: two to three times any other division and sometimes more than half the revenue of the firm. This was a big transition from the late 1990s and early 2000s, when investment banking (things such as mergers and acquisitions and corporate finance) had been an equal or greater part of Goldman's profit engine. On Wall Street, often the power goes to the person bringing in the most profit.

Lloyd had become the golden boy of Goldman Sachs. Within the firm, he had developed an aura of being a prescient genius who just couldn't put a foot wrong. People admired him, feared him, respected him. He was equal parts intimidating and self-deprecating, but he came across as a regular guy with a good, sharp sense of humor. When you met him you were won over by him.

Hank, on the other hand, was an old-school banker: a little gruff, straightforward, and conservative, even abrupt at times. (Rudy once played Hank in a prank video for the Goldman holiday party; they resembled each other very closely in height and appearance. Ironically, they were not completely dissimilar in personality, either.) You wouldn't catch Hank getting loose at a company party; he was a teetotaler—and a bird-watcher, ardent environmentalist, and exercise fanatic. I had worked out next to him in the company gym, watched him put up some pretty impressive weight on the incline chest-press machine. (My one other experience with a Goldman CEO in the gym was the time I saw Lloyd "air-drying," that is, walking around the changing room au naturel to dry off from his shower. But this was not uncommon among a generation slightly older than mine. I don't think it was a show of power.)

Hank had gotten in some hot water during the firm's rough period in 2003, when at a Salomon Smith Barney investor conference, he cited the so-called 80-20 rule—that in any business, 20 percent of the people produce 80 percent of the profits. His remark, which was seen as very antagonistic to Goldman's teamwork culture, triggered a large and immediate backlash within the firm. To his credit, Paulson then sent out a mass voice mail saying he was sorry and making no excuses. He said, "It was a glib, uncalled-for remark, and I apologize," and people forgave him.

But now the wheel had turned. The banking world had become a trading world, and that was Lloyd Blankfein's world. And Goldman was in the process of merging FICC and Equities, the latter now under the leadership of Lloyd's fellow trader (and fellow pre-IPO partner) Gary Cohn. It was a move that would have a huge impact on the firm and on the entire financial world.

Lloyd and Gary went way back. They'd first met in 1990, when Gary moved over from trading metals in the pits of the New York Mercantile Exchange to join J. Aron, Goldman Sachs's commodities division. Lloyd was a rising star, a gold salesman. Every good salesman needs a go-to trader, and Gary became Lloyd's guy.

Gary was a brilliant trader—legend had it that he'd single-handedly cornered the aluminum market—with an interesting background. Severely dyslexic, he'd been continually told as a child that certain doors would be closed to him, but he made it his business to open them all. At six foot three and 220 pounds, he looked imposing and determined. At American University, he found he liked financial markets a lot more than he enjoyed studying; he literally talked his way into his first job on the commodities exchange by sharing a cab to the airport with a commodities trader and persuading the trader to hire him. He succeeded there on cunning, instinct, and emotional intelligence. Trading is a human business. When you're in the pit, you see the fear in people's eyes. (This was what Gary had seen when he started buying up aluminum.) The guys who get to the top are the ones who are book-smart enough, but who have an instinct about what motivates other people. Gary Cohn was a genius in that regard.

Cohn took a pay cut to go work for Goldman Sachs, but with his human intelligence and gut instinct for commodities, he quickly rose through the ranks, almost in parallel with Blankfein, but always a notch or two below. Lloyd looked out for Gary. They became close friends and took family vacations together.

The skills that had made Gary a great trader also helped him succeed as a manager. When Lloyd (who's five or six years older than Gary) became Goldman's number two under Hank Paulson, he appointed Gary cohead of the Securities division, with a particular focus on equities.

Many saw this as a strange move: Gary was a commodities guy. But Lloyd said, "You know what? If he can figure out aluminum, he can figure out stocks." There was a lot of this at Goldman Sachs: great managers and gifted traders were considered nimble enough to transfer their skills to any region, asset class, or job function.

I first encountered Gary while I was still on the Futures desk, just after Corey Stevens was transferred out to work under Michael Daffey and the merger with FICC was happening. A guy who came over to the Equities floor in the merger had once been Gary Cohn's broker in the commodities pit, and Gary, who was still new to the division and didn't know anyone else on the Equities floor, used to come over to talk with him.

Gary had a very distinctive signature move, one he had become famous for within the firm; I must have seen it ten or fifteen times in action. It didn't matter if the person he was talking to was male or female; he would walk up to the salesman or saleswoman, hike up one leg, plant his foot on the person's desk, his thigh close to the employee's face, and ask how markets were doing. Gary was physically commanding, and the move could have been interpreted as a very primal, alpha-male gesture. I think he just thought it was comfortable. And what came out of Gary's mouth was not what you'd expect.

He was friendly. He was low-key. He'd say, "How are you doing? How is your day going?" All in very soft tones. What I began to notice as he stopped by the desk was that he almost never talked about business. Instead, it was chitchat of the "How 'bout those Yankees?" variety. In later years, when I heard Gary speak about leadership at Pine Street, Goldman Sachs's leadership-development program, he would always emphasize the importance of walking the floors, letting your people know who you were. He also talked about consistency of mood, needing your people to know you were even-tempered—you weren't going to flip out every two minutes—and predictable.

To his credit, this was how I always saw Gary—and Lloyd, for that matter: always upbeat, never negative or intimidating. They were (and are) very skilled at human interaction. They understood how to win people over, how not to scare people, how to put on the pressure when they needed to. It made them great leaders. Now that Hank had gone to Treasury, Lloyd and Gary were the future.

————————

Trading, not banking, had become Goldman Sachs's present. In 2006 it seemed that every business magazine ran a cover story about how Goldman was at the summit of Wall Street, doing double and triple the business of the other investment banks. I kept an April 27, 2006, copy of the *Economist* that proclaimed in a cover story that Goldman Sachs was "On Top of the World." The cover even had a picture of a mountain climber so high up that it looked as if he were in the clouds. I was proud to see this. This was a far cry from the dark days of 2001, when people were saying that maybe Goldman had lost its luster and that the bigger banks, with bigger balance sheets, were going to eat us alive.

How was Goldman Sachs achieving these astounding profits? Not through investment banking, not through the traditional methods of raising capital for companies, some of the articles pointed out, but by taking its own positions with its own money: trading for itself. This is called proprietary trading. What these magazines (and some investors) were saying was that Goldman Sachs was becoming a hedge fund, and as part of the evolution, the bank was getting into new conflicts of interest. This new direction was a significant departure from what Goldman Sachs had become known for.

From Goldman's first days until its 1999 IPO (130 years), it had prided itself on serving as an adviser to its clients, with fiduciary responsibility. A fiduciary stood in a special position of trust and obligation where the client was concerned. This role was applicable when the firm was advising the client about how the client should best invest its money versus pushing the client into investments that generated the largest fees. It was also true in investment banking, when the firm was telling a client whether it should merge with another company. This ideal of doing what is right for the client, and not just what is right for the firm, was there, prescribed in the 1970s by former senior partner John Whitehead in his set of 14 Principles. These principles were drummed into our heads when we were summer interns, and I felt idealistic about them. At one point, I pinned up a copy of them next to my desk. The principles that referred to fiduciary responsibility were:

1. Our clients' interests always come first.

*Our experience shows that if we serve our clients well,
our own success will follow.*

5. We stress creativity and imagination in everything we do.

*While recognizing that the old way may still be the best way,
we constantly strive to find a better solution to a client's
problems. We pride ourselves on having pioneered many
of the practices and techniques that have become
standard in the industry.*

12. We regularly receive confidential information as part of
our normal client relationships.

*To breach a confidence or to use confidential information
improperly or carelessly would be unthinkable.*

14. Integrity and honesty are at the heart of our business.

*We expect our people to maintain high ethical standards in
everything they do, both in their work for the firm
and in their personal lives.*

There it was, all written down: clients' interests coming first; our constantly striving to find better solutions to a client's problems; not using clients' confidential information improperly; maintaining the highest ethical standards in everything we do. So how on earth did proprietary trading fit in with these ideals?

As the power base at Goldman shifted from investment banking to trading—a shift embodied by Lloyd Blankfein's rise in the firm, which coincided with a huge rise in trading revenue relative to banking revenue—the client increasingly came to be regarded as a counterparty, merely the other side of a transaction, rather than an advisee. A counterparty was on its own; its goals might or might not match up with those of the investment bank (the other counterparty) facilitating its transactions. Advisees are more like children: you have a responsibility to look out for them and defend them from their own worst instincts. Counterparties, however, are adults, and in full-frontal capitalism, anything goes between consenting adults.

There was another new nebulous role for Goldman: that of co-investor. In the old days, the firm would advise a client to invest in something; in the new universe, the firm could now invest its own money in the same thing. Where this practice of proprietary trading (or "prop trading") turned morally ambiguous was when the firm changed its mind (or masked its intentions) and made a bet in the other direction from the client's.

In early 2005, when Lloyd Blankfein was still Hank Paulson's number two, the two of them, in their annual letter to shareholders, addressed the subject of conflict of interest in the brave new world of investment banking. The letter marked a sea change in Goldman's attitude toward its clients. Conflicts between bank and client were inevitable, they argued. Moreover, such conflicts were to be embraced. If a firm wasn't generating conflict, it wasn't pursuing business aggressively enough.

"It is naïve to think we can operate without conflicts. They are embedded in our role as a valued intermediary—between providers and users of capital and those who want to shed risk versus those who are willing to assume it," Hank and Lloyd wrote.

Not long afterward, Goldman brokered a $9 billion merger between a client, the then–privately held New York Stock Exchange, and a much smaller, publicly traded electronic exchange called Archipelago. The problem with the merger, in the eyes of the outside world, was that Goldman, which was the second-largest stockholder in Archipelago, was on both sides of the deal, which netted the firm some $100 million,

all told. Also, the chief executive of the NYSE at the time was John
Thain, formerly Goldman's president and COO. Goldman's spin on the
transaction—presented with a completely straight face—was that it was
promoting stability in the financial markets by managing conflict. To
questions about these conflicts, then–Goldman spokesman Lucas van
Praag responded, "Life is filled with conflicts, some real, some imagined."

At the time, I bought into the spin. When I and many other people
at Goldman read Lloyd Blankfein's very convincing arguments about
embracing conflict, we even felt a certain sense of pride: The firm was
charting new territory. We'd figured out inventive ways of walking the
line and helping clients. My instinct, for a long time, was: *Let's give the
firm the benefit of the doubt.*

The summer of 2006 was an exciting time for me: business was
cranking, the markets were strong, and I was doing well in my job. I
was loving life in New York City. And sometimes it's when you are
happy that you meet a girl. Nadine and I had been set up on a blind
date the week before I left for Connors's bachelor party that spring, and
I'd been very eager to get back to New York to see her again. I'd even
told Bill-Jo about her in my drunken state by the blackjack table. She
was a dietitian, smart and attractive, and we had a similar Jewish upbringing. We shared a love for wine and restaurants, sushi in particular.
On some of our first dates, we went to Sushi of Gari on the Upper West
Side; Cube 63, on the Lower East Side; and the new Asian-fusion hot
spot Buddakan, in the Meatpacking District.

Also that summer, Goldman had asked me to comanage the summer
intern program. This was a particular point of pride for me. The firm
saw me as a culture carrier, someone who embraced and championed
all that was excellent about Goldman Sachs. I felt honored to represent
the firm in this capacity. I happily mentored new analysts; I captained
Stanford recruiting. Twice a year, I'd fly out to Palo Alto with a team of
five or six people, speak at the Stanford Career Fair, and interview the
kids who were interested in Goldman Sachs.

In interviews, I always looked for the same few things. I was not so
interested in how much someone knew about finance, or what students'

GPAs were. I was more interested in their judgment and enthusiasm for the business. On Wall Street, it's very easy to teach someone the theoretical aspects of finance. It's almost impossible, though, to teach someone good judgment and awareness. Will he know when to ask for help? Will she admit when she's made a trading error? Will he be willing to work his butt off even if the job isn't always intellectually challenging, but still needs to be done? Will she be able to juggle several tasks at the same time? Is he interested in the markets, with a desire to learn more?

I always felt that just chatting with someone for five minutes would give me a much better sense for all this than asking hard questions about finance. Most important, though: Was the person pleasant? Did we like him? Would he get along with people? Arrogant budding finance gurus did not often make it through the Goldman interview process.

Once we had picked our kids on campus, I always did everything I could to help them get in the door. Admittedly this was biased, but I felt that Stanford kids were better rounded and more easygoing than the Ivy League kids, who could be more serious and cutthroat. I'd seen this contrast between East Coast and West Coast very clearly when I was a summer intern.

I felt proud, at the end of the summer of 2006, that of the internship managers, I had the highest percentage of kids—more than half of my group of twenty-five—who were asked to join the firm full time.

Also that summer, Goldman chose me as one of ten Goldman employees to appear in a documentary-style recruitment video that was made that summer. The firm brought in a production company that filmed me on the trading floor interacting with other employees, then interviewed me on-camera.

The cherry on the sundae for my summer was an offer that came out of left field. Laura Mehta, the managing director of our desk, had a house on the North Fork of Long Island—it was only a two-bedroom, but it could have come straight out of the pages of *Architectural Digest*. Pristine white, perched on the edge of the bluff overlooking the water, the place was fitted out with all the goodies: full chef's kitchen, Sub-Zero fridge, surround sound. Laura e-mailed Connors and me, saying that either of us could stay there on the weekends she wouldn't be there. "You guys have worked very hard," she said. "You're welcome to use it." Nadine and I had just started dating, and nothing could have been more romantic—or, frankly, more impressive—than taking my new girlfriend to a managing director's house overlooking the Long Island Sound. Laura went out of her way to recommend all the best places in town—we went to the Frisky Oyster in Greenport for dinner, got the egg-and-cheese croissants that she recommended from the farmers' market down the street. I was twenty-seven years old, and it felt as though a lot was going my way.

————

Going my way in a big way. At the end of November, Laura called me into her office, smiling, and said, "Well done, Greg."

I was smiling, too. I knew what was coming.

"We're promoting you to vice president," she told me.

I was extremely proud; at the same time, I have to put this promotion in perspective. A little later that day, Lloyd Blankfein sent out an e-mail to the whole firm saying, "These are the new vice presidents; we'd like to congratulate everyone." There were more than a thousand people on the list.

To sharpen the picture further: in a given year, depending on market conditions, Goldman Sachs could fire roughly that same number of employees—one to two thousand people. So being promoted to vice president is as much a tribute to your survival skills as anything else. Many in my analyst class had fallen by the wayside; many more were still to fall.

A Goldman Sachs vice presidency does not mean a bump in total compensation. In theory, if the firm has a bad year, it's possible for a newly minted VP to earn less than he or she earned as an associate. Nor are Goldman vice presidents an elite minority: out of thirty thousand people in the firm, some twelve thousand are VPs. They are in the trenches. They are the people who do most of the work and, in my mind, who understand better what the culture really is than someone stuck in a corner office with glass walls.

Still, I was very proud. Everyone started congratulating me. I must have gotten seventy-five or eighty e-mails—from people above me and below me, from clients, even from friends outside finance altogether who had somehow heard the news—saying, "Well deserved," "May you go from strength to strength," and the like.

As 2006, that Year of Wonders, wound down, did I also feel uneasy about some of the things that were going on at Goldman Sachs? Things such as the Archipelago deal and proprietary trading, not to mention some of the new structured products I had started seeing—derivatives so complex that only the firm's smartest quants and strats (and perhaps not even they) truly understood them?

Maybe. But some of those things were happening on another side of a wall as tall and as strong as the Great Wall itself, in an area whose doings I was not even privy to. And from a compliance standpoint, Goldman was the most legally rigorous of all investment banks. We were constantly being reminded about how careful we should be; how thoroughly we should check things; how, if we weren't sure about something, we should speak to the lawyers. We were trained in securities law and precedent every few weeks. *Surely*, I (and many others) thought, *we must be doing everything right.*

The year ended strangely. In early December the Securities division (the name for the new entity that combined Equities and FICC) held its holiday party in a massive hall near Chelsea Piers. It was an unbelievably ostentatious affair. There must have been three thousand people in attendance, and nearly as many ice sculptures. The cavernous space was packed with crowds milling around and visiting food stands catered by some of the city's best restaurants, such as Blue Smoke and Landmarc. Rock music exploding from giant speaker banks ensured that conversation would be impossible—basically, all you could do was eat, get hammered, and gape at the sheer spectacle of the thing.

The most gape-worthy sight of all was the entrance of Gary Cohn. Our new president had earned something like $50 million that year, and his stratospheric new status had clearly pushed him into bizarro world, for he walked into the hall surrounded by beefy guys wearing earpieces. This was an internal party, and here was friendly Gary Cohn—who was as big and as beefy as any of the beefy guys—ringed by bodyguards. Who, exactly, were they protecting him from? If a lowly associate or VP attempted to walk up and make party chat, would the presumptuous underling have been tackled and tased? Fortunately, this didn't happen. Gary, surrounded by his Praetorian Guard, made his way from food stand to food stand smiling and sampling the goodies.

A few days later, I went into Laura's office again, for my compensation discussion.

This was an annual ritual at Goldman Sachs. In mid-December every employee at the company, high or low, was called into his or her manager's office and, in a ten-minute meeting, told the amount of his or her PATC ("per annum total compensation"). The amount combined base salary with bonus; bonus per se was never discussed. You did the math yourself, in your head.

Nevertheless, the meetings were known as bonus meetings, and the day was known as Bonus Day, because for everybody above analyst status, the bonus was the Main Event, the big deal, the bulk of your compensation. A lot of people who have been on Wall Street for a long time start getting used to a certain amount of bonus every year, and factor this into the planning of their family lives—things such as private schools, summer houses, nannies, vacations. So when the number doesn't measure up, it can mean unpleasant conversations when they get home, about things that, to the rest of the world, are considered extreme luxuries. People anticipated the meeting for the whole year; on the day itself, everybody would arrive fifteen minutes early, at 6:30 A.M. rather than 6:45.

It was an interesting day if you were a student of human nature. The bonus meetings were much like the firings. People were called into a partner's glass-walled office, and everyone outside could see exactly what was happening. The difference with Bonus Day was that the meetings usually proceeded from the most senior people to the most junior. The partner in charge of your group would sit in his office and, outside, at around 6:45 A.M., the phone lines would start ringing. The most senior person's line rang first. He'd go into the room and then emerge ten minutes later with a poker face. The next person would go in and then, ten minutes later, come out with a poker face. And so on, down the line.

There was an absurd amount of emphasis placed on these meetings. For many people, the session determined a person's entire self-worth. In many cases, the meeting inflated (or deflated) an already exaggerated ego. But however arbitrary the number handed down by the partner might be, there was also a real poignancy to the bonus meeting. Many people had spent the year working eighty-five-hour weeks, killing themselves for the firm. They expected something in return.

Therefore, as you might imagine, Bonus Day was an emotionally charged time for almost everyone, and not everyone was able to manage the customary deadpan. You saw a lot of antics: You saw people slamming the door as they walked out. You even saw people so upset that they came out and left the office for the day, at 7:00 A.M. It was the one day in the year that such behavior was acceptable. It was a given that some people were going to be disappointed and some elated. Bobby Schwartz was notorious on our desk for not being able to hide his emotions after a positive bonus meeting. A couple of times, Corey Stevens swore to me, he had actually seen Bobby click his heels.

The one rule that was hard and fast was that the meeting lasted ten minutes, and not one minute more. If you were disappointed with your bonus, you could speak your piece—and then, at the ten-minute mark, the partner would say, in effect, "Thank you, the meeting is finished. Accept it."

My hopes were high when I entered Laura's office. They were quickly dashed. Or, to put things into proper perspective, I should say that they were dampened.

She told me that for 2006, my PATC would be close to half a million dollars. By the logic of the outside world, I was being absurdly well compensated for work whose chief benefit was to maintain the robustness of the world's capital markets—work whose benefit to mankind was limited to the pensioners and foreign governments in the pension and sovereign wealth funds I serviced. By any measure, I should have felt exceptionally lucky and grateful.

But by the warped logic of Goldman Sachs and Wall Street, I was being screwed. Our desk had brought in millions of dollars in revenue that year, and I was well aware that a vice president or managing director could have been paid between 5 and 7 percent of that total, assuming the firm was having a good year overall—which it was. It was true that I had just been promoted from associate to vice president, but, I told Laura, I didn't think that that fact should have been held against me when it came to compensation time. I had, as she well knew, done at least 50 percent of the heavy lifting on the desk, along with Connors. I could only imagine what he had been paid. He hadn't clicked his heels when he came out of Laura's office, but he might as well have.

Laura smiled sadly. "I'm sorry, Greg," she said. "You're just too junior at this point for us to compensate you at that level. If we do as well next year, it'll be a different story."

The meeting was over. I stayed and worked for the rest of the day.

CHAPTER 6

Hunting for Elephants

While the world started seeing a financial crisis only in 2008, my clients were the canary in the coal mine. On our desk, we started seeing a crisis in 2007. Unbeknownst to the broader world, a significant portion of my clients started blowing up in the summer of 2007, in what became a huge "quant meltdown," and was a foreboding sign of what was to come just one year later.

On Wall Street, the term *quant* typically refers to a geek who has a PhD in a field such as physics, applied math, electrical engineering, or economics. Within the investment banks, quants do all the intellectual heavy lifting: they build financial models to manage risk; they test formulas to price complicated derivatives, sometimes designing structured products so complex and opaque that, even though they may be designed to meet a specific client need, their true worth is impossible for the client to assess. In the meantime, these structured products can generate millions of dollars in revenues for Wall Street firms. It is not the most glamorous work, but make no mistake: quants can be worth their weight in gold; the best ones get paid millions of dollars. Sadly, that's why actual rocket scientists and engineers leave their professions for the allure of making ten times as much money in finance.

Some quants have gone out on their own and started quantitative hedge funds, relying on their smarts and the models they've built to generate outsize returns for themselves and their investors. (When you hear someone on Wall Street talk about a "black box," there isn't an actual box. It is the computer model that one of these quants has built.) It was my job to cover the biggest quant funds on the Street—in particular, Goldman's flagship fund, Global Alpha, run by Mark Carhart and Ray Iwanowski; AQR Capital, run by Cliff Asness; and Bridgewater Associates, run by Ray Dalio. I mostly dealt with the trading desk at each of these hedge funds. In 2007 these three managers alone had close to $100 billion in assets, and saying they ran into a little trouble in the summer of 2007 would be a huge understatement.

The name Global Alpha was very Goldman Sachs. *Alpha* is not just a term that primatologists use to describe the big swinging monkey who rules the pack. In finance terminology, *alpha* indicates the excess return of an investment relative to its benchmark.

Global Alpha had been created in the 1990s by Cliff Asness, who had an aura of being so smart that some people said he could bend spoons just by looking at them. He'd studied under the libertarian economist Eugene Fama and had a doctorate in finance from the University of Chicago. Asness had developed a black-box computer model that combined, in powerful ways, the ideas of value investing (buying stocks, bonds, currencies, and commodities at less than their intrinsic value and holding on till the price rises) and momentum investing (buying or selling securities according to their movement over a certain period). The model, which was designed to seize on anomalies (mispriced securities), produced such impressive results that in 1997, in the midst of the inflating dot-com bubble, Asness left Goldman to start his own hedge fund, AQR Capital.

After he left, the running of Global Alpha fell to his two deputies, Carhart and Iwanowski. They more or less kept Asness's quant model and tried to improve on it over time. This computer program could decide, more quickly than any human, when to buy and when to sell. For most of the next decade, even during the 2002–2005 recession, Carhart and Iwanowski's black box kept minting money for the firm, month after month after month. The media speculated that Mark and Ray were earning $20 million a year. Global Alpha became a source of huge pride and revenue for the firm—to the point where our detractors were enviously likening all of Goldman Sachs to a giant hedge fund.

I had a front-row seat to this world: quant hedge funds were a substantial part of my client base in Derivatives Sales, and one of my most important clients was Global Alpha. This may seem strange—how could I have had a client relationship with another part of the Goldman Sachs empire?—but the rigorously enforced Chinese wall between divisions at Goldman Sachs made it possible. On behalf of Global Alpha, I was allowed to execute "agency" business—transparent, commissioned trades of futures, options, or stock on an exchange such as the CME or the NYSE. For compliance reasons, however, I was not allowed to execute "principal" business—transactions in which Goldman Sachs would have to commit its own money to take the other side of a Global Alpha trade. Principal trades might carry an embedded fee, known as the "bid-offer spread," instead of the flat commissions that agency business carried.*

For a long time, though, the commissions generated by Global Alpha—which ran into the millions of dollars because of the size of the fund and the magnitude of the trades—were big business for our desk, and for me. And what I saw in the summer of 2007 was that, for one day, then two, then three, then for an entire week, Carhart, Iwanowski, and Asness's excellent black boxes suddenly stopped working.

The fundamental problem with computer models for trading securities is that they don't effectively take the outside world into account. They don't have human thoughts, so psychology can never figure into their calculations. Unlike Gary Cohn in the commodities pit, they can't look into the whites of people's eyes and see their fear. And as Gary discovered so successfully, a large part of trading is based on understanding other traders' emotions. Are they scared? Are they panicked?

In the summer of 2007, fear had started to creep into the markets, and the computer models simply couldn't pick it up. My colleagues and I began to worry about Global Alpha and AQR when we saw something curious going on with the funds' vital signs. We used to track how closely these funds' performance correlated to a benchmark such as the S&P 500 Index (a collection of five hundred stocks that acts as a kind of

---

* In a continuing war against the Volcker Rule, which seeks to end proprietary trading, the investment banks defend principal trading, saying they need to hedge themselves after they've facilitated a client trade as a market maker. In fact, what often happens is banks use the cover of this "hedging" to then express their views via proprietary trades.

blood pressure gauge for the stock market). Normally, the quant funds traded within 10 to 50 basis points of the S&P. (A basis point—"bip" for short—is a unit equal to a hundredth of a percentage point: 100 bips equals 1 percent.) In the summer of 2007, AQR and Global Alpha were showing a variance of greater than 250 bips from the S&P 500. Highly abnormal.

We needed to figure out what was going on, and to understand what's really going on in a quant meltdown, you need to talk to a quant. I was fortunate to have had a great one on our team. Like Cliff Asness, Helga had an economics PhD from Chicago. She spoke with her fellow geniuses at other banks and hedge funds and deduced that the quant funds seemed to be falling victim to their own success: there were just too many of them using the exact same model.

It wasn't just AQR and Global Alpha that used the model. There were other big funds run by PhDs working with variations on Cliff's special sauce: there was James Simons's Renaissance Technologies, and there was D. E. Shaw, among many smaller imitators. As a result of all these companies working off similar models, investment opportunities in heavily capitalized mainstream companies were becoming crowded, so the computers were increasingly seeking out more illiquid and less widely held investments. The more out of the way the security, the fewer buyers and sellers for it, so it can be hard to unwind one of these investments. Although quants do think about the dangers of illiquidity a lot, the mistake they made this time was to fail to imagine that everyone would want to get out at the same time. They were so hypnotized by all the relentless success that they just kept doing most of what the computer model was telling them to do.

If the computer spat out, "Buy 10,000 shares of Lukoil," the fund's traders went out and bought the Russian oil company. If the computer said, "Sell May wheat futures," the traders started selling. The programs kept looking for freakier securities that displayed the anomalies the model was looking for—and the fund managers kept trading. Not enough questions were being asked.

Then, suddenly, everybody's model was saying, "Sell." Ironically, this fear in the market was actually being driven by something completely different: emerging jitters in the subprime mortgage market. Nothing to do with math; everything to do with emotion.

But the computers didn't care. They had known before what to do, and they knew now. Selling made sense to the computer model, and it is very rare that quants overrule the model. The problems were twofold, and they were massive: First, the out-of-the-way securities that the computer models had chosen to unwind were illiquid. Second, since everybody's model was saying the same thing, there were few buyers.

It was as though somebody had yelled, "Fire!" in a crowded theater and the exits were blocked.

All at once that August 2007, the quant hedge funds' computer models began imploding. Everyone was trying to unload the same securities at the same time, and as prices went lower and lower, the funds began to hemorrhage money. In addition, investors in these funds panicked and demanded to be cashed out. The one-two punch of the black boxes going haywire and investors making mass redemptions gutted several of my desk's biggest clients. AQR survived because the firm had launched other, nonquant funds that appealed to retail investors. But Goldman's own quant fund was not as fortunate. Global Alpha lost more than 30 percent that summer, and the fund never really recovered. Its comanagers quit in 2009, and the firm shut it down in 2011.

The summer of 2007 was highly unnerving. *What is happening here?* everyone wondered. *This market makes no sense.* Colleagues canceled vacations, afraid to be away from the desk until the volatility died down. Wall Street likes predictability, and all at once predictability had gone out the window. Confidence evaporated. Clients stopped trading. It was sad to see the order flows of clients such as Global Alpha decrease slowly but surely, and significantly. Some of these quant funds went from being among the biggest commission payers on the Street to the smallest, with annual commissions plummeting from the millions of dollars to the thousands. The business environment after the summer of 2007 was tough. We were all looking for ways to keep the lights on.

One solution, according to management, was to go elephant hunting. In quarterly internal "town hall" meetings conducted by the heads of the division, there was often an entire segment devoted to giving kudos to salespeople who had done elephant trades.

In good times, transparent, flat-fee commission business was steady and paid the bills; it was a volume business. But if the register wasn't ringing, as was now the case, new types of business had to be found.

What could make up the fastest for lost revenue? Products that were quick hits, that had very high margin embedded in them. As a general rule on Wall Street, the less transparent a product is, the more money is in it for the firm. Over-the-counter derivatives (OTC, meaning not listed on an exchange) and structured products (complex, nontransparent derivatives with all sorts of bells and whistles) were the trades to go for.

As I've mentioned, Matt Ricci, my boss's boss, had coined the term *elephant trades* to signify those trades where Goldman made $1 million or more in discretionary profit. When you executed one of these trades, the revenue would go next to your name in the form of a gross credit, or GC, another favorite Ricci term. (Matt Ricci had left the firm by early 2007 to go to another bank, but many of his catchphrases remained.)

One client that did an elephant trade was the government of Libya, which gave Goldman $1.3 billion to invest in a product that bundled a bet on currencies with call options on big liquid stocks such as Citigroup, UniCredit, Santander, and Allianz. Placed just before the financial crisis, this bet was one Libya would come to regret. Its $1.3 billion was vaporized in short order—gone. I had to wonder why Goldman Sachs would want to get in bed with Muammar Gaddafi and his exchequer. This was business that the firm probably would have turned away a few years ago, due to the possible reputational damage of dealing with a nation once officially declared a terrorist state by the U.S. government. But now the margins were just so big that it was hard to say no.

But no matter who the firm was dealing with, Goldman and Wall Street were getting really smart at playing on clients' fear and greed. The sales pitch went something like this: "The world is falling apart. You need a magic fix to protect yourself and help you outperform your peers. You should trade this structured derivatives product that we have specially tailored for you."

The problem: there was no magic fix. Sure, these clients were foolish to trade these products, but I don't believe they were educated enough to understand them, and I don't believe the risks and rewards were presented objectively to them.

———

It was a climate like this one, a climate of fear, that allowed my old colleague Bobby Schwartz to go from zero to hero at Goldman Sachs.

I first met Bobby when I was a second-year analyst, at the beginning of my tenure with Corey Stevens on the Futures desk in late 2002. The Jewish John Kennedy was a third-year analyst, a year older than me, and a bit of a strange guy. He was athletic, with a head of thick dark hair (hence his nickname), but was somewhat inept socially—a lot of what he said came off as just plain goofy. He had an amazing ability to do complex calculations in his head. At the same time, he was extremely absentminded. He was like a numbers nerd in a jock's body: both halves of the Nutty Professor combined.

Bobby had had a rocky start at Goldman, showing up late for work and occasionally making trading errors—sometimes forgetting about orders, buying instead of selling, miscalculating quantities. If you'd seen him then, you'd have thought, *Here's a guy who's bound to get fired.* I thought this. And yet somehow he hung on, slowly learning the art of social interaction and getting a few senior people to like him.

When the clients started panicking in the summer of 2007, Bobby was their guy. His quantitative skills made it easy for him to persuade smart but scared people to do things that made the firm significant amounts of money: dive into extremely complex, structured-product trades. If the client said, "Can you explain that to me?" Bobby could say, "Sure—here's the math formula." Then he would walk the client through it—but he would often skip steps because his mind worked so quickly.

As the markets fell, Bobby's fortunes rose. He didn't have to call clients with ideas much; the clients were calling him, frightened, and he was charging them significant embedded spreads—which were not always transparent to the client—for the privilege of trading with us. And as his business swelled, so did his head.

He would come in at 9:00 A.M., when everyone else had shown up at

6:45; he would leave at 4:16 P.M. on the dot, one minute after the U.S. equity futures markets closed. There were two young guys who backed him up on the Derivatives desk, and they always used to complain about how he would go AWOL. Plus they were doing all the hard work, yet he was getting all the glory, and the money.

But money talks. Once Bobby started bringing in all these revenues, he could come and go as he pleased. No one would ever know where he was. If anyone asked him why he'd come to work at noon, he would tell them, with a completely straight face, that he'd been at physical therapy. He was a marathon runner, so it could have been true. But it also became an inside joke: "Where's Bobby?" "Physical therapy." Cue eye roll. He did whatever he wanted, and the firm said nothing about it because they worried that if he left, his revenues would disappear.

Just like that, Bobby had turned from the goofy guy into the cool guy. He was on the charity benefit circuit in Manhattan and out in the Hamptons. He dated a lot of models. For Tim Connors's wedding, he flew in a beautiful girl from London to Martha's Vineyard as his date. I heard her accent and realized that she was from South Africa—then found out she was an Oppenheimer, the daughter of one of the richest families in the world. He rode a Vespa to work, and bought a share in the Surf Lodge, a club that was then the new hot spot in Montauk.

The partners ate this up. A few of them tried to tag along when Bobby went out (almost every night of the week), because they wanted to live vicariously through him. And he believed in his press. He had become a Master of the Universe while the financial markets were cratering, a rainmaker in the midst of a hurricane.

———

On March 16, 2008, I was watching my TiVo-ed recording of *Meet the Press* when I saw the news on my BlackBerry that JPMorgan Chase had bought Bear Stearns for $2 a share. At first I thought the number was a typo. As late as January 2007, Bear Stearns had been trading at $172 a share, and at $93 just the month before, in February 2008. The firm had recently erected a shiny new tower on Madison Avenue; the building itself was worth $5 a share.

But it wasn't a typo. The background was that the Federal Reserve Bank of New York was making a $30 billion loan to JPMorgan Chase (still collateralized by Bear Stearns's unencumbered assets) to buy the firm at $2 a share, 7 percent of its market value before the weekend.

People put two and two together and immediately realized the reason behind the fire-sale price: the assets on Bear Stearns's balance sheet were so toxic that JPMorgan was actually taking on billions of dollars in immediate losses. But the deal had a sweetheart fragrance about it, and soon the financial world was accusing the Federal Reserve of giving Bear Stearns to JPMorgan on the cheap because of the latter firm's robust balance sheet. Ultimately, Jamie Dimon of JPMorgan raised the purchase price to $10 a share: still pretty sweet.

Even then, though, with the subprime mortgage market teetering, the official view was that the fall of Bear Stearns had just been a glitch.

On the Goldman trading floor that Monday, the consensus was that Bear was a firm that had gotten a little over its skis. The then-chairman of the SEC, Christopher Cox, said that the cause of Bear Stearns's demise had been a crisis in investor confidence rather than a lack of capital: in plain terms, a run on the bank. There was a certain amount of truth to this, but to be honest, on the desk, we thought Bear was a firm with an irresponsible appetite for risk, and that what had happened to it could not happen to Goldman. We were smarter and better.

Still, Bear's fall infected the marketplace with fear that the same thing could happen to someone else. Everyone needed cash, but no one wanted to lend it. Long-term, secure borrowing costs suddenly became very expensive for the remaining pure investment banks: Lehman Brothers, Merrill Lynch, Morgan Stanley, and Goldman Sachs. Investment banks did not have depositors or offer checking accounts to Mom and Pop; nor did they have access to very cheap financing through the Federal Reserve's borrowing window.

So, as a way to get cash in the door—to use as a security reserve to stabilize its balance sheet, or to "rehypothecate" (reallocate) for whatever business purposes the firm had in mind—Goldman Sachs (and the other banks) devised the *funding trade*.

It worked this way: a client—say, a German or Dutch or U.S. asset manager or pension fund, or an Asian or Middle Eastern sovereign wealth fund—would commit a substantial amount of cash (say $500 million) to the firm for one year. In exchange, the firm would guarantee to pay the client the returns of whatever benchmark the client chose (say, the S&P 500 Index, or the Russell 2000 SmallCap Index), plus an additional, very large (say, 2 percent) "coupon," a rate the client would not be able to get elsewhere. In effect, Goldman was getting to borrow large amounts of money at 2 percent or so, as opposed to real borrowing costs of, say, 4 percent.

That was the upside for Goldman; the catch for clients was that they were taking what's called *counterparty risk*—completely fair in the Lloyd Blankfein, we're-all-big-boys world of investment banking, but dicey nonetheless. The risk was simply this: if Goldman Sachs went bankrupt, the client's money might vaporize.

And what were the chances of Goldman Sachs—*Goldman Sachs*—going bankrupt? Wasn't going to happen. Bear Stearns had been foolish to tie up so much of its business in subprime mortgages. (What had been *really* foolish was betting so much *on* subprime mortgages, rather than against them...)

I told my clients, "Look, you have to make a determination. Do you think Goldman Sachs is going to go bankrupt? If the answer to that is yes, you should not do this funding trade. However, if you believe that in a year's time Goldman Sachs will still be around, you should do this trade, because you will outperform your benchmark by two percent, and that two percent will make your year." It was easy for me to make this pitch with a straight face back in the winter of 2008. Despite what had happened to Bear Stearns, I thought Goldman had as much chance of going down as the sky did of falling. Other dominoes might tumble, but we would be the last one standing.

Many of the clients who did the funding trade would come to regret doing so before the year was out. In the depths of the crisis that fall, as each week saw a new financial institution circling the drain, a number of clients wanted their cash back early. Some banks took a measured approach, telling their clients, in effect, "We'll give you the money back at seventy-five to eighty cents on the dollar—we will make some money on this to reflect the turmoil in the world, but we're not going to rip your eyeballs out." Goldman Sachs made it much harder, almost impossible, for clients to get their money back. Putting an extremely stringent interpretation on the "break clauses" in the funding trade contracts, Goldman offered the clients far less than the other banks. This burned bridges with a number of important institutional clients. Even today, there are large clients across Europe, the U.S., and Asia who hold a grudge against the firm because of its behavior then.

"Our assets are our people, capital, and reputation. If any of these is ever diminished, the last is the most difficult to restore." That is Goldman Sachs's second business principle. But a comment made during the crisis by a European partner summed up the latter-day evolution of Goldman's business principles. A number of sales colleagues had grown frustrated with our traders' unwillingness to make a fair price for clients who wanted out during the teeth of the crisis, so they approached one of the partners in charge. "If I have to choose between my reputation and my P&L, I choose my profit-and-loss," the partner said back to them. "Because I can ultimately recover my reputation, but if I lose a lot of money, I can't recover that."

———

In April 2008, a couple of weeks after the fall of Bear Stearns, I got on a plane and flew across the Pacific to visit several important clients in Asia. I traveled with another Goldman VP and with a partner named Brett Silverman. Brett had joined Goldman after business school and had made his name trading blue-chip technology stocks, such as Microsoft, during the peak of the Internet bubble. He was a culture carrier who had made partner by age thirty-seven.

After the customary formal greeting, we met with the first set of clients in their offices, high above the Asian capital, with amazing panoramic views all around. As usual, the clients—five of them in all, heads of portfolio management and risk management among them—lined up on one side of the table. The three of us were on the other side. We waited for them to sit down before taking our seats.

The head of the fund seemed uncertain. "What does Goldman Sachs think?" he asked Silverman. "Are we out of the woods? Is the worst over?"

Brett looked the client in the eye. "I'm very bullish," he said. "I think this is an anomaly. I think things are going to get much better. I'd be buying the market if I were you."

Meaning he'd be buying stocks.

I sat there surprised, thinking about the strangeness of Brett's statement: from all I'd seen and heard, there was not a lot of evidence to suggest such optimism.

Was he being naïve? Strange to apply that word to a Goldman Sachs partner, a man ten levels above me, making (at a guess) at least $5 million a year, but that was how it seemed to me at the time. *One of the five biggest investment banks in America has just been swallowed alive, and you're giving clients the all-clear?* It made no sense to me.

If he truly was being sincere, and I think he might have been, he couldn't have been more wrong, given what would happen that fall.

I was on the road with Silverman for two days, and he seemed genuinely (if not strangely) calm. That night, he took me and the other VP and a couple of Asian clients out to dinner at a traditional restaurant in the capital. We sat at a low table, on floor mats. Before the clients arrived, Brett took out his iPhone. (This was not long after the iPhone had first come out, and being able to watch a video on one was still a novelty.) He had something very special to show us. Every year, he was the partner who made a famous prank video—an elaborately produced hoax, along the lines of *Candid Camera* or Ashton Kutcher's *Punk'd*—that was screened at the Goldman holiday party in December. What he showed us now was one of the funniest things I had ever seen and was definitely worth watching again while we had some time to kill.

For the prank, Brett had planted hidden cameras in one of the firm's conference rooms and brought in a professional actor impersonating a major potential hire for Goldman to be interviewed by several partners (including Matt Ricci) who were not in on the joke. The scenario was that the "candidate" had just made $100 million for another bank, and we were trying to lure him away. Brett had told all the partners that this was a terrific guy, and that we really needed to hire him. But when the partners came in, the "candidate" acted like a complete asshole, propping his feet up on the desk, interrupting the interview to ask if he could order some food. When he got a sandwich, he tucked his napkin into his shirt. These were very senior partners, and they began to get flustered, red-faced, and angry.

One of them asked the guy, "What are your goals?"

"My ideal lifestyle would be to have two helicopters," the guy said, with a completely straight face. "I'd like to be at a ski slope and have one helicopter at the bottom of the mountain to take me to the top, and then, after I ski down, another to take me back up."

Finally the interview came to an end. "Do you have any questions for us?" one of the partners asked.

"I have a lot of mental health problems," the guy said. "How's the firm's psychiatric coverage?"

By the time the clients showed up to the restaurant, the three of us were rolling on the floor. We had a wonderful, lighthearted dinner— with little in the way of business discussed. Maybe everything was all right after all.

———

The markets went into a weird period of calm in the summer of 2008. Everyone was waiting for the other shoe to drop; no one—including Treasury Secretary Hank Paulson and New York Federal Reserve President Tim Geithner—knew what was going to happen next. In hindsight, Paulson and Geithner should have been doing some more intensive contingency planning. There were research analysts on the Street predicting a chain reaction in which the markets would go after each bank, one by one, from the smallest and weakest to the biggest and strongest. Some even foresaw which dominoes would fall next.

By Friday, September 12, 2008, everyone knew it was the day of reckoning for Lehman Brothers—either it would go bankrupt or someone would save it. Deep down, I didn't think it would be allowed to go bankrupt, but part of me thought this may have been the right thing to happen. Dying animals should be allowed to die. I left the office that day knowing that the events of that weekend would be crucial, but that there was nothing I or any of the other hundreds of thousands of people on Wall Street could do but stay glued to the TV and our Black-Berrys. We were awaiting news from the New York Fed, where the heads of the country's most powerful financial institutions were huddled with Paulson and Geithner trying to solve the hardest brainteaser of their lives.

That Saturday night, September 13, Nadine and I were out to dinner with another couple, at a favorite Italian place of mine called Supper, in the East Village. It was a schlep from the Upper West Side, but this was a weekend for good, rustic Italian food. The other couple also worked in finance: he in private equity, she at a hedge fund. The mood wasn't one of panic; it was one of astonishment. We all couldn't stop saying how surreal the world we were living in had become. It felt as if we were in a movie. I remember saying that night that if you had told me a few years ago that Bear Stearns and Lehman Brothers could both vaporize within months of each other, I would have called you crazy. This was the stuff of the weirdest science-fiction movie any of us could think of.

Things would get stranger.

Over that weekend of September 13 and 14, Merrill Lynch and Lehman Brothers—both of which turned out to have been as badly exposed in the subprime mortgage market as Bear Stearns—toppled. On Sunday, Merrill Lynch was acquired by Bank of America, and in the early hours of Monday morning, Lehman Brothers filed for Chapter 11 bankruptcy. It was then (and still is) the largest bankruptcy in U.S. history. With two investment banks down, it was only a matter of time before the rest of us were in the crosshairs.

And the hits just kept on coming. The Dow lost just over 500 points on Monday the fifteenth, the biggest single drop since 9/11. Money market funds—the safest investment around, with minuscule rates of return—began notching negative returns. If you put your funds into a money market at that point, you would have gotten less back than if you'd stuck them in a mattress. The term for this is *breaking the buck*. No one thought this could ever happen. It happened.

With three investment banks gone by Monday, September 15, both our stock and Morgan Stanley's got pummeled. On Tuesday of that week, the stock of AIG, the world's biggest insurance company, dropped 60 percent, after already having dropped more than 95 percent from its fifty-two-week high of $70.13. AIG was an insurance institution that affected millions of lives in almost every country in the world, and because of some reckless gambling in credit-default swaps,* it was on the brink of collapse. The Federal Reserve stepped in and gave AIG an initial $85 billion bailout. This would grow. After people saw what was going on with AIG, the reaction was: *Holy shit!* Wall Street likes predictability, and the way the government was flip-flopping between bailing out companies and letting them fail was not helping the markets.

Uncharacteristically, we were rooting for Morgan Stanley, our closest competitor—as they were for us. We were in this together.

There was a lot of talk about mergers. People up to the highest levels in the government were saying Goldman needed to find a partner, a bank with a lot of deposits, one to make us more stable. Who was the right partner? Was it Wachovia? Washington Mutual? Citibank?

Screw the mergers was what everyone on the trading floor was thinking. *We will survive this thing. We are Goldman Sachs.* Outsiders would probably have called us arrogant, but everyone felt that what made Goldman special would be lost if we merged.

It had been a brutal week. Lehman, Merrill, AIG—it felt like an environment where almost anything could happen. Nothing seemed out of the realm of possibility. Several of us went in to the office on Sunday evening, September 21, because a lot of news had been breaking over the weekends, and because the U.S. futures markets open at 6:30 P.M., New York time, on Sunday, just as the Asian markets are opening on their Monday morning. I had seen how, after the 2003 blackout, futures were the first place people looked to get a sense of whether the market was panicked. If there was any big news that weekend, the futures markets would take the financial world's temperature on it.

My colleagues and I were phoning and e-mailing clients who were reachable on a Sunday evening, giving them updates, trying to reassure

---

* A credit-default swap is a type of derivative that acts like an insurance policy against the default of a company or sovereign nation.

them that we were there for them if they needed us. But at the same time we were also worried about ourselves. Uncertainty hung heavily in the air. We were just trying to figure out what was going on in the world, and most of us stayed till quite late to see how the Asian markets were trading.

By 9:15 P.M. nothing much had happened, so I left, along with a younger colleague. We got into the elevator on the fiftieth floor. As the doors were closing, a big hand reached between them, and they opened again. The hand belonged to Gary Cohn, who stepped into the car with us.

It was the strangest thing to happen at 9:15 P.M. on a Sunday, when only a few people had been on the trading floor. The doors closed. Gary looked very tired and scruffy: he was wearing jeans and a sweater; he hadn't shaved in a couple of days. He nodded to me—I think he recognized me from the days when Equities and FICC had first merged on the Futures desk and he used to come over and visit his friend from the old days in the commodities pits. "Crazy world we live in," I said, in the blandest, most neutral tones I could find. It was a touchy time, and I was just trying to be friendly.

"Tell me about it. I've been here the whole weekend, and I haven't gone home much," Gary said. He looked as if he could have slept on his office couch the previous night.

I knew, and I'm sure my associate sensed, that this was the end of the conversation. We knew the world was in turmoil, and even if there wasn't a specific reason for Gary to be there, he'd probably just been strategizing. We would very soon learn the truth.

As I got into a cab outside One New York Plaza to head back uptown to the Upper West Side, I checked my BlackBerry. A fresh work e-mail caught my eye. "The Federal Reserve Board approved the applications of Goldman Sachs and Morgan Stanley to become bank holding companies." *Holy shit!* So that was why Gary Cohn had been working around the clock in the office all weekend. This was huge.

In a single weekend, the institution of the investment bank, as it had once been construed, had vanished forever. The Goldman Sachs of Sidney Weinberg, Gus Levy, and John Whitehead had vaporized—cleverly converted, through the eleventh-hour labors of desperate men (Lloyd Blankfein, Gary Cohn, and Morgan Stanley's then-CEO, John Mack, among them), into an institution that could borrow money from the government at zero interest and then invest it at government bond rates, in essence making free money. Goldman Sachs and Morgan Stanley were now effectively getting paid by the government just to stay in business.

CHAPTER 7

Looking into the Abyss

Out of the corner of my eye I saw Lloyd Blankfein, the CEO of the company, walking toward my group, Derivatives Sales, with a throng of people. They were on the other side of the football field–size trading floor, but steadily moving in our direction. A couple of photographers and someone with a video camera were walking along with them. This was a strange sight. You never saw photographers on the trading floor, especially not during what felt like financial Armageddon. The markets were melting down, and Lloyd was smiling from ear to ear, as was everyone in the crowd. Then I saw that the group moving closer to my desk was full of bigwigs: the global head of the Securities division, Harvey Schwartz; the head of North American sales, Enrico Gaglioti. There must have been seven or eight partners, but none of these bigwigs was as big as the man they were walking with.

The Oracle of Omaha, Warren Buffett. Indisputably the greatest investing mind of his time, and possibly of all time. His Berkshire Hathaway had become legendary in its ability to see value and generate returns for its investors year after year after year.

This was a good day for Goldman Sachs amid a storm of bad ones: Warren Buffett had come to save the firm from extinction. We were all taken by complete surprise: only two days after we had converted ourselves into a bank holding company, Buffett had extended us a lifeline, in the form of a capital injection of $5 billion. It was an incredibly attractive deal for him, one he couldn't refuse. He would receive a 10 percent annual dividend—Goldman Sachs would pay him an extra

$500 million a year above and beyond his investment—plus he had the right to buy $5 billion of additional stock in the firm at a discounted price in the future, through warrants (similar to call options) the firm had granted him. An expensive deal for Goldman, but the stamp of approval of Warren Buffett was like gold. It also gave us momentum quickly to go out and raise an additional $5 billion in capital from our clients, some of the biggest institutional investors in the world. What was more important than the Oracle's $5 billion investment was the powerful shot of confidence it gave us, and the message it sent to the market: both the money and the gesture had made us more stable.

As the group headed down the long row that ran down the middle of the trading floor, Warren looked around, smiling; Lloyd was pointing things out to him. Then they decided to stop—directly by my desk.

"Lloyd, let me say a few words," Buffett said.

An associate quickly scrambled and got Buffett connected to the handset at the desk directly next to mine, so he could speak over the Hoot, reaching each and every one of the six hundred traders on the floor.

The moment Buffett started talking, applause erupted. It was the kind of applause I had heard only one other time in my career: on the one-year anniversary of September 11 when everyone cheered New York's resilience. Everyone on the floor was now standing, beaming, clapping for what felt like minutes.

"I want you to know that I have always admired Goldman Sachs," Buffett said, holding the speaker of his handset close to his mouth and the receiver to his left ear, "from the time my dad brought me to New York City when I was ten years old and we came to visit Goldman Sachs. I met Sidney Weinberg, and I have admired the firm ever since."

You couldn't make this stuff up.

"Goldman Sachs has the best people, you are the best firm, and I couldn't be prouder or more happy about my investment."

A roar of applause erupted again. It didn't stop until Lloyd and Warren had left the trading floor.

It was a moment I will always remember. I still have a photo that a colleague snapped on his iPhone: me, in my white shirt and bright blue tie, standing to Buffett's right, Lloyd to his left, and dozens of my colleagues crowded around the Oracle, every single one of them beaming with pride, and some hope. For a brief moment, all was right with the world.

A few days before Buffett's visit, treasury secretary Hank Paulson famously went to Speaker of the House Nancy Pelosi with a three-page proposal—Paulson had wanted to keep the proposal short, to facilitate its quick passage through Congress—for TARP, the Troubled Asset Relief Program, a $700 billion program to save the banks. People were stunned at Paulson's audacity: both for requesting an unprecedented amount of money, and for doing so in such a short proposal. TARP was a way for the federal government to purchase toxic, illiquid assets from the banks in the hope that the move—in effect, the biggest bailout in financial history—would revive the catatonic capital markets. There was a lot of back-and-forth in Congress, a fuller proposal was asked for, and as the program was about to go up for a vote, the Jewish High Holy Days approached.

I'm not extremely religious, but I have always been traditional, and the Jewish holidays are important to me. I had always taken off work and gone to shul on Rosh Hashanah and Yom Kippur, with no questions asked by my managers. My girlfriend's family, who lived in Dallas, had invited the two of us down to celebrate the Jewish New Year. Nadine and I had been dating for two years by now, and would alternate holidays between my cousins in Chicago and her family in Dallas. Nadine had left already that weekend, but I changed my ticket so I could wait until the last possible moment. Now, however, the earth was shaking. It was Monday, September 29, 2008. Rosh Hashanah was to start at sundown, and Congress was to vote on Paulson's proposal that afternoon.

I went to an observant Jewish managing director on the floor to get some guidance. Should I leave the ship when it felt like it was sinking?

"I need your advice, man," I said. "I'm supposed to leave now to catch a flight to Dallas for Rosh Hashanah. It feels like the whole financial system as we know it could collapse any minute and take us down with it. I have never worked on *Yontif* before, but are these exceptional circumstances? Do I stay?"

He didn't hesitate. "It's not even a choice," he said. "I don't care if Goldman Sachs goes bankrupt this minute; you and I are not going to change the outcome. Rosh Hashanah is the biggest day of the Jewish year. Go."

He had put the world into perspective for me. I got in a cab and headed to the airport.

I was running late for my flight, and the whole way, I was on the phone with my associate on the desk, asking her how the markets were looking ahead of the congressional vote. "It's looking okay," she said. "The market is holding in; the market is expecting TARP to pass."

I got to the airport and rushed through security, worried I was going to miss my flight. I made it through. Running to the gate, I phoned my associate again. TARP was the only thing the market was hanging its hat on to instill some stability and provide a way forward. "So, what's the latest?" I asked.

"You're not going to believe this," she said. She repeated it: "You are not going to believe this."

"What? What?" I said.

She sounded stunned: "They did not pass the bill."

Now, this was very unexpected. Everyone thought Congress had realized that the patient was about to die, and that TARP was essential. But the House Republicans had revolted, had changed their minds at the last minute and voted down the bill.

"Holy shit," I said. "What's the market doing?"

"It's tanking, it's tanking, it's tanking," my associate said. She meant the S&P 500: between our two phone calls, it had fallen something like 6 percent. A bad day on Wall Street is a drop of 1 or 2 percent, which doesn't happen often. A terrible day is a drop of 3 percent, which happens maybe a few times a year. Markets don't drop 6 percent while you are on a five-minute conversation. This was panic. The Dow Jones Industrial Average dropped 777.68 points that day—its single largest point drop in history.

When I got to the gate, I had to turn off my phone, which, in one respect, was a good thing (since I could now spend three and a half hours unplugged from the anxiety), but in another respect, was bad (since I could think about little else). When I landed in Dallas, I checked on the markets, which had since closed. Blood in the streets.

I got on a train to Nadine's parents' house, in the Dallas suburbs. As I stared out the window at the unfamiliar landscape, my phone rang. I jumped, then smiled when I heard the voice of my best friend Lex on the other end.

After Stanford, my path and Lex's had diverged: while I had gone to Goldman Sachs, Lex had stayed in Palo Alto, worked for and founded various start-ups, and done well for himself as an entrepreneur. Despite the fact that he was an atheist, he always called me on Rosh Hashanah, to wish me *Shanah Tovah*—Happy New Year. And while this Rosh Hashanah was anything but happy, I was comforted to hear from him.

Ever since the financial world had started coming unglued, I'd been getting a lot of texts and e-mails from friends wanting to make sure I was okay. "I hope you're surviving," one friend had texted me the day before. Everybody knew I was in the center of the storm, sitting in the front row. After acknowledging the holiday, Lex asked the same question. I told him I was hanging in there.

Then the conversation took a turn.

Instead of saying what I wanted to hear from him in the brief time we had to chat—which was basically "I hope everything turns out okay with Goldman and that things calm down"—Lex started firing questions at me.

"Do you think TARP is justified?" he asked. "After all, wasn't it the banks who took such irresponsible risk and got us into this mess?"

"Yes, Lex, but that isn't us. Goldman Sachs didn't have the same kind of toxic assets on our books. We made smarter decisions."

I was looking for someone to be on my side, not for questions.

"What about the people whose 401(k)s are getting decimated? Where's their bailout coming from?"

"I don't know, Lex. I'm right in the middle of this thing."

Now, Lex is one of the most decent, moral people I know. But he is also a very analytical guy—hence the atheism. So at the moment, Lex was just being Lex. He always likes to try to find a counterargument to every argument. Later he admitted that, to a certain extent, he was playing devil's advocate. His questions were good ones, but not necessarily the best questions from your best friend at that moment.

"And what about Lehman Brothers?" he said. "What were they up to?"

"Lehman Brothers went down because there was a witch hunt," I told him. "People were speculating that Lehman was running out of cash, therefore it became reality. People started pulling their money out; it became a run on the bank. That's all it was."

"Well, was this a run on the bank or was Lehman Brothers taking bad risks? I read that they had some really bad stuff on their books."

I knew about that, too, but I felt that the whole disaster was still too fresh for anyone to make snap judgments. "Lex, I'm right in the middle of all this right now," I repeated, "and I'm really stressed out. I can't believe some of the stuff I'm seeing. I'm worried."

I meant it. My whole career was in the balance; my future was in the balance. And not just my future. Over the summer I'd helped my sister move in for her freshman year at college in Illinois—an education I was very proud to be able to pay for. I was also trying hard to convince my mother to move to America from Johannesburg, where the crime rate seemed to be rising every day. (My dad was already planning to come over to take his pharmaceutical exam and work here afterward.) That, too, would take money—money I was glad to have, for now. If Goldman Sachs went belly-up, so would all my plans. What about my relationship with Nadine? I loved America and wanted to stay here. Could I get a visa to work somewhere else? Would I have to go back to South Africa?

Also, as corny as it may sound, I was worried about the firm. I was very proud of Goldman Sachs, and I did not want it to go down. In my mind, that would have been a terrible, unimaginable thing. Even though I knew that the financial crisis was not life or death, it felt as if we were fighting a war.

"Lex," I said. "We have only five minutes on the phone—I don't need an inquisition. I need you to be a friend."

He apologized. If I had nothing else, I thought, I would still have friends and family.

———

In mid-October, Hank Paulson summoned to Washington the heads of the nine biggest banks and told them that, whether they liked it or not, the government was going to give them a lot of money: more than $100 billion on that day alone. The banks were, in the phrase that became famous, "too big to fail." Some of them—including Goldman Sachs, in the person of Lloyd Blankfein—told Paulson they didn't need the cash. Paulson told Lloyd and the others that whether they thought they needed it or not, they were going to take it.

And take it they did—all of them. The rationale was that if some banks took the money and others didn't, the TARP funds could be seen as a stigma for those that accepted them: *This bank is in such deep trouble that it needs a bailout*, the world could think. Treasury figured the best way to keep the playing field level was simply to make everyone take the funds. (Most of these banks would also pay their executives substantial bonuses that December—on the backs of taxpayers, many taxpayers felt.) And what the world wanted to know was, wasn't the fact that the government had to give hundreds of billions of dollars to banks that had made a lot of bad investments not just a bad thing, but a *really* bad thing?

Throughout the mayhem, there was a sense of pride on the trading floor about one of our own being appointed to head Treasury. Because of his background at the helm of Goldman Sachs, I think there were few people in the world who would have been better equipped to make real-time decisions on such difficult financial problems as Hank Paulson. At times I have shuddered at the thought of what it would have been like for either John Snow or Paul O'Neill, Paulson's two immediate predecessors, to have been running Treasury during the peak of the financial crisis. I think history will judge Hank well.

As the markets continued to crater that fall and winter, it continued to feel as though the whole financial system might fail at any minute. A persistent feeling of doom hung over the trading floor, where very little trading was going on. To their credit, Lloyd Blankfein and Gary Cohn were proactive in trying to rally the troops during the crisis: they were frequently present on the trading floor, and they showed strong leadership. But true leadership was coming from only the very top of the firm. Our immediate leaders, the partners, were a completely different story. Many seemed to be holed up in their bunkers.

I remember a period of several weeks when one of my bosses, Paul Conti—a guy who, by title anyway, was a leader—did not seem to be calling clients, was not talking to his employees, did not try anything (as far as I could tell) to pump up the troops. The most impressive thing I saw him do during the crisis was put himself through one of those weeklong juice cleanses that had been trendy among the senior people at Goldman that summer and into the fall.

Most people did it to lose weight. Conti, a weightlifter who went to the gym every day, seemed to be undertaking the program as an act of supreme self-discipline. I remember sitting right behind him when he decided to start his regimen. It was Sunday evening, September 14, and we were all in the office waiting to see if Lehman would go under. I thought, *What kind of hardened motherfucker puts himself through this during the biggest financial crisis since the Great Depression?*

Every day for a week—through Lehman, Merrill, AIG, and "breaking the buck"—Conti took delivery of "six 100% organic vegetable and fruit juices" from the BluePrintCleanse company, and every day he dutifully drank all six bottles. He didn't have one bite of solid food for seven days. This did not help his mood.

Mr. Cleanse was Brooklyn-born and raised, a former college football player, equal parts intensity and passivity. During the crisis, unfortunately, it was the latter quality that surfaced. In retrospect, I can understand that he was scared, but did he think a partner's only responsibility was collecting big bonuses when times were good? Everyone on the team talked for weeks about how disappointing the partners on the floor were during the darkest days of 2008. Now was the time to step up and show everyone why they made the big bucks, why they had been appointed leaders. Instead, Mr. Cleanse sat frozen at his terminal day after day, anxiously tracking Goldman Sachs's stock price, which for the partners on the floor correlated significantly to their net worth. His passivity was particularly demoralizing to the junior analysts, kids who had been at Goldman all of three months, and who were really frightened. At one point, a partner from another floor came by and did the best he could to say a few encouraging words.

Smiling, he said, "Come on, guys. I know things are scary. But this is when Goldman Sachs rises to the occasion. The best thing we can do right now is not to retreat, but to stay in front of our clients." Magic—that's all that was needed.

This rare show of leadership on the part of a partner was such an isolated incident that people talked about it for days afterward.

The lack of leadership on the floor disappointed me sharply. I had looked up to the institution of the partnership; I had aspired to be a partner one day. I could only hope that, had I been one at the time, I would have acted differently.

With trading slowed to a crawl, Goldman began another of its periodic rounds of firings. Every couple of weeks, more people were let go. One week, the rumor on the trading floor was that one person in every group on the floor would have to be terminated. Mr. Cleanse chose to fire a new associate who had recently joined our group. The associate, in his early thirties, had been trying hard, but at that point, he probably had the fewest client relationships on the desk: he simply wasn't as valuable as others, in commercial revenue terms. There was nothing to be done about it. As he walked off, an associate named Becky began crying, right in the middle of the trading floor.

This was not a common sight in what was supposed to be a tough environment. You were supposed to suck it up on the trading floor—if you really needed to cry, the unwritten rule said, you went to the bathroom. But especially in the midst of that scary time, it was traumatic to see someone you liked get fired in front of your eyes, to pick up his things and leave the building.

Mr. Cleanse went up to her and said, "Becky, what did you major in at Villanova? Was it emotionalism? Cut it out." And that was it—the shock of this remark stopped her. That line got talked about a little bit afterward. Mr. Cleanse, it was agreed, had acted like a douche bag. In his defense, he did later help the fired associate find another job, a gesture I was impressed with.

———

Three subway stories:

1. One afternoon that October, a managing director named Doug Miller and I had a meeting scheduled with a client in Midtown, a large asset manager with about $200 billion in holdings. The client was very conservative—hence the relative health of the fund—and the topic very straightforward. We were to discuss the basics of a trading product on which the client was a little behind the curve: ETFs, or exchange-traded funds.

ETFs, which were developed decades ago, are essentially souped-up, highly targeted investment funds that trade just like stocks. If you want to get broad exposure to banks, for example, you could buy each individual banking stock (such as Bank of America, Citigroup, Wells Fargo, JPMorgan Chase), or you could buy shares in an ETF with the ticker symbol XLF, which holds shares of all these banks and gives you a composite performance for the banking sector as a whole. While ETFs are not without their fair share of critics because of the outsize market impact they can have, and the disappointing returns versus benchmark they can sometimes show, it felt almost comical to be sitting down to talk about this relatively simple investing strategy in the midst of a crisis caused by ultracomplex derivatives. Maybe black comedy was more what it felt like. Times were tough; Doug and I worried that the clients might be in a bad mood. We briefly considered canceling the meeting.

But then we decided to go. For one thing, it felt like a necessary distraction. Plus, there wasn't much we could do to fix the turmoil going on around us. Why not go visit a client, stay in front of them, show them that we weren't holed up in our bunker down in Lower Manhattan?

We decided to take the subway uptown. It was very unusual to use the subway to get to a meeting, especially among managing directors; usually you'd call for a town car. But it was rush hour, the client's office was near a station for the number 4 train, and Doug was a good guy who didn't feel the need to put on airs.

The meeting was scheduled for 5:00 P.M.; we waited for the market to close at 4:15, then hustled out to try to get there on time. Walking out of the office together, we were both a little shell-shocked. Every day that fall, institutions that had existed for a hundred years were disappearing in seconds. The markets weren't rational. It was a frightening time.

As we got on the packed subway—the two of us were standing, holding on to a pole—I said to Doug, "What do you think?" He was a decade older than me, more experienced, and I was looking for a voice of wisdom about what was going on—especially since Mr. Cleanse, the partner running my group, wasn't talking to anyone. I also thought Doug might have some insight into what the firm had in mind.

I didn't get the answer I was looking for.

Instead, Miller stared down the length of the subway car and said, over the roar of the train, "I spent almost my entire day on the phone with my wife, moving our money around." I instantly knew what he was talking about. The FDIC protects bank deposits up to $250,000: this guy had been opening new bank accounts, trying to make sure none of his savings was exposed to the wild winds howling around the markets: $250K here, $250K there. This was the banker's version of stocking up on ammo, drinkable water, granola bars, and an inflatable raft to get you west of the Hudson.

"I'm just wondering what's going to happen if the whole ship goes down," Doug said. He was talking numbly, still staring, as if he were in a trance. "All these guys in finance making two million a year—where are they going to go? What's our value to society? What skills have we developed?" He shook his head. "Society doesn't need us," he said. "We'll be lucky if we can find something for eighty grand a year. I'm going to tell my kids to go into the sciences."

It was surreal. On the one hand, we were on a crowded subway; we had to be careful about what we said. I'm sure Doug was as aware as I that some people around us were half-listening, and that the words *Goldman Sachs* should not be uttered. On the other hand, he was speaking the kind of unfiltered truth you never hear on Wall Street. It really felt like a moment of reckoning, as if the whole industry and the economy were about to die. And in a strange way, our talk on the subway felt like one of those movie scenes where two people are in a plane that's about to go down, and they can finally say—they *have* to say—what's really on their minds.

2. One day not long afterward, Nadine and I had The Talk. We'd now been going out for a long time, and in all fairness, it was time for us to think about staying together for life if we were going to stay together at all.

She initiated the conversation. Nadine is a direct person, and she began directly, at a quiet moment, one night smack in the middle of the crisis, when we were in bed and about to go to sleep. The background was, I think, that she had been advised by some of her friends that when you're thinking seriously about marrying someone, you need to have a checklist of how they're going to behave financially: what the plans are, what the goals are. This was where she was coming from. But she began fast. Very fast.

"How will you dress our kids?" she asked me.

This took me by surprise, since what was on my mind was the chaos I had seen in the markets that day.

"I'm not sure," I said. "I, uh—"

"Would you want the kids to go to private school?" Nadine asked.

"Why are we talking about this now, Nadine?"

"Do you see me working when we're married?" she asked me.

The cross-examination rubbed me the wrong way. But, in all fairness, the backstory was that she was sensitive to how involved I was in supporting my family financially: paying for my sister's college education in America, sending money to my parents. I think she was, quite fairly, wondering if that would change if and when we were married. Would my focus be on supporting our family? She clearly wanted to make sure that it would be. What I would always tell her was "Please, God, I'll be making enough money that this won't be an issue either way. I'll be able to do both." But Nadine was adamant that she didn't want to work when she had kids. The ironic thing is that I agreed with her. I've always felt that whoever was the mother of my children should—at first, anyway—work exclusively at raising the kids. I saw this to be a very special thing that I hoped to be able to provide for my wife and our family. But she wanted an explicit commitment, in no uncertain terms, almost in writing.

I felt put on the spot. So, once more, I said what I'd always said: "Well, it would depend on whether we're in a financial position where it's okay for one person not to work."

The look she gave me said: wrong answer.

I tried to recover and elaborate—I was trying, as Nadine was, to be as honest as possible. "I just want a teammate who is going to support me in the right ways, and I would support her in the right ways," I said. "That doesn't mean we both have to be working. It just means we'd both contribute to the relationship."

Another look. She'd clearly wanted answers that were as concrete as her questions. But the conversation continued, and we came around to the (quite natural) conclusion that, in the midst of wild market irrationality, in the thick of the worst financial crisis since the Great Depression, we were both freaked out about money—not to mention whether I'd have a job next week.

We decided to cut back on restaurants and taxis. (Many Wall Streeters can spend north of $10,000 a year on taxis alone.) Instead of going out to eat two or three nights a week, we said, we would try to do it just once a week. We started cooking more—and Nadine, being a dietitian, cooked very well. We started finding little ways to conserve money. At times we went overboard: penny wise, pound foolish.

On a cold Saturday night in November, my close friend Adam—whom I'd first met when we were summer interns together—had a birthday party at a bar on the Lower East Side. And not the gentrified part of the Lower East Side, but deep in Alphabet City, a good ten- to fifteen-minute walk from the nearest subway stop. (Adam had a great head for numbers, I always told him, but a lousy head for picking party venues.) The party was to begin late, around 11:00 P.M. Nadine felt too tired to go. My place was on the Upper West Side, at Eighty-First and West End. It would have been the easiest thing in the world to step out of the building and hail a cab, but the fare to First Street and Avenue

Z (or wherever the hell the thing was) would've been thirty bucks. And when the party was over, at 2:00 or 3:00 A.M., who wants to get on the subway then? There goes another thirty.

I decided to kick off our austerity plan and take the subway: the number 1 train to Times Square; the Shuttle crosstown to Grand Central; the 6 train down to Bleecker Street; the F east to Second Avenue. Three transfers. Three long waits. A fifteen-minute walk to the restaurant. The whole thing in reverse to get back home at 2:00 A.M., on a very cold night in November.

I saved sixty bucks.

I was making between $400,000 and $500,000 a year.

But who knew if I'd still be making it come January? It could all end any second.

3. My parents were coming over from South Africa, my father to take his American pharmacy exam, my mother to visit. I had persuaded my father, at the age of fifty-eight, to study for the exam; I was gently but steadily trying to pressure both my parents to come to America and escape the crime of Johannesburg. This was December. They were landing at JFK on a Sunday afternoon, and Nadine and I were going to meet them. Being very grown-up and rational about sticking to our frugal economic plan, we decided to take the Train to the Plane: the subway.

This was no jaunt to the Lower East Side. This was a number 1 train to Columbus Circle, then a transfer to the A train, and then a long, long ride on the A train through Brooklyn and out into Queens, way past Howard Beach, to John F. Kennedy International: an hour and a half in all. We felt virtuous taking the subway. I felt a little more ambivalent when we met my mom and dad, who'd just gotten off a twenty-hour flight from Johannesburg. My father had two huge suitcases full of heavy textbooks to study for his exam. Surely we could take a cab from Kennedy to the Holiday Inn in Brooklyn where the pharmacy chain administering the exam required candidates to stay?

My mother, who always worried about how much money I was spending on the family, would have none of it. Nadine agreed. I was outvoted. So we schlepped their bags onto the subway and rode through the wilds of Brooklyn—where we had to make two more transfers, schlepping the suitcases up and down subway steps. It was madness. But we saved $120 that day.

————

Goldman didn't go down. But the storm kept raging. Those who wanted to survive had to reinvent themselves. One way to do it, if you were a salesperson fortunate enough to still have a few great clients left, was to go into overdrive and simply do more bread-and-butter business than anyone else. This was tough, since clients were unwilling to take risks. They were frozen, sitting on their hands, waiting for the next shoe to drop. Another way was to try to convince your clients to buy structured derivative products (black boxes) that might temporarily give them some hope: "Look, the markets are really panicked, but if you buy our GoldDust2000 product, instead of losing ten percent, you're only going to lose two percent." Since these structured products were created by the bank that sold them and not widely traded, they came with the markup one expects from any bespoke product. These kinds of murky promises were legally okay, because in the twenty pages of disclaimers on the document, somewhere there would be a line that read, "This may or may not be accurate; we may or may not believe what we're telling you; we may or may not have the opposite view..."

Throughout the 2000s, Wall Street structured complex derivatives to help European governments such as Greece and Italy mask their debt and make their budgets look healthier than they actually were. These deals generated hundreds of millions of dollars in fees for the banks, but ultimately helped these countries kick the can, and their problems, down the road. Failing to address these problems culminated in the European sovereign debt crisis that the world is trying to deal with today.

But it doesn't end with state governments. Municipalities and cities also get pulled in. Goldman sold a derivative called a swap to the City of Oakland to help it protect itself against rising interest rates. The product ultimately backfired, and is now costing the city millions of dollars a year. In 2009, JPMorgan Chase was forced to pay the SEC $700 million to settle a probe into the sale of structured derivatives that pushed

Jefferson County, the most populous in Alabama, to the brink of bank-ruptcy.

There was tremendous potential for short-term profit in structured derivative products—also tremendous potential for short-term loss. But when clients are scared, you're not telling them about possible down-sides. Those are buried in the fine print of the ten-page disclaimer at the end of the contract. Most clients pay as close attention to that as you do when you hit the Accept button before downloading music from iTunes.

Buying one of these structured derivative products is a bit like going into a store and buying a can of tuna. The can clearly says, "Bumble Bee Tuna," and features a cute little logo. You go home, and most of the time you enjoy some delicious tuna. But let's say you get home one day and find dog food inside the can. *How can this be?* you wonder. *They told me it was tuna.* But then you look at the back of the can. There, in print so tiny as to be almost unreadable, is printed something like "Contents may not be tuna. May contain dog food." The govern-ments of Greece and Italy, the Libyan Investment Authority, the City of Oakland, the State of Alabama, and countless other endowments and foundations have all opened their cans and found dog food.

And somewhere along the way, Goldman Sachs stopped being the market maker it used to be, a firm that stood up and took risk in order to help clients, no matter how tumultuous the environment. The firm became pickier about what business it did, and did not, want to facili-tate. It was willing to take reputational hits, as long as it kept its profit and loss intact. This was a long way from the days, weeks, and months post-9/11, when the firm's main priority had been to facilitate client po-sitions and get the markets up and running again. Back then, it was not the time to exploit our clients' and competitors' weaknesses—as now should not have been.

Back then, we were saying, "Come to us. We're ready to get our hands dirty. This is why we're here." Now a client would call in and ask us to help them ("Can I get a price on ten thousand Vodafone put options?"—a strategy to protect their Vodafone stock holdings), and we were saying, "No, I'm sorry. The markets are too tough. It's too risky right now." We had pulled in the drawbridge, leaving our clients to fend for themselves. (Remembering the crisis, one salesperson I knew said, "Clients would call in and we would effectively be telling them, with our unwillingness to facilitate their business, to go fuck themselves.")

Finally, Goldman really had become more like a hedge fund, concerned more with helping itself than helping clients, with doing only the business we thought could make us a lot of money and ensure our survival. A perfect case in point was the lucrative fiefdom of Bobby Schwartz.

There was a whole segment of hedge funds that had the wrong trade on before Lehman Brothers went belly-up. These funds were almost always short volatility: in other words, they'd bet that, on average, markets would remain fairly calm, even though there might be some hiccups along the way. Academic studies had shown this strategy to work over prolonged historical periods. The problem was that these hedge funds were not anticipating "Black Swan" events, a term coined by Nassim Nicholas Taleb to explain once-in-a-thousand-year-type events that people do not expect and that models can't predict.

What we saw in 2008 and 2009 was a series of Black Swan events that the statistical models would have told you were not possible, according to history. Instead of the S&P 500 Index having average daily percentage swings of 1 percent, for a sustained period the market was swinging back and forth more than 5 percent per day—five times what was normal. No computer model could have predicted this.

The markets exploded in volatility, and the funds got crushed. They were actually going out of business because the pain on their portfolios was so great. Suddenly they needed to unwind everything; they needed to get out of all their derivatives positions. This was where Bobby came in.

A client would call him and say, in a panicked voice, "I need to get out of this immediately. What's your price?" And Bobby would quote them a substantial price. Goldman was taking significant fees on these clients. During one period in the midst of the crisis, Schwartz was bringing in $2 million a day on his trades. In a sense (a very cynical person would say), Goldman was hastening the rates at which the clients were going out of business, because of the amounts we were charging them. But then, the market was in turmoil; of course we had to charge high fees, because we were taking a big risk by facilitating this business. However, there is such a thing as a middle ground.

It was almost like a fire sale. And the firm rewarded Bobby for doing this business. At the end of 2008, a year when very few people were getting promoted, a year with the smallest MD class in a long time, Bobby's name was on the list of new managing directors. One couldn't begrudge him his monetary success: After all, he was just doing his job, and he was really good at it. But I remember thinking, *Welcome to the changing world of Goldman Sachs leadership.*

Company culture and morale seemed to be bygone values. To paraphrase that great sage Puff Daddy, it was all about the Benjamins now. If you were in the right place at the right time, if you were the trader with the "hot pad" (credit-default swaps, for example), or if you were the salesperson with the clients who were running for the exits, and if you had the instincts to know how to capitalize on this, then—*boom!*—the firm promoted you and paid you well and you were now a leader of the firm. This was the new model of Goldman Sachs managing directorship from about 2008 onward.

Bobby gave a big figurative click of the heels at his bonus that December. There was a story that back in 2004, at our Derivatives team-building clambake in the Hamptons, Daffey had seen Bobby tossing a football around in the afternoon and joked, "Dude, you throw it like a girl. That's gonna cost you ten grand this year," the joke being that because Daffey determined everyone's bonus, he could easily subtract $10,000 at the end of the year. Fast-forward four years, and ten grand had become a rounding error for Bobby. He was now playing in the big leagues. He used part of his 2008 bonus to buy an apartment on Park Avenue.

———

I was as scared as everyone else that fall. My solution was to embark on a self-reinvention plan of my own. During lulls in trading—there were a lot of lulls in trading—I began trying my hand at market commentary.

My idea was to jot down my thoughts about the markets—how I believed they might react to certain news items, what sort of patterns I was seeing, whether there was any hint of a recovery—and send out my short essays as Internal e-mails. I wanted to take an approach that was completely unbiased by what Goldman Sachs was saying. I decided to write down exactly what I thought, without fear of consequences. The worst that could happen was that people would disagree with me.

My models were two managing directors in Derivatives Sales who had been writing similar reports for years. These two guys were the gold standard as far as I was concerned: I admired their unbiased way of presenting content. They would always include a few charts to illustrate their concepts; they would cite public sources to ensure objectivity, as opposed to referencing Goldman's internal information. And they would add humor, to make something as arcane and dry as derivatives sound interesting.

In October and November, I tried my first couple of pieces. I spent three or four days writing each, sometimes during those lulls but mostly at night, after work. After condensing the pieces, I got our Compliance department to sign off on them. Though I originally meant these commentaries for Goldman eyes only, there was no telling which clients they might be passed along to. The worst thing you could do would be to reveal a confidential client name or a specific trade, so I worked hard to make everything I wrote observational, using publicly available information, packaged in a way that formed a thesis.

Then I showed the pieces to my two MD mentors, asking for advice and constructive criticism. I said, "What do you think of the way I'm making this argument? Is there a way to strengthen it?" Or, "Can you help me spice this up a little bit?" I wrote in my own style, but I wanted to learn everything I could from them.

They both believed in me from the start, and both started sending my commentaries to their biggest clients, which was very gratifying. One of the MDs sent a piece of mine to Paul Tudor Jones and his team, saying, "This is from the real-money guru on my team—you'll like this." (*Real money*, a term I liked, referred to the category of long-term-oriented institutional investors I covered—asset managers, mutual funds, and pension funds—and to sovereign wealth funds. Some also called it *slow money*—as opposed to *fast money*, which referred to hedge funds, which dealt in more leveraged instruments and quicker ins and outs of positions.) Tudor Jones actually wrote back, saying only, "Thanks," but indicating that he'd actually read the piece. Coming from a hedge fund icon, that felt cool. What was cooler, though, was that the MD had had enough confidence in me as a commentator to endorse my piece and send it to his most important client.

My ambition was to become the Real-Money Guy, the spokesperson for what the real-money clients were doing—in the same way that one of my MD mentors had become known for writing about what the macro hedge funds were doing and thinking. I tried to build a niche and become an internal expert at understanding flow of funds, a topic many people cared about. Who was buying and selling the market? Were retail investors adding money to mutual funds? Were pension funds reweighting their asset class distribution from fixed income to equities? Were hedge funds increasing their speculative short positions in E-mini futures? Could volumes or trends at certain times of day tell us anything about what direction the market might head in? I had found a way to consolidate these types of metrics into a thesis about what effect they could have on capital markets.

By nature, the macro hedge funds were very interested in what real money was doing: Even though hedge funds do a lot of turnover (trading in and out of positions often), they represent only about 5 percent of ownership in U.S. equity markets. The real whales in the market are the mutual funds, pension funds, and sovereign wealth funds, with trillions and trillions of dollars in assets under management. *The real money.* When real money starts moving over a period of time, the whole market starts moving with it. And in similar fashion, my clients were very interested in what the hedge funds were doing because of the funds' ability to impact the market over minute-to-minute or day-to-day periods.

Then I struck gold. Writers everywhere will tell you they're always surprised when something they've done catches on in a big way. This is especially true for someone who's just a beginner, as I was. On December 11, 2008—my thirtieth birthday—I sent out my third piece of market commentary, and it got more attention both inside and outside Goldman than I ever would have imagined.

It was a month after Obama's election, and despite his promises of hope and change—and his closeness to important Wall Street players such as JPMorgan Chase CEO Jamie Dimon and Robert Wolf, then UBS's chairman in the Americas—the mood in the markets was still apocalyptic. I was looking for hope myself, and I had a solid idea about where to find it.

My piece focused on something that many people had an intuition about but didn't fully understand: the concept of dry powder. During the crisis, the first thing all the mutual funds and pension funds started doing was selling—and they kept selling, deepening the crisis. As a result, the funds built up a huge cash base, also known as "a wall of money," or "dry powder." (The term is an old military one, from the days when it was important to keep gunpowder supplies safe from moisture.) Hundreds of billions of dollars were just sitting on the sidelines.

The piece was built on the thesis that even though everyone was still selling, eventually this cash supply was going to become so big that it would have to come back into the market in search of returns, with—no matter how good or bad the world happened to be at the moment—a significant impact. So I came up with a framework for showing how to track when the dry powder was actually getting deployed, and what that said about the direction of the markets.

The reaction at Goldman was electric. When I discussed the piece on our internal morning call that day in a conference room on one side of the trading floor—at which all the partners and managing directors were participating—one of the most respected salespeople on the whole trading floor immediately chimed in. "Guys, this piece is going to be essential reading today," he said. "Everyone on Wall Street is going to be talking about it. I've already sent it to my three biggest clients, and they love it. I want everyone to send the piece out to all their clients."

Everyone did: it got sent out to hundreds, maybe even thousands, of clients. Over the next few days, several partners came by the desk and patted me on the back. "This is great stuff," they'd say. "Let's do more of this." They all seemed to be in agreement: commentary like this was a way to stay in front of our clients, to show them we were looking out for them.

I think another reason the piece caught on was that people were scared and looking for hope that the markets might recover, and in a calm, objective way, my dry powder thesis had provided some.

I e-mailed the salesperson who'd given me that surprising endorsement in front of everyone: "Thank you, man—that truly meant a lot to me."

"It's well deserved," he wrote back. "In the new world we live in, content is the way we will differentiate ourselves. Keep it up."

CHAPTER 8

The Four Clients

Passover, April 2009. Goldman Sachs had come through the wilderness
of the financial crisis a changed firm. From a simple structural perspective, we were now a bank holding company instead of an investment
bank, but the mind-set was changing, too, and the part of the business
where this was becoming readily apparent was in how the firm dealt
with its clients.

Every Jewish kid who was half awake during Hebrew school knows
at least a few things about the Passover Seder, a Jewish Thanksgiving
meal of sorts where we read from a book called the Haggadah about
the liberation of the Israelites from slavery in Egypt. There is the matzah
(unleavened bread), the bitter herbs to commemorate the hard times,
the four cups of wine, and some delicious matzah ball soup. But every
April, when I conduct the Seder at my cousins' house in Chicago for the
twenty-five jabbering adults and twenty screaming kids who come every
year, I particularly like the part of the text that discusses the reaction
of the Four Sons to Passover: one who is wise, one who is wicked, one
who is simple, and one who doesn't know how to ask questions.

And as it was told in ancient Egypt about the Four Sons, so, too, it
was on Wall Street that there are Four Types of Clients: the Wise Client,
the Wicked Client, the Simple Client, and the Client Who Doesn't Know
How to Ask Questions. I had seen all four types in action over the years,
but coming out of the market meltdown, I was learning the new roles
that each would be expected to play.

The Wise Clients are the large hedge funds and institutions that have access to all the resources their bankers and traders have to offer. This includes research; communication with the management teams of the companies they are looking to invest in (or short); first looks on deals that are coming to market, such as IPOs and capital raises; their own unbiased derivatives pricing models, to determine what opaque products are *actually* worth; but most important, human capital: really sharp people working for them. For a client to be wise, its managers must fully understand the conflicts of interest that are rife on Wall Street—in IPOs, in structured products, in proprietary trading. Therefore, many of the people at the helm of the Wise Client firms have previously worked at Wall Street banks and understand all the tricks of the trade.

As Goldman started looking more and more like a hedge fund, the Wise Clients were important allies. They'd get looped in early about the various trades Goldman Sachs liked, so they could invest alongside the firm and use their muscle to propel the firm's investing ideas into self-fulfilling prophecies. Goldman would never try to push some high-margin financial product on our Wise Clients. The people who work at these firms are too smart. They also have the tools to spot when a trader is trying to play games. In the newly constituted Goldman Sachs, these multibillion-dollar hedge funds and institutions would be handled with kid gloves.

Which brings us to the Wicked Client. This is often a very smart client who pushes the envelope. Some funds engage in rumor mongering to drive down the prices of companies they are shorting. Some funds "spray their flow all over the street"—they try to game Wall Street banks against one another to get the best price for themselves. While this is not illegal, Wall Street firms don't like to get played—they like to be the ones doing the playing. At worst, some clients—like Raj Rajaratnam, founder of the $7 billion Galleon fund and always highly charitable with his personal wealth—show bad judgment and trade on inside information. In October 2011, he was sentenced to eleven years in prison.

Then there's the Simple Client. You would be appalled at how backward and badly run certain large asset managers and pension funds can be. There's a huge discrepancy between the sophisticated ones and the unsophisticated ones, even though they may be of equal size and look almost identical to the outside world. The bad ones are big and bureaucratic, have outdated systems, and still use fax machines for trade confirmations. They generally move very slowly—sometimes too slowly. These are perfect prey for Wall Street, and after they get fed one cup of wine, they are forced to eat bitter herbs. An example of a Simple Client would be a client whom a longtime salesperson on the floor dubbed the Queen of Wall Street. She was a piece of work: volatile, quirky, and given to peculiar utterances and outbursts. She liked to break in the new kids—once, when a scared first-year analyst named Jonah was doing some trades for her, she shrieked, "Jonah, if I could, I would reach through the phone line and bite your fucking head off!" Poor Jonah wasn't the same for a while after that.

Though the Queen was responsible for trading billions of dollars in futures, options, and other derivatives, she was strangely unsophisticated about the business. She had a special paranoia about trading the incorrect amount of futures contracts. She would say crazy things like "I don't care what the price is; I just don't want to overtrade"—that is, accidentally trade too many contracts, an error on her part that could get her into trouble with her boss. For anyone on Wall Street, this was an insane thing to hear, since getting the right amount of contracts is the most basic of calculations; a rookie should get it right every time. The important thing is, what was your execution? Did you buy low and sell high? What was the price? The Queen's wackiness was especially egregious in light of the fact that thousands of people's pensions were tied to her decision-making processes.

We used to hold the Queen's hand, and treat her like a queen. We assumed a fiduciary responsibility to tell her when she was doing something wrong or making poor decisions. But, sadly, the Queen of Wall Street is the type of client many people on Wall Street are looking to prey on.

The fourth? That would be the Client Who Doesn't Know How to Ask Questions. This is the sorriest of the lot, because not only are these clients simple, but they are also trusting. They often are the investment managers who are meant to look after the pensions of cops, firemen, and teachers, or they might be running the portfolio of a charity, an endowment, or a foundation. In the brave new Wall Street that was coalescing during this time of market turbulence, these would be the target clients for elephant trades.

As an example, imagine a client who lived in the mountains of Oregon, running billions of dollars in state pension fund money. In his world, he was a big fish and thought of himself as a sophisticated investor, but he had never worked inside a Wall Street firm. He lacked the infrastructure to figure out exactly what he was buying, and after the crash of 2008, he was under pressure to make up for lost returns. He was the perfect target to sell a type of derivative known as an exotic—a very complex product that could be made to look much simpler for the client when dressed up with enough bells and whistles as a structured product. These were similar to the cans of tuna that Greece, the City of Oakland, and Jefferson County in Alabama had bought.

They are called exotics for good reason: these products are so complicated that often the clients don't understand how much money they've paid to the bank. Exotics require very complicated financial models to value them accurately, and often the smartest quants within the bank are assigned to create and price them.

A certain Goldman cachet came into effect with the Client Who Doesn't Know How to Ask Questions. He was dealing with the smartest guys on the Street, he figured, so why did he need to do the math for himself? And guys such as Lloyd Blankfein, Gary Cohn, and CFO David Viniar really were the smartest guys on the Street. They truly understood derivatives: they knew the risks inherent in them; they understood their theoretical underpinnings. On the other hand, Bear Stearns, Merrill Lynch, and Lehman Brothers all got into trouble by not understanding the risk they had on their books.

What the Client Who Doesn't Know How to Ask Questions failed to grasp in 2009 was that Goldman's sense of fiduciary responsibility was eroding. And every year, one or another of these clients probably shows up on the list of Goldman Sachs's top twenty-five clients—these are clients ranked by *fees generated*, not assets under management or return on investment. There is something highly disconcerting about seeing a global charity or philanthropic organization or teacher's pension fund in the top twenty-five of a firm's clients.

———

When I returned to work after Passover, the gloom that had hung over the trading floor seemed to have lifted slightly. In March (before the holiday), the markets had hit new lows, and the banking stocks, ours included, were still getting hammered. Even with the government injecting hundreds of billions of dollars into the biggest banks, there were still significant worries about the scope of toxic assets still lingering on each balance sheet. But Goldman was navigating through the crisis, thanks to brilliant risk management. Derivatives desks make the most money when the markets are volatile, and in 2008 and early 2009, Goldman's Derivatives desks across the firm made a killing. And this windfall didn't come from taking bullets for clients; rather, a large part of it came from collecting large fees for unwinding panicked clients' failed trades.

Once it seemed as though the last of the panicked trades had been unwound, Wall Street did what it does best: it saw a huge dislocation in the market and started figuring out how to act on it. Baron de Rothschild, the famous eighteenth-century British financier, captured what Goldman Sachs and other banks on Wall Street would soon start doing: "The time to buy is when there is blood in the streets."

To put it in layman's language, Goldman Sachs was ready to wager a lot of its own money that the markets were going to calm down very quickly. In mid-2009 before it was obvious that the markets were going to start recovering, a number of the smartest traders at Goldman Sachs started noticing an anomaly in the derivatives markets: derivatives prices were implying that for the next ten years straight, we were going to continue to see the levels of unprecedented volatility that we had been seeing in the nine months since Lehman Brothers went bankrupt. Could this kind of turmoil and unpredictability continue for ten years, unabated? Surely things would calm down—maybe not immediately, but sometime soon. A ten-year period of constant turmoil had not occurred since the Great Depression. And by now the government had shown the will to step in and support the system through capital injections to banks and an $800 billion stimulus package to help the economy. No one thought the mistakes of a passive Herbert Hoover would be made all over again.

So Goldman Sachs and other banks on Wall Street, plus a number of the Wise Clients, started implementing a bullish bet: that the markets would start rising, and that volatility would start falling. The way many investors put this trade on was through shorting a derivative called a ten year S&P 500 variance swap—an over the counter, opaque product with very little liquidity.

Famously, another smart investor had thought of a similar idea. Warren Buffett, the Oracle, who had previously called derivatives "financial weapons of mass destruction," also noticed this dislocation and made a similar bet (albeit using a different tactic).

This trade made banks and clients all over Wall Street hundreds of millions of dollars from mid-2009 until mid-2010 as the markets rallied and volatility compressed. In many ways, betting that the markets would calm down was a brilliant move. It was certainly a daring one. After Bear Stearns went bankrupt in early 2008, a lot of people had thought that the firm's fall was just an anomaly and that the worst was over. A number of hedge funds went bust at the time by getting the timing of this return to calm extremely wrong. Having the right investing thesis is only half the battle; knowing when to put the idea into practice is arguably more important. And the beauty part was, the more Wise Clients Goldman could line up behind the short, the more long-dated volatility would go down.

But the strategy backfired significantly in the summer of 2010, when there was a huge short squeeze—a lot of people got wind of these positions and all started buying at the same time. On Goldman's second quarter earnings call on July 20, 2010, CFO David Viniar would offer a mea culpa: "As a result of meeting franchise client and broader market needs, we had a short equity volatility position going into the quarter. Given the spikes in volatility that occurred during the quarter, equity derivatives posted poor quarterly results."

The real question though, is this: Was this trade formulated primarily in the service of clients, as Viniar says? Or was it being driven by Goldman Sachs's and other Wall Street banks' desire to implement a proprietary bet? I would argue the latter.

It was in the context of pondering this type of question—of whether the firm saw its customers as "clients" or "counterparties"—that I attended the exclusive Goldman Sachs leadership program called Pine Street. Based on Jack Welch's pioneering Crotonville Management Development Center at General Electric, Pine Street started during the Hank Paulson era as a way to ensure that the leadership and cultural tenets of the firm weren't diluted after Goldman Sachs went public. In the beginning, the series of seminars was reserved for managing directors, but later VPs and even select clients were allowed to attend. I took the president of my largest client.

At Pine Street, thought leaders such as Bill George, the former CEO of Medtronic turned Harvard Business School professor, the author of *Authentic Leadership*, and a Goldman Sachs Board member, talked about how leaders are meant to behave. A scientist talked to us about the Stanford marshmallow experiment—the one where children were left alone in a room with a marshmallow. Some gobbled up the marshmallow; others waited and then ate it; still others waited until the tester returned to the room. The subjects were tracked over the next forty years, and the researchers found that the ones who had delayed gratification the longest ended up growing into leaders; the little piggies, not so much. It occurred to me that back on the trading floor I was seeing more little piggies and instant gratification than I was seeing under the old Goldman model of "long-term greedy."

———

Right about this time, I was experiencing some volatility in my personal life. On March 15, 2009, the equity market hit rock bottom, its lowest point in the crisis. Coincidentally, that was also the day that my three-year relationship with Nadine hit rock bottom. We broke up. I had felt it coming for a while, and increasingly knew in my heart that we probably were not meant to be together in the long run. We were very good at having fun together, at laughing together, and enjoying each other's company; we shared the same Jewish background, and it seemed that it should have been right. But it wasn't. We just kept on disagreeing on too many important things and could never find middle ground on anything. It was wearing us both down.

That doesn't mean we hadn't been talking a lot, though. As the financial crisis deepened, so did our respective concerns about the future. I worried about my career, my livelihood, and how our relationship would work out. Nadine worried about whether I was husband material. She was thirty; she felt it was time for her to settle down. With increasing frequency during the dark early months of the year, she asked me whether I was thinking along the same lines.

The selfish part of me, the part that needed someone to hold onto while the world was coming apart, would have liked for us to continue as we had been. But she kept asking—and she was right to do so—where we were going with this. I finally had to tell her that I didn't see us getting married, and that was that. It is an unfair thing in life that something can be so good and so much fun, but just not the thing for you, and you have to let it go.

It was the worst possible timing—or at least it seemed so then. Between my business life and my emotional life, things were in turmoil. I had put on weight, I was eating terribly, and hadn't been to the gym all year. The thing that helped me most in those subsequent months was a healthy routine: I started exercising almost every day (running; not Zumba), cut out all alcohol for weeks, and stopped eating all the beef lo-mein and pastrami sandwiches that had become the staples of my diet while I was glued to my desk during the crisis. An older salesman had years earlier dispensed some great advice to our team: Eat Light, Feel Right. Slowly, I started to feel right.

David Viniar, the chief financial officer of Goldman Sachs, is an extraordinarily impressive guy—the guy who, every quarter, when Goldman releases its earnings, is the public face of the firm. Tall and thin, a Bronx native, he went to Union College and then Harvard Business School and has been at the firm for thirty-two years. Periodically, he gets on a conference call with all the business journalists and research analysts and opens himself up to interrogation. He has to be able to answer any question—has to have all the numbers in his head and at hand, but also has to be careful not to put his foot in his mouth, not to incriminate himself, not to say anything stupid.

This is a process that, as you can imagine, can potentially go very wrong—if you're not Viniar. Lehman Brothers had had a CFO named Erin Callan—charismatic, polished, and attractive—whose badly botched conference call with a hedge fund manager named David Einhorn only firmed Einhorn's resolve to short Lehman stock and escalate broader rumblings that the firm was in trouble.

On March 19, 2009, David Viniar held a two-hour conference call with journalists and research analysts to explain the firm's involvement in the government bailout of AIG. I listened in; everybody at Goldman did. It was a masterful performance under extraordinarily difficult circumstances. As the experts peppered Viniar with questions, he succeeded in making a two-pronged, essentially self-contradictory argument: that Goldman Sachs, which was owed billions of dollars related to credit-default swaps with AIG, had hedged itself to such a degree that we would have been just fine if AIG had gone bankrupt—but also that Goldman had been completely justified in accepting $12.9 billion, a hundred cents on the dollar, in AIG's bailout money. You see, AIG had insured Goldman's mortgage securities, and when the mortgage market crashed, Goldman wanted to get its insurance money—even though we were shorting the market. The firm had doubled down on the collapse, and like any policy holder, we wanted our money.

People within the firm and on Wall Street say Viniar is the best CFO in the world. I've often thought that if I had to send someone into the arena for me, David Viniar would be right at the top of the list. He has a ploy that he's famous for, the verbal equivalent of Gary Cohn's in-your-face, foot-on-the-desk move: when some research analyst asks him a tough question—"David, do you think these numbers and those numbers equate to four billion dollars?"—Viniar will just give a one-word answer: "No." Or, "Yes." Or, if he feels like being more exact: "Actually, it's three point eight billion dollars." No further elaboration.

A deep silence follows. Then the same thing always happens: the poor analyst gets so flustered with the silence and lack of detailed response, that he eventually thanks Viniar. To which Viniar always gives the same two-word response: "You're welcome." Which a lot of people at Goldman consider corporate-speak for "Fuck you." Viniar has given the guy nothing; now he's telling him to go fuck himself. Anytime Viniar did a conference call, I dialed in. The guy was a gladiator.

Everybody on the trading floor had listened in, enraptured, to this particular conference call: Goldman was still struggling for its life, and this was the man we'd sent into battle to fight our fight. Wartime Britons hearing Winston Churchill must have felt much the same way. And I'm sure everyone else felt the same triumph I felt at Viniar's ability to tackle these insanely complex questions calmly and cogently. In the heat of the crisis, the instinct of every Goldman employee was still to defend the firm.

But a funny thing happened: as time passed, Viniar's argument began to emit a certain odor, and it wasn't the fragrance of roses, freshly baked bread, or crisp hundred-dollar bills. It was the distinct odor of conflict of interest. The CFO's contention that taxpayers would've been hurt if Goldman Sachs had taken less than a hundred cents on the dollar for AIG's debt sounded less and less convincing as 2009 ran its remarkable course.

From their nadir on March 15 (also known in my world as Nadine Break-Up Day), the markets would climb smoothly and steadily, with few hitches, until year's end. It was crazy. The market commentary I had written a few months earlier about dry powder coming back was proving true. In retrospect, I should have headed directly to Atlantic City, since clearly I had found some luck in my prediction.

At first, nobody could see it happening: things continued to look bleak. But every day, there were little signs of improvement, and soon it became clear that the change was for real. It took many people by surprise. And this was not Mom and Pop deciding, "Let's get back into the stock market." These were the vast cash reserves that the big funds had amassed in the sell-off slowly making their way back into the market, week after week, as spring turned to summer and summer to fall.

Instead of going to Atlantic City, the manager at one of my biggest clients told me that they had actually acted on my prediction early, as the train was leaving the station, profiting with some very big and well-timed trades. A senior partner, and one of the global heads of trading, came by my desk and told me he had used my commentary in his recent presentation to the firm-wide risk management committee. All this was nice for my ego. I should have been breathing more easily. (After all, my waistband was looser.) The problem was that my fans in upper management and my clients had more knowledge of the work I was doing than my direct managers, who were sitting a few seats away from me.

In early spring, before the recovery was evident, one of my bosses, Beth Hovan, the partner who was cohead (along with Paul Conti, Mr. Cleanse) of my group, called me in for a meeting. Beth was dark-haired, attractive, very smart, and, like most who had ascended to management at Goldman Sachs, very tough. With her, though, the toughness included a certain callousness. ("Let's be honest about the reason we're all here—it's to make a lot of money," she told me once.) She also struck me as an example of someone who managed up, meaning that she often seemed unaware of what was going on beneath her. When I walked into her office, she looked concerned. "So how are things going?" she said. "I notice the clients aren't really paying the firm a lot."

I admitted that business had been declining because clients were panicked and frozen. "But," I said, "I've been trying to add some value for the clients, and bring more people to the franchise by writing these pieces." She seemed to have only the dimmest understanding of what I was talking about. "Oh yeah, I've heard something about those," she said, vaguely. "Why don't you reforward them to me." Her tone said it was all the same to her whether I sent them to her or not. Adding value for clients seemed to be the last thing on her mind.

———

In the fall of 2009, Goldman finished erecting a magnificent monument to itself: a gleaming, $2 billion, forty-three-story glass-and-steel headquarters at 200 West Street, just a stone's throw northwest from the World Trade Center site. The building was also right across the way from my old place at 41 River Terrace. Back in my days as a young analyst, my roommates and I used to go to the movies at the West Street multiplex, which had a smallish parking lot next door. Goldman Sachs had somehow managed to shoehorn this gigantic new tower into that little parking lot space. Amazing what a couple of billion can do for you.

Construction had begun in 2005, when the recession was ending and times were flush again—and Goldman had an incentive from the U.S. government: for spearheading the revitalization of the area, the firm was issued $1 billion in Liberty Bonds, a tax-free bond program that provided below-market financing. Goldman was making a bold statement by setting up shop right across the street from where the World Trade Center once stood.

The building was significant in many ways. For one thing, Goldman had never built or owned a structure before; previously, the firm had leased buildings and rental space. The very fact of the new headquarters, not to mention its sheer in-your-face splendor, ran directly counter to the understated ethos of the old Goldman Sachs. (The one understated tradition that did remain was that the firm did not put its name on the door. It just said "200 West Street"). To temper the ostentation somewhat, architects Pei Cobb Freed and Partners had designed the tower on state-of-the-art, environmentally "green" principles, with features such as an ice-cooled under-floor air-circulation system. But to underline the ostentation, Goldman had paid abstract artist Julie Mehretu $5 million to paint an eighty-by-twenty-three-foot mural for the lobby. The swooping lines and stretched geometrical forms flying over the huge painting's surface were meant to suggest, in an abstract way, the history of finance capitalism. The sheer size of the mural certainly suggested the mighty wealth of Goldman Sachs.

The building's first seven stories were occupied by gigantic trading floors, each larger than a football field, and significantly bigger than the fiftieth floor at One New York Plaza. (The Derivatives desk, along with the rest of the six-hundred-person Equities Sales and Trading division, was on the fourth floor.) Above were Goldman's executive offices, Research division, and Investment Banking division. On the tenth and eleventh floors, under a beautiful high glass ceiling, were a 54,000-square-foot gym and an enormous new cafeteria. There was a lot of excitement and pride within the firm about the new headquarters.

And the place to get the latest information on when we would be moving in was Salvatore's Barber Shop in the basement of One New York Plaza. A significant proportion of the guys on our trading floor used to go down for a quick "wig adjustment" and a hot towel after the market closed. A lot of honchos and power players also used to go there, including Hank Paulson and Duncan Niederauer, former Goldman partner and then CEO of the NYSE. I was once having a haircut and then–New York Attorney General Andrew Cuomo pulled into the chair next to mine for a snip. As October turned to November, my barber, Mike, was tracking the move-in date closely. "Mr. Cohn was in here yesterday, and he said two weeks," he'd tell me. Or, "Harvey Schwartz [cohead of Global Securities] said no later than Thanksgiving."

Much of the anticipation about the move centered on the new cafeteria. The cafeteria on the forty-third floor of One New York Plaza had been, to put it mildly, uninspiring if not outright unappetizing. The new facility, with its high, glorious ceiling and sparkling fixtures, looked like a cathedral by comparison.

From the moment we moved in, however—the Equities division, the guinea pigs, moved over just after Thanksgiving—we realized that something was terribly wrong with the new cafeteria. Maybe it was poor management; maybe it was bad feng shui, but the place turned out to be absolute chaos. There was some flaw in the design or layout that no one could ever quite figure out. People were constantly running into each other, literally knocking each other over. There were frequently multiple lines at the grill, salad, sandwich, and omelet stations. There were always long lines to check out. It was all very strange. Clearly, no expense had been spared on the facility; the space was tremendous. Crowds formed anyway. Things got so bad that, at one point, Human Resources sent out an e-mail saying that anyone who came for lunch between 11:00 and 11:30 A.M. or between 2:00 P.M. and 2:30 would receive a 25 percent discount. (Believe it or not, there were a couple of managing directors, earning $1 million-plus a year, who were always very eager to take advantage of these savings.) This same e-mail also encouraged people to use the "external" options (aka takeout) in the World Financial Center, so as to reduce crowding and chaos in the Goldman cafeteria. The firm never seemed able to fix this problem.

Some employees seemed to relish the Early Bird Special. Indeed, one of my colleagues got in the habit of lunching at 11:15 A.M. every day, but he was also the sort of managing director who once took a client skiing, bought a ChapStick at the bottom of the mountain, and then put in a one-dollar expense report to cover the cost of the lip balm. This parsimonious behavior did not go unnoticed by our boss, who upon seeing the one-dollar expense report, started berating the fellow.

"Are you fucking kidding me? A one-dollar ChapStick? How much money did you make last year?" yelled our boss.

"Fair point. Fair point. Fair point..." was all the managing director could mutter in his defense.

The new gym was a different story. As was the case with the old cafeteria, the old Goldman gym, at 10 Hanover Street, had been merely functional: a windowless basement that nobody really loved for itself. The new gym, grandly titled the GS Wellness Exchange, was simply spectacular, with amazing vistas of New York Harbor and the rivers from the treadmills and weight rooms. In fact, it was such a great gym that from the moment we moved in, people started hitting it as early in the day as possible, often right after the markets closed. Junior people couldn't really get away with this (though some tried), but for VPs, MDs, and partners, late afternoon was workout time. Mr. Cleanse was there between 4:00 and 5:00 P.M. most days.

Therein lies a tale. One day, the whole Derivatives team received an e-mail (and apparently everybody on the fourth floor got a similar message) reading, "No one should be in the gym with a 4 handle." A bit of translation is called for here. People in finance often like to couch everyday conversation in trading terminology. "Handle" is a term for where a particular index or asset class is trading: for example, if Google stock is at 634, someone might say, "GOOG is trading with a 6 handle." So what the e-mail was saying was that nobody should be in the gym between 4:00 and 5:00 P.M.

The word on the floor was that Mr. Cleanse was the reason for the prohibition.

The rumor mill had it (and this was never confirmed) that Harvey Schwartz, Mr. Cleanse's boss's boss, was always in the gym between 4:00 and 5:00 P.M., and he was sick of seeing Mr. Cleanse there at the same time every day. So the time slot then got banned for everyone. Sometimes Wall Street can be a little like high school.

———

My total compensation for 2009, including bonus, came to more than $500,000. The year had been a tough one, and I was proud and felt lucky to be earning this kind of a living. I was fortunate to have a job, given how brutal the layoffs had been throughout the crisis.

Half a million dollars is a significant amount of money. But it should be noted that partner compensation is in a different stratosphere completely. From the $16 billion in compensation that Goldman paid out in 2009, 47 percent above the previous year's total, a disproportionately large share went to the 1 percent that sat right at the top of the heap: the partners. The thing about being a partner is that, by virtue of being a partner, you're guaranteed a minimum amount no matter what you do—usually in the millions of dollars. The risk is that if your bosses eventually figure out you're doing nothing, they'll get rid of you. But for at least a year or two before they figure this out, it's a very nice ride.

———

My thirtieth birthday, the previous December, had been an intense time in my life. Nadine and I held a big joint birthday party—her thirtieth was two weeks after mine—at Freemans, a place with a vintage speakeasy vibe that sits at the end of an alley on the Lower East Side. We rented the private room and invited about thirty of our friends: half hers, half mine.

Toward the end of the meal, Nadine surprised me with a cake. When they brought it in, people started calling for a speech. So I stood up and gave one. I'd had a few drinks, so I waxed a bit philosophical. I said something like "I know life seems tough for many of you right now, when the world is in turmoil. But let's take a few moments to put things into perspective and just enjoy each other's company, and not let the tumult of the world affect us too much. Let's try to get some rest over December, and let's toast to a better 2009—let's be rejuvenated and go into the New Year with a more positive outlook."

At the end of the night, I decided to pay for everyone. The bill came to over $3,000, but I was happy to do it—I like treating people; it was a milestone for both Nadine and me, and we were with our closest friends. I wouldn't have had it any other way.

Flash-forward a year, to my thirty-first birthday. Nadine and I had broken up; the world had turned—a lot. The year 2009 had been more complicated than I ever would have imagined. Exactly one of the thirty people from the previous year's party, a friend from my freshman year at Stanford, flew in from Detroit to help me celebrate this nonmonumental occasion. I was lonely after the breakup, but I now felt in a better place: healthier, stronger. Work was going well; the markets were still headed upward. My friend and I went out for a quiet evening; we met a couple of girls, one of whom I quite liked...

The office was open but quiet between Christmas and the New Year. Almost all the partners had left for vacation; the most junior partner drew the short straw and stuck around. On the desks, the hierarchy worked the same way: the senior VPs leave, one junior VP stays; the senior associates leave, one junior associate stays. I'd reached a point in my career where I'd paid my dues for a number of years: I was now comfortable taking the week off.

I flew to Cape Town to meet my mother and brother. It was beautiful there, and summer had just begun. The city was full of excitement about the coming soccer World Cup; the big new stadium built for the event, on the water in Green Point, had just opened. My mother, brother, and I went to the wine country in Stellenbosch. It was nice to spend some time with them in the hot sun, and think about the girl I'd just met. So much of life is about anticipation. And though I had no reason to think the world had gotten any less complex, I couldn't help but feel that 2010 was going to be a very good year.

CHAPTER 9

"Monstruosities"

On April 16, 2010, I went to the South African consulate in Midtown Manhattan to renew my passport; in a few days I would travel across the Pacific to visit a number of clients in Asia. After some haggling to expedite my application, I walked outside into one of those crisp early spring days that make you love living in New York. I took my time finding a cab to get back to the office, enjoying a few minutes of sunshine, and started thinking ahead to my trip. It seemed that slowly, though excruciatingly so, the world was healing.

I was looking forward to visiting some of my clients whom I had not seen in a number of months. We would discuss the latest developments in the markets, but we would also go out for dinner and drinks and have some fun. A big part of this business is face-to-face interaction; there is a human element to it. That was probably the thing I always liked most about being in sales. Some people in investment banking find traveling ten thousand miles around the world to have a few meetings to be a chore. But it never got old for me. Business-class flights with wine and sashimi at thirty thousand feet. Ritz Carlton or the Four Seasons? Three-star dinners with a $150 per-person budget when dining with clients. If I had time: a stop at a tailor in Asia to get some quality suits hand-tailored (for less than you would pay for one at Brooks Brothers). Also, a short ferry ride to the Wynn Hotel in Macao (a crazy sight—an almost identical replica of the one in Vegas, but smaller). What part of this is a chore? These are things I always tried to savor and appreciate.

A quick glance at my BlackBerry put an end to my Asian daydream.

My eyebrows rose. The markets were not rallying. In fact, Goldman Sachs's stock was down more than 10 percent, and volume was ten times what was normal. Something was wrong. Badly wrong. I started scanning my e-mails. The same word showed up in every subject line of every e-mail on the screen: SEC, SEC, SEC. The Securities and Exchange Commission. The federal agency responsible for enforcing the securities laws and regulating the financial industry.

I jumped in a cab and hustled back to the office at 200 West Street.

Riding back downtown, I started reading the e-mails. I couldn't believe it. It was the worst possible thing you could read.

FOR IMMEDIATE RELEASE

SEC Charges Goldman Sachs with Fraud in Structuring and Marketing of CDO Tied to Subprime Mortgages

I read further...

The SEC alleges that Goldman Sachs structured and marketed a synthetic collateralized debt obligation (CDO) that hinged on the performance of subprime residential mortgage-backed securities (RMBS). Goldman Sachs failed to disclose to investors vital information about the CDO, in particular the role that a major hedge fund played in the portfolio selection process and the fact that the hedge fund had taken a short position against the CDO.

My immediate reaction: this must be a witch hunt. *The SEC has been asleep at the wheel for the last two years and now it needs to show the public that it's doing something? Why isn't it going after the bad guys, the ones who caused this mess, the ones who took the irresponsible risk, blew up their companies, and brought the entire global economy to its knees?*

My immediate feeling: anger.

The cab finally pulled up in front of Goldman Sachs. I paid the driver, walked into the lobby, scanned my ID, and took the elevator to the

fourth floor. When I walked out onto the trading floor, I found the familiar hum of activity in the vast and sparkling space muted. Every face
I saw was pale with shock. People were staring open-mouthed at their
screens. I could instantly see on the tape running across the bottom of
a nearby monitor that Goldman Sachs stock was down close to 13 percent. (It was by far the largest and most precipitous percentage decline
in our stock since the dark days of late 2008 and early 2009.) A drop of
13 percent in this calmer climate could mean only two things: panic and
disaster.

I quickly went to my desk and pulled up my Bloomberg screen.
Whenever Bloomberg News reports a vitally important story, the news
scrolls up on the screen from bottom to top in red. It is not a frequent
occurrence. My entire screen was red.

What kind of misrepresentations was the SEC alleging? I started talking to my colleagues; everyone was trying to piece it together. The
chatter on the floor was about one of our products built on CDOs
(collateralized debt obligations, basically a sausage stuffed with subprime mortgages). *Why now? Why us?* Everyone, including me, was
on the defensive. Ever since the federal government had bailed out the
banks thanks to TARP, there had been murmurings in the world at
large that someone needed to be held accountable for the crisis; for
months there had been the sense of a gathering lynch mob. A series of
big articles—in *Rolling Stone, New York* magazine, and *Time*, among
others—castigated Wall Street in general, and Goldman Sachs in particular, for surviving and thriving on the backs of U.S. taxpayers, for using
bailout money to make big bets, then using the winnings to award executives obscenely big bonuses. When I heard the term *vampire squid*,
popularized by Matt Taibbi in *Rolling Stone*, I was repulsed by it.
Propaganda, I thought. It angered me. *Why don't they ever write about
10,000 Women or 10,000 Small Businesses, and the way the firm is
helping to nurture the next generation of entrepreneurs, or any of the
other philanthropic endeavors we fund and lend our expertise to?*

Everybody on the trading floor, myself included, had the same reaction to whatever it was that the SEC was cooking up: *What the hell
are these guys doing? Why aren't they going after Dick Fuld for crater-*

ing Lehman, or Stan O'Neal of Merrill Lynch, or Jimmy Cayne of Bear Stearns, who all ran their firms into the ground—some of them, while they were on the golf course or at the card table? They just want to get us because we're the only ones doing okay...

Clients began to call, wanting to know what was going on.

Management had been very quick to anticipate this. Don't say anything substantive, we were told; don't be defensive. Just say, "We're not sure; we're looking into this." We'll have a list of talking points for you later in the day.

Within an hour or two we got an internal e-mail that gave us some very general talking points and a slightly better understanding of what had been alleged. The SEC was charging Goldman with materially misstating and omitting facts in disclosure documents for a synthetic CDO product that we'd originated. The product was called Abacus 2007-AC1.

Abacus 2007-AC1. I had never heard of it. Nor had anyone sitting around me. Nor had any of my clients. It sounded like something from another planet. These CDO deals and other customized products in the derivatives space were always given enigmatic, important-sounding designations. It was marketing. It turned out that Abacus was an entire class of CDOs that Goldman had been marketing since 2004—a product that had come back to haunt us. The number referred to the date of issue.

Goldman Sachs responded quickly, and in no uncertain terms:

"The SEC's charges are completely unfounded in law and fact and we will vigorously contest them and defend the firm and its reputation."

The firm hired a prominent lawyer, Greg Craig, President Obama's former White House counsel, to spearhead its defense. *Good,* I thought, not knowing anything about Abacus or what the facts of the charges were. *Let's fight back. Hard.*

Amid the chaos and the flurry of client phone calls and internal e-mails, Mr. Cleanse was marching up and down our row. "We want to hear what clients are saying," he said emphatically. You didn't have to do much reading between the lines to see that senior management was freaked out that clients were going to start panicking and pulling their money.

At that point I was in the process of booking my trip to Asia. "Should I still go?" I asked Cleanse. "Absolutely," he said. "Now is a very important time to make this trip. We need for clients to see us, and we need to be in front of them. We need to defend ourselves in exactly the right way."

I decided to go to Asia and stand up for Goldman Sachs.

———

The SEC's complaint was rough. It said that a Goldman VP named Fabrice Tourre, working out of the New York headquarters in 2007, had put together Abacus 2007-AC1 in collusion with John Paulson (not to be confused with Hank Paulson), the hedge fund manager who since early 2006 had been raking in huge sums by shorting the mortgage market. According to the SEC suit (which was lodged against both Goldman Sachs and Tourre), Paulson had personally selected the mortgage securities that went into the product, using a single criterion: which were most likely to fail. The fall of Abacus netted Paulson a cool $1 billion.

The complaint painted Tourre in a terrible light, and a number of his more callous e-mails were made public. The fact that he was French seemed to delight the London and New York tabloids. In January 2007 he wrote in an e-mail to his girlfriend about the imminent downfall of Abacus: "The whole building is about to collapse anytime now...Only potential survivor, the fabulous Fab...standing in the middle of all these complex, highly leveraged, exotic trades he created without necessarily understanding all the implications of those monstruosities [*sic*]!!!"

There, in a nutshell, was a valid description of much of the complex structured-product market, one often not fully understood by its creators or its customers: "monstruosities."

The funny thing was, when I saw the name Fabrice Tourre, I vaguely remembered meeting the guy about a decade earlier. It was at a Goldman team-building dinner for Stanford graduates, when I was either a first-year analyst or a summer intern. The idea was for some of the more senior alumni to meet and possibly mentor their junior counterparts. Tourre was sitting a couple of seats away from me that night. He worked with a friend of mine who was in Fixed Income, so I chatted with him for about thirty seconds.

I didn't know or remember him from college, because he hadn't been an undergrad at Stanford, and we generally didn't speak to grad students, who were considered huge nerds. Fab had done his undergraduate work in France and gotten a one-year master's degree at Stanford, in management science and engineering—something thoroughly quantitative.

Tourre struck me, in the very brief time I spent with him, as being a classic quant: slightly goofy, socially awkward. He clearly hadn't been hired on the strength of his charisma. I realize this is an unfair thing to say. Quants, by definition, are not meeters and greeters. Cliff Asness hadn't conquered the world with his charm. The quant's job is to come up with complicated mathematical models, the black boxes that, clients can be made to believe, turn old rags into crisp new hundred-dollar bills.

In an ideal world, the quant would be objective, would work on behalf of the client as well as on behalf of the firm. But quants usually work for the traders, who live for quick hits and big revenues, instead of for the salespeople, who have to maintain client relationships. So the quants tend to focus on developing ways of advancing the firm's agenda that seem sexy to the client but wind up benefiting only one party: the firm. The Fabulous Fab was a perfect example of this, and he had found a perfect ally in John Paulson, and perfect clients in ABN AMRO and IKB, the two big European banks that lost the $1 billion Paulson gained.

In the days after the SEC filed its charges, the world piled on Goldman Sachs. One commentator in the *New York Times*, Michael Greenberger, a professor and former regulator, said that if the fall of Lehman Brothers in September 2008 was like Pearl Harbor, the SEC's enforcement action against Goldman was like the Battle of Midway, when the U.S. Navy redeemed itself by neutralizing the Japanese fleet. Harsh stuff. Accountability had arrived at last, the writer said. U.S. taxpayers were finally going to get answers to some of the questions they'd been asking all along.

And they would get them soon. As I was flying to Asia, Lloyd Blankfein, David Viniar, and Fabrice Tourre, among other representatives of

Goldman Sachs, were headed to Washington to appear before the Senate Permanent Subcommittee on Investigations to "vigorously contest [the SEC's accusations] and defend the firm and its reputation."

———

It was a strange time to be distancing myself from the main office, especially by ten thousand miles.

The Asian capital was sweltering when I arrived. I'd purposely come a day prior to my meeting to try to acclimate, however slightly, to the time difference and the heat. It had to have been a hundred degrees; the air felt like a microwaved sponge. Even the short walks between air-conditioned oases were punishing. As luck would have it, one of my clients, Taku—who was a native but worked in the fund's New York office now—was back home, here in Asia, partly working and partly on vacation visiting his family. We'd already made dinner plans for that evening, by e-mail. I gave him a ring, and was happy to hear a friendly voice.

I liked Taku. We'd both come from overseas to go to college in America, and we'd both fallen in love with our adopted country. He was someone I could talk to. We chatted for a couple of minutes about the SEC-Goldman tempest, both of us expressing great interest in seeing how the Senate would treat Lloyd and the boys, and what kind of defense Goldman would mount. C-SPAN was going to broadcast the hearings live, beginning that night, local time, in the Asian capital. Suddenly the same idea hit both of us: why not cancel our dinner plans and watch the hearings instead?

"Why don't you come over to my mom's house?" Taku said. "We'll have some snacks while we watch."

I got settled in my hotel, took a nap and a shower, then headed over to Taku's mother's place. I knew they were quite a wealthy family, but I wasn't sure what to expect. It turned out they owned an eight-story apartment building in a beautiful part of town, and various members of the family lived on different levels of the building. It was a stylish, solidly built structure—not crazy-opulent, New York style, but elegant and understated. It had a lot of space, wide open rooms, and the ceilings were high. Taku welcomed me inside his mom's place. I was surprised to see two servants, a man and a woman, standing by, silent but watchful. Taku smiled. "Come—sit down," he said.

The hearings hadn't started yet, but C-SPAN was turned on, on the flat-screen. One of the servants started bringing in snacks: a plate of fresh fruit, a platter of exotic hors d'oeuvres. The food kept coming. Everything tasted delicious, but sometimes that's what jet lag and hundred-degree weather does to you. Then Taku's mother came in; she was a quiet lady with exquisite manners, and was dressed that day in traditional attire. I shook her hand politely. Everything suddenly felt more than slightly surreal: it was as though I were visiting a friend instead of one of my most important clients. And we were about to watch Goldman Sachs being grilled by the subcommittee chairman, Senator Carl Levin. I felt comfortable and uncomfortable at the same time: pleased to be watching in comfort and luxury in an exotic destination— at my client's mother's house, of all places!—but wary and defensive on behalf of my firm.

The next couple of hours proved to be every bit as weird as the circumstances promised. As Taku and I watched intently, his mom kept popping in, chatting distractingly. I had to try to be polite to her and focus on the screen at the same time.

ME: Yes, my flight was great, Mrs. Taku. By the way, you have a
    lovely apartment...
LEVIN ON THE TV (yelling at one of my colleagues): You got no re-
    grets? You ought to have plenty of regrets...

Levin was ready to rumble. Among the other senators who took the microphone, some were challenging and well informed about finance, while others were angry, volatile—and almost unbelievably uninformed. The Goldman witnesses—David Viniar; former Mortgage department head Dan Sparks; and three of Sparks's former subordinates, including the Fabulous Fab himself—looked about as comfortable as anyone facing a televised Senate subcommittee hearing could be expected to look. In a moment that became famous, Levin, grilling Sparks, quoted verbatim an internal Goldman e-mail from Sparks's boss, about a CDO called Timberwolf: "'Boy, that Timberwolf was one shitty deal.'" Levin then asked Sparks, "How much of that shitty deal did you sell to your clients after June 22, 2007?" Levin couldn't seem to get enough of the word *shitty*, which he said at least five more times, right on live international television, in a proceeding of the U.S. Senate. *Shitty* deal. *Shitty* deal. *Shitty* deal. Again and again and again.

Late at night, in a sedate living room ten thousand miles away, the effect was both comic and tragic. Taku and I laughed, but my laughter was nervous. While we could make fun of some of the senators who had little idea of what they were talking about, the fact that Goldman Sachs was on the stand was no joke to me at all. It was about the worst possible thing that could happen to a firm that had prided itself on maintaining its golden reputation.

At a certain point, I felt a need to defend myself and my firm to Taku. But it wouldn't have helped: Taku was out cold. The hearings had by now bored him to sleep. Hmm. Sitting in your client's mother's house watching your firm on trial, in a foreign land, when everyone else in the household had gone to sleep—a strange circumstance I could not have predicted. But I quietly kept watching.

Finally, Lloyd came on. Viniar had looked somewhat shell-shocked under Levin's verbal barrages; Lloyd struggled in a similar fashion. Goldman Sachs was not good at this: appearing in public, in the limelight, under interrogation, was not our strong suit. These were muscles we had never exercised before. There was a sense that this was a no-win situation for Lloyd and the other Goldman people getting grilled that day. It was a show trial. The best they could do was come out alive having not said anything too bad or, in a nightmare scenario, too incriminating. You could tell that Lloyd was annoyed to be there. But he was doing his best to fight back as hard as he could. The thing I kept thinking about was the argument Lloyd kept making: that in a sales and trading business, there is no fiduciary responsibility; that we are not obliged to do what is in the client's best interest; that we were not *advising* the client; that we are just there to facilitate trades between big boys (i.e., large institutional investors). The two things I thought were: *No one ever told me this.* I was advising my clients every day, telling them what I thought was right for them. Why did we have salespeople with clients if we were just trading monkeys matching up buyers and sellers? And second, that the argument about "we're all big boys here," that the markets are a level playing field, rang hollow. *Surely it's obvious that Goldman knows the most in any situation because it can see what both buyers and sellers are doing.*

I looked over at Taku, who was still asleep. I nudged him gently and said, "Hey, I'm going to get out of here. Thanks for having me." I took a cab back to my hotel and stayed up till the early hours of the morning watching the rest of the hearings. Even though I was exhausted, I kept watching until the sun rose.

———

The meeting the next day was to be a formal sit-down with Taku's boss's boss's boss, the head of the fund. I'd met the man several times over the years. He was middle-aged, dignified, formal—reserved in the way his culture called for.

It was an important meeting, so I spent the morning at Goldman Sachs's local office going over talking points with the local partner, a native of the region. He'd been with Goldman a long time, but what was puzzling to me, and to quite a few of my colleagues, was that this guy wasn't especially conversant with the fund or its personnel. A lot of people wondered, *How can this guy be a partner?* But it turned out he was a trading partner, and traders, as I've said, tend to be somewhat introverted, managing risk but not dealing as much with the clients as the salespeople do. He just happened to be the most senior guy in the office, and (a bit embarrassingly for him) I, a South African Jewish guy living in New York, was going to be introducing him for the first time to the head of the fund that was Goldman's client, even though the two worked ten blocks apart.

We went into the meeting. In our preparation, the local partner and I had gone over several possible scenarios for ways we thought the talks might go—clearly the SEC investigation was going to come up—but we didn't know exactly how things would go down. After handshakes and niceties all around, the head of the fund immediately brought up the SEC charges against Goldman Sachs. No bullshit on his part.

The normally extremely dignified and guarded head of the multibillion dollar fund did not mince words. He looked at the partner and then at me and said, "Let me be clear with you guys. You don't need to worry. We're not going to stop doing business with you. The truth is, we haven't trusted you guys for a long time, because we think Goldman Sachs is a hedge fund; we know you have exclusively your own interests at heart. Yet we also recognize that you're the smartest guys on the Street, and there are times when we need to trade with you."

I tried to keep my mouth from falling open. He went on. He was not unsympathetic, he said. He was with us in thinking that the hearings were a bit of a witch hunt. He was taking the tack that some people in the media had also begun taking: Of course Goldman Sachs advances its own interests. This shouldn't be a surprise to anyone. We know it. There's nothing illegal about that. The firm is just matching up buyers and sellers—and often, the firm itself is one or the other. But, he said, we're not naïve enough to think that Goldman is always going to do right by us, either.

The meeting continued. We spoke a little bit about the markets; the local partner, finally seeing a place to jump in, gave some opinions about what Lloyd was saying and thinking in that regard. The senior client said, quite politely and mildly, that given the length of his relationship with Goldman Sachs, he was slightly surprised not to have heard directly from Lloyd. I cringed. Then, after parting handshakes, we left. I felt extremely deflated. I hated not being trusted. My instinct was to think, *How can we fix this? How can we make this client trust us again?*

But the local partner's reaction was one of relief. "Thank God they're not going to cut their business off," he said. "This is a good outcome! I thought it was going to be much worse."

I shook my head.

In the days that followed, I kept shaking my head, trying to adjust to the new reality. Here was a Goldman Sachs partner expressing relief that business with a client was going to continue even though the client's top guy didn't trust us to do right by him. Partners used to take on themselves the mantle of stewardship of the firm, but this partner was not acting like a steward of the firm at all. It was demoralizing for me to see so senior a person act in such a totally self-interested and short-sighted way. In effect, he was saying, "I'm not going to get into trouble; I'm going to keep making money. And if this client stops doing business with us five years down the line, I'm probably not going to be here anyway." Maybe this was an isolated example, but it was not what I expected from a partner.

What had become of the 14 Principles—specifically, principle 2: "Our assets are our people, capital and reputation. If any of these is ever diminished, the last is the most difficult to restore"? We seemed to have entered some strange Future Zone, where the last asset wasn't merely tarnished; it had vanished. It appeared that a Goldman Sachs employee now had to accept as a fact of life that we were no longer to be trusted. This was not a great fact for me to think about. I expected the leadership of the firm to try hard, to do whatever it took, to fix this. But would they?

———

As soon as the SEC charges hit the tape, Goldman started to lose the momentum it had been building steadily since March 2009. When investors saw the regulators going after the most profitable bank on Wall Street, they couldn't help wondering, *What's coming next? When will the next shoe drop?* The financial world was already more than a bit shaken up when May 6, 2010, came along.

I remember it very clearly. The markets had been down all day on worries about the Greek debt crisis. Early in the afternoon, I stepped away from my desk to go to the bathroom. I remember chatting with someone who was at the urinal next to mine, our futures strategist, and then going back to my desk to find that the market had plummeted an extraordinary amount: the Dow had been down 9 percent at one time and quickly recovered. This swing of 1,000 points was one of the largest moves in Dow Jones history. Everyone was gawking at their screens. What the hell was going on? Another thing people noticed is that stocks such as Accenture, CenterPoint Energy, and Exelon had, for a brief moment, lost the entirety of their value, and had traded as low as one cent per share. This wasn't possible. How could a stock instantaneously lose its market cap in less than a second? This was unprecedented, to say the least.

This was the flash crash.

Between 2:42 and 2:47 P.M., the Dow Jones dropped 600 points beyond the 300 it had fallen earlier, for a loss of almost 1,000 points on the day. By 3:07 P.M., the market made back most of the 600 points.

Whenever there is a very big and precipitous drop in the market that cannot be explained by any one news headline, investors almost always speculate: "Oh it must be a fat finger in the E-mini S&P futures"—meaning some clumsy trader accidentally sold off a massive amount of volume, far more than he intended, wreaking havoc in the process. In the early 2000s, there were a few famous fat-finger issues as the E-mini was taking over the big futures contract that had been traded in the pit. We used to joke on the desk that the guy who kept "fat-fingering" was a mysterious character known as the "E-Mini Bandit."

But was the flash crash the E-Mini Bandit's work?

What actually happened was never clear to me—nor, I think, to anyone else. Various theories were offered, but the one thing a number of people started saying was that the crash had been triggered by a large sale of E-mini S&P 500 futures, the very product I had traded years ago on the Futures desk with Corey, the most liquid futures contract in the world. In the midst of this bizarre twenty-five minutes, a number of senior people, remembering my experience with these futures, came up to me for an analysis of what was going on. I told them I didn't think it was caused by the E-minis. There was just not enough volume going through to cause such a crazy move.

What was so disturbing to me—and to millions of people around the country who invest in the stock market—was the utter fragility the flash crash revealed in a market that had become insanely complicated. There were interlocking technologies and backup systems, none of them necessarily able to communicate with the others when things went wrong. High-frequency trading—computers making millions of trades per second—had become a massive proportion of the daily trading volume. Eventually, the SEC and the media settled on a trade made by the mutual fund company Waddell and Reed as the catalyst. No one will ever convince me that a mutual fund manager selling $2 billion in E-mini futures was responsible for what happened that May afternoon. When I was on Corey's desk, I would routinely trade $3 billion of them myself. I never caused a flash crash. To an outsider, the mini-disaster may have looked reasonable: a big sale triggering a sell-off. To me, it simply looked scary—one more sign that the global capital markets were officially out of balance.

Investors felt the same way. With the flash crash following hard on the heels of the SEC charges, clients were rattled. And being rattled, they stopped trading. They froze. Things turned dead quiet once more; the layoffs recommenced. The mood on the Goldman trading floor was dire.

In July, Goldman Sachs agreed to a settlement of $550 million in the SEC suit: $300 million to go to the government and $250 million to investors. Fabrice Tourre was not included in the settlement, further reinforcing the impression that the firm had hung him out to dry. As to the SEC's charges, Goldman neither admitted nor denied any wrongdoing. Many people found this very strange. What was a settlement of $550 million if not an implicit admission of wrongdoing? The spin doctors at the SEC crowed that it was a huge victory, the biggest settlement of all time. Skeptics on Wall Street said, "This is a huge victory for Goldman Sachs; they got away unscathed." For anyone in America, $550 million was a mindboggling amount of money. But for a corporation whose Securities division was bringing in $5 billion a quarter, $550 million was a parking ticket.

————

After the settlement, a lot of people at Goldman felt relieved. *Maybe,* they thought, *with all this out of the way, we can move on.* Yet business didn't get a lot better: the firm's reputation had been damaged with some clients. A lot of clients were no longer comfortable taking counterparty risk with Goldman Sachs. They would be willing to trade only listed, transparent products that went through a clearinghouse. That way the clients' money, and market exposure, would be safe, irrespective of what happened to the bank they were trading with. Not the case with OTC derivatives or structured products, with which you would be subject to the fate of the bank with whom you did the trade.

As the pressure for revenues increased, so did bad behavior of various kinds inside Goldman Sachs. There was more pressure to steal a colleague's client or to try to persuade unsuspecting clients to do things that weren't in their best interest. People who had risen to leadership positions during the crisis, elevated for their ability to bring in cash rather than lead, now consolidated their power. Right and wrong had become a thing of the past; the new watchword was "GC or not GC?" Gross credits: they're what people cared about, talked about, measured themselves by, and got paid for. More and more people in the firm carried this banner, and these people were now the managers setting an example to their teams.

The smarter among their ranks must have known how the optics of this would play out. After the Senate hearings, Mr. Cleanse forbade the mention of GCs in office e-mails, for fear that such messages might, like those of the Fabulous Fab, someday become public. Or, just as bad, that a client might see such an e-mail and begin to understand what kinds of hidden charges it was paying.

Jack Welch, the iconic former CEO of General Electric, wrote that once an organization starts rewarding bad people for generating profits, the good people become demoralized, the culture gets ruined, and some of the in-between people (those on the fence) get lured into thinking they have to act like the bad people. And the more this happens, the more it continues to happen, until it becomes the norm. This moral erosion was swiftly becoming the norm at Goldman Sachs.

Welch (in Reuters) on culture:

It happens to be one of the most immutable rules of business. Soft culture matters as much as hard numbers. And if your company's culture is to mean anything, you have to hang—publicly—those in your midst who would destroy it. It's a grim image, we know. But the fact is, creating a healthy, high-integrity organizational culture is not puppies and rainbows. And yet, for some reason, too many leaders think a company's values can be relegated to a five-minute conversation between HR and a new employee. Or they think culture is about picking which words—do we "honor" our customers or "respect" them?—to engrave on a plaque in the lobby. What nonsense.

An organization's culture is not about words at all. It's about behavior—and consequences. It's about every single individual who manages people knowing that his or her key role is that of chief values officer, with Sarbanes-Oxley-like enforcement powers to match. It's about knowing that at every performance review, employees are evaluated for both their numbers and their values...

With the squeeze on, the old-fashioned kind of business (making flat commissions on transparent exchange-listed trades) was increasingly seen as not profitable enough. Around the time of the SEC settlement, a Goldman quant came up with a sexy new black box with a very unsexy name. Call it Clorox. The real tag is even more generic—the firm was very concerned, post Abacus, that new structured products be designated as blandly as possible, I suppose to avoid drawing undue attention to them.

Clorox was what is known as a "multi-asset-class momentum product"—a fancy term for "Give us your money and we'll reallocate your funds based on historical models (taking a big markup on every reallocation)." This product was a bit like a jazzed-up version of basic portfolio management. It was like taking a baloney sandwich and offering it to a client as a Panino di Bologna. The first is worth fifty cents; the second, you can sell for eight dollars.

Some clients went for it, especially the kind I mentioned earlier: the simple ones and the ones who didn't know how to ask questions. There were a number of endowments, foundations, and philanthropies out there who took the bait and bought Clorox.

When my bosses pressured me to try to sell Clorox to some of my bigger clients, I knew immediately that it would not be up their alley. They would have been offended, in fact, had I broached it with them, because they can do asset allocation and portfolio management themselves. Why on earth would they need a complex black box called Clorox that generated outsize fees for Wall Street? They could achieve the same thing using exchange-listed stocks, futures, and options. I pushed back on pushing Clorox to my clients. It was not in their best interest.

As the sales force went out flogging Clorox to philanthropies, state teachers' retirement plans, and small hedge funds that were just getting up and running, I wondered, *Is this reflecting any lessons we've learned from the Senate hearings or the crisis?* And I couldn't help thinking, *No, this is not reflecting any new direction. In fact, the rhetoric around GCs is increasing constantly.*

Then the firm commenced its "Business Practices Study." Goldman took it upon itself to say, "All right, we haven't done everything right; let's start investigating." All the top people at the firm were put on the Business Practices Committee. The guy in charge of it was a long-standing partner named Mike Evans, who was supposed to be old-school, up-front, and high on the list to take over the firm one day.

I was hopeful about the study, hopeful that Goldman could start repairing this trust deficit it had with clients. I had a vision of going back to my client in Asia and saying, "Look, we've studied these things. We know it is going to take us time to fix this. But we're determined to get it right."

But as the study proceeded, I began to wonder whether it was all just for show. I would have liked to contribute to the study, offer some opinions, but I wasn't contacted. I didn't know anyone who was contacted for their input. Was the study being conducted in a back room somewhere?

————

I had developed a real money niche. Thousands of clients and internal Goldman people were on my distribution list when I sent out my market commentaries. I had built up a track record of thoughtful content, and had been more right than wrong in my market predictions. This was part luck, but since my early days with Rudy and then Corey, my market instincts had improved. They had become sharper. I had a sense for how markets might react under different circumstances. After all, in my decade-long career so far, I had seen multiple bubbles and busts; I had seen how market cycles work. My little essays were becoming dialogue-starters. People would say, "Did you see the 'Real Money' piece?" or, "Did you see Greg Smith's latest?" They forwarded them around to their clients. I was proud that I was producing original content. Very few salespeople were doing this on a regular basis, aside from me and my two MD friends.

I was also proud to maintain a level of objectivity. I said what I thought, rather than parroting the company line. This didn't go down well in all quarters. One day, toward the end of the summer of 2010, my co-boss Beth called me into her office for yet another worried conference about how slow business was and what she wanted me to try to do about it. When I mentioned a recent piece I'd written, she made a face.

It was probably ill advised, but I had to say something on my own behalf. "I don't want to make too big a deal of this," I said, "but some of the biggest clients in the division are reading and responding to my pieces, and we are gaining mind share with them in a tough climate."

She shook her head a little sadly, as if I were a particularly dense grade-school student. "Content and ideas are not going to lead to success at Goldman Sachs, Greg," she said. "The only thing that matters is the numbers."

———

Every September 11 since 2002, Wall Street has observed three moments of silence to commemorate the attacks on the World Trade Center: one at 8:46 A.M., when the North Tower was hit; one at 9:03 A.M., when the South Tower was hit; and one at 9:30, when the opening bell on the New York Stock Exchange rings.

For the first few years after 2002, somebody would always pipe up on the Hoot, "Guys, moment of silence coming up; everyone keep it down." The trading floor would go dead quiet. But after the five-year anniversary, in 2006, I began to notice that people were no longer paying attention.

The moments of silence would be going on in the background—on the monitors, you could see the observances on CNBC—yet people just carried on with their business: calling clients, checking their Bloombergs. I don't think they were being intentionally disrespectful; I think they were just being young.

By the mid- to late part of the first decade of the 2000s, the average employee tenure at Goldman Sachs, in a workforce that now numbered thirty thousand, was approximately five years. So, when it came to September 11, people simply didn't have the context. They hadn't been here then; they'd still been in college, or even high school. Aside from the brief annual commemoration, Goldman's institutional memory had sealed over and walled off the trauma, so that we could go on with business as usual.

By September 11, 2010, we were in a new world altogether at the firm. It made me feel old, and sad. But I also felt proud to have stuck around so long.

Also, in September 2010, something monumental happened.

My green card. I got it! Fourteen years after I landed in America as a college freshman with a thick South African accent, I was now a permanent resident of the United States of America. What a feeling it was to open that envelope and see that card. A mixture of wonderful emotions: freedom to stay in America, flexibility, relief, happiness. People born and raised in America have no idea how hard it is, and how long it takes, to get that magic card. And I was thrilled. My adopted homeland had been good to me, and I could not have felt prouder. Lex and I—buddies in Jo'burg, buddies at Stanford, buddies when he had stayed in Palo Alto and I had flown off to New York—were both now full-fledged permanent residents of this great nation. When we saw each other a few weeks later, we toasted our achievement, feeling proud of how far we had come, that we had been able to stay in America. Jo'burg seemed a long way away now.

I have always sought out mentors. After my market pieces began to gain traction, I formed a bond with a very senior 2006 partner who seemed to take a genuine interest in my career. He liked my writing, which meant he liked my ideas. As an upper-echelon partner, he knew what was going on in the organization, and he felt I was on track toward taking the next step up, to managing director. He also had ideas about what I might do to facilitate the move. "I've heard good things," he would say. "This is how you need to position yourself."

I was about to turn thirty-two in December; I had been a vice president for four years. Most new MDs were promoted in their mid- to late thirties. There were people such as Dave Heller who had made it under thirty. So it would not have been unheard of for me to move up now, but it would certainly have been considered quick. My partner mentor had also said, "The good guys around here always finish first, but it usually takes them longer"—meaning that the bad guys did well and rose fast, but the good guys ultimately outlasted them.

In truth, I was never very good at the political game. I always (perhaps stupidly) wanted to let my work speak for itself. But I could tell that, in the Goldman Sachs world I was living in now, it was essential that I look out for myself, find sponsors, make sure to speak up and ask for what I wanted. That's why I was happy to have found a senior partner mentor.

A few weeks later he asked me to swing by for a follow-up meeting. "How are things going?" he asked. "How's the year progressing?" He mentioned my last couple of market commentaries, and said, once again, "These pieces you're writing are great—it's really good stuff."

I thanked him. "But I have to say—" I hesitated.

"What is it?" he asked.

"It's a little bit hard for me to hear from my boss that these pieces are almost irrelevant," I said, and then I told him about my unsatisfying discussion with Beth.

To his credit, he was very disturbed to hear this. In fact, he got quite angry. "Gary is very concerned about this kind of stuff," he said. He told me that Gary Cohn had worried aloud to a number of the partners that the good guys in the organization, meaning the culture carriers, weren't succeeding as much as the people who were selling ice in the Sahara Desert—say, unwinding distressed positions for panicky clients—and racking up huge fees. My mentor said Gary realized that throughout the mortgage boom and the subsequent crisis, Goldman had promoted a lot of people for selling ice, putting a lot of the wrong people into leadership positions. "Gary is very worried about this, and is very focused on getting it right," he told me. "I'm going to talk to somebody about this."

Two days later, at 7:45 A.M., Beth asked if we could have a chat in her office.

I have to say that I wasn't especially worried. On a spectrum of people Beth hated and loved, I was probably somewhere in the middle: I didn't ever have a sense that we had a bad relationship. My first thought was that my complaint to my mentor had gotten back to her, and she wanted to rough me up a little bit. I also wondered, since she knew he had been mentoring me about the managing director track, if she wanted to assert her power as my boss and take control of that conversation. As I walked into her office, I imagined her saying something like "Look, your mentor has spoken to me, and first of all, you need to be careful about how you portray things. But also let's talk about the MD track. We see it as being maybe two years out for you. Here's what you need to do; here's what you don't need to do."

But there was none of that. Instead, she smiled and (very unexpectedly) said, "How would you feel about moving to London?"

She looked especially pleased with herself, as if she were presenting me with a terrific gift. But my heart sank immediately. I had no desire to move. I loved New York, I loved America, and I thought I was doing well in my career here. The environment was tough, but I felt I could succeed.

My face must've betrayed my unhappiness. "I'd never really thought about it," I said.

"We're going to start a U.S. equity derivatives business in Europe," she said excitedly, "and we think you might be the right guy to go start it. We think you're at the right point in your career. You're responsible, you have a lot of experience in derivatives, and we think you're enough of a grown-up that you'll be able to travel the Continent and the Middle East and do a good job for us figuring out this business."

I wasn't as excited as she was. Beth now found herself in the unwelcome position of trying to foist a prize on an ingrate. Her smile hardened. "We could have chosen anyone for this," she said.

Just then, Mr. Cleanse walked in. As coheads of the group, he and Beth shared a big office. Remembering that he had been previously stationed in the London office, I said, "Conti, you spent six years in London. What do you think about this?"

Beth was looking unhappier by the second. It suddenly occurred to me that she had met with me solo, rather than together with Cleanse, because she was trying to show me that she was the one who'd thought of me for this role, the one who'd put me forward and put herself on the line. She wanted gratitude, she wanted ownership, and she wasn't getting it.

Mr. Cleanse sat down. "Dude, this is a great opportunity," he said. He was a salesperson, and he was selling me. "I understand you're happy here, but this could be a good thing for your career."

But as he talked, I felt more and more shell-shocked. Beth was talking about a three-year commitment. The first thing that came to my mind was my hope and plan to move my mother to the States from Johannesburg, which was crime-ridden and dangerous. The plan had been in motion for a couple of years. I'd helped move my sister over to America; my dad had by now passed his pharmacy exam and moved over. But my mother was hesitating. My transferring to London could throw a wrench into the works.

"Look, most of my family live here," I said.

"But you're a single guy," Cleanse said. "How hard could it be? London is only seven hours away."

I shook my head. "I don't know," I said. "I really need time to think about this—I'm not sure it's up my alley."

Beth frowned. "You really need to tell me if you're serious about this," she said. "I'm not going to send you over there to meet with Daffey [who was now in charge of Securities division sales in the London office and Global Head of Equity Sales] if you're not. There are a lot of other people who want to do this job—in fact, would kill to do this job."

As fate would have it, a fairly close acquaintance of mine from the London office, a managing director named Georgette, was in New York that week. I invited her out to lunch to ask her what she thought.

I'd known Georgette since we were both junior analysts, and we'd come up together as futures traders, talking on the phone almost every day. She usually came to the States twice a year, so we'd met a number of times. She was dark-haired and striking, always elegantly dressed. Cleanse had mentored her in London; rumor had it that she was more Cleanse than Cleanse himself. Word had also crossed the Atlantic that she'd become a vicious boss and ruthlessly power-hungry, with a penchant for trying to get colleagues fired or transferred—one MD had dubbed her the Black Widow. I found all this strange: Georgette and I had always respected each other and gotten along well.

When I mentioned Beth's offer at lunch, Georgette seemed taken aback. I assumed she'd been in the loop on the offer, possibly even involved in deciding who should get the job, but it was now clear that she wasn't senior enough to know about it. She clearly didn't like hearing about it for the first time from me, and she tried to save face: "Well, I'd heard some rumblings about this," she said. I would also find out, soon enough, that she was threatened by the idea of someone moving in on her territory.

At the moment, however, I trusted her enough to be honest with her. I told her about my family situation and my reservations about the transfer. I said I was afraid I'd reacted badly to Beth's offer.

Georgette appeared completely calm and reasonable—it was hard to imagine how she could have gotten her evil-sounding nickname. "Well, I also would have reacted badly," she said. "If you're shocked with something like that, what are you supposed to do?"

———

When I came to work the next morning, Corey Stevens came by my desk and said, "I've got to see you immediately." He pulled me into a room and shut the door. "You really, really fucked up with Beth," he said.

"I thought she was unhappy," I said, "but I didn't know she was that unhappy."

"This is very serious," Corey said. "You gave her the impression you weren't grateful; that was insulting to her. This could be big trouble. You don't want to be on her bad side, because she's not someone who forgives easily. You need to figure this out quickly. You need to either unwind this thing very quickly and say, 'I'm sorry, family issues, I'm not able to do this,' or very quickly and diplomatically and sincerely apologize to her and say you want to really consider it seriously, and you're grateful that she thought of you, and that she's gone out on a limb to recommend you when she could have recommended anyone."

I later found out that Corey had been considered for, and wanted, the job. But he was an MD by now and was deemed slightly too senior to leave his post in New York. Now he was looking out for me.

CHAPTER 10

London Calling

Then came the groveling.

Putting my family worries on hold for the moment, I decided to give this opportunity serious consideration—or at least make a very good show of doing so—and eat humble pie.

The problem was, Beth wouldn't let me. She was a major league grudge holder, and I'd clearly pissed her off big time. Every time I asked her for ten minutes, she looked at me as if I were a fly on her food. "Speak to Brigitta, my assistant," she'd say. "Try to see if you can get some time."

Finally, after she'd decided I'd squirmed and sweated sufficiently—and since her desk on the trading floor was only four seats from mine, she had a very good view—she budged. When she was off the desk and in her office, I got an e-mail from her saying, "I have a few minutes now." I was on the phone with a client. I got off. When I walked into her office, I found her staring distractedly at her terminal. "Take a seat," she said. I sat. Then she looked at me, stone-faced. "So what's up?" she asked.

My move. There was no way forward but to tell the truth—humbly. "Look," I said. "I realize I didn't act in a way that showed how grateful I was to you. But once Corey explained how far out on a limb you went for me, I began to understand what a big deal this was." Mentioning Corey was purposeful. She knew he was my mentor, and I knew that she and he were close. And I was telling her the truth. Corey had made it clear that she really had extended herself on my behalf.

According to him, she had actually told Daffey, "Greg is the guy we want to send."

I admitted that the idea of leaving New York had seemed shocking at first. I told her how much I loved the city. I told her I did have some family issues, repeated that most of my family lived here in America, but didn't spell out the situation in great detail. "But," I said, "now that I've thought about this, I am excited, and I just want to ask you to give me another chance. I'd love to go over there and meet the people in the London office. I'll give it the most serious possible consideration and look at it as a potentially great opportunity."

It was a pretty stirring speech, but Beth still had her poker face on. She didn't want to let me off the hook just yet. "You know, I have to tell you, I was really taken aback by how you reacted," she told me.

"I'm sorry," I said. "I was just really shocked by the thought of moving to another country. It was a human reaction. I understand I didn't convey the right sense of appreciation."

But she wasn't giving an inch. Still, she nodded to show she'd heard me. "Let me speak to Conti," she said, referring to Mr. Cleanse. "Let me think about it a little bit more, and then we'll let you know." Just a few days earlier, I'd been her fair-haired boy. Now, for all I knew, she had ruled me out.

That night I had dinner with a client who was in town from overseas and, oddly enough, Mr. Cleanse ended up coming along. It was just four of us—the president of the New York office of the client, the client's head of trading, Cleanse, and me—at a three-star Italian restaurant called Alto, in Midtown. Poking mild fun at me, Cleanse brought up my table tennis history. It turned out that the client trader was a good player, so, strangely, we talked about that for quite a while. Mr. Cleanse couldn't get enough of it. The evening flowed freely, and was mostly social, with little shop talk. In an effort to impress everyone at the table, Cleanse ordered a $400 bottle of wine—significantly over the Goldman Sachs allowance. (He would end up paying for it out of pocket.) At the end of the night, he sent me an e-mail saying, "Great dinner—well done, well organized." The London opportunity never came up.

Two days later, though, Beth said, "All right, get your visa. We're going to send you over to meet some people." It was no longer "We think you're the right guy for this"; the strong implication was that I would have to win London over. It was all right with me. Beth wanted to put some pressure on me and exact some further revenge, not to mention save face. I was very deferential. I even asked her for advice about the different personalities in the London office. I could sense her warming ever so slightly.

Before I left, I had another conversation with Corey. "All right, you almost blew it," he said. "Now you've made it all the way back to neutral. Beth's not sold on you; Daffey isn't, either. You're going to have to go over there and really crush it with London. You're going to have to sell them on why you're the right person, and what you see as the opportunity."

My suspicion meter flickered a little at that. How could Corey have known that Daffey wasn't sold on me? Had Beth put him up to saying this? But it was clear that he was trying to light a fire under my ass.

"And by the way," Corey said, looking me in the eye, "you should want this." He mentioned the example of the guy who had expensed the ChapStick, who was doing in New York the same job I was being considered for in London. "Look what happened to ChapStick," Corey said. "He was nowhere, and he took this role, and now he's on the partner track. The same could happen to you. This wouldn't just put you on the managing director track. If you get this right, this puts you on the partner track. The fact that Daffey and all these partners are focused on this—this is no joke."

So I got on a plane and headed to London. One thing I hadn't told anybody: I'd never been there before. I didn't want to look like a rookie or anything.

American Airlines, business class, red-eye. I arrived early in the morning to a typically rainy, gray London day. The sky looked bleak: low-hanging clouds, no visibility. I went outside to stand in the drizzle and wait for a cab. I had arrived a day early so I could see my brother, who'd been in London for a few months, working as a lawyer—a nice coincidence. I also wanted to rest a bit: I needed to bring my A-game to the office the following day.

"Where to, guv'nor?" the cabbie inquired, in his Cockney accent.

"I'm going to the One Aldwych Hotel, please," I answered, in my South African accent.

"One *the* Aldwych, is it?" he said, adding a *the* right in the middle of the name. "No problem, guv."

I felt like I was in a movie. The cab ride cost £120, the equivalent of almost $190, and took more than an hour. I was glad Goldman Sachs was paying. (I would later learn that taking a cab was a rookie mistake: the Heathrow Express train gets you in to London in fifteen minutes.)

———

The position I was being considered for was head of U.S. Equity Derivatives Sales in Europe, the Middle East, and Africa—which meant I would be selling options, swaps, derivatives, and other products to foreign hedge funds, mutual funds, sovereign wealth funds, and asset management firms. In the beginning, I would have to build the business, but Beth and Mr. Cleanse had told me that, within a year, I could probably hire another person if I found the business that I believed was there. My title would be executive director, the equivalent of vice president in New York.

I was scheduled to meet with nineteen people over two days in London, mostly managing directors and partners: my assignment was to persuade them, one by one, that I was the right guy for the job. If and only if I managed to do so, I would get a twentieth and final meeting, this time with Michael Daffey.

The audition would be strange.

The weather outside was cold and rainy, but the action on the trading floor at the Goldman Sachs offices on Fleet Street was hot and heavy: intense, dramatic, in your face. The offices were housed in two adjacent buildings, Peterborough Court and River Court, connected by a sky bridge. Both buildings had belonged to newspapers and dated to the early 1900s. The trading floor was noticeably smaller than its New

York counterpart, with a significantly lower ceiling, and the traders and salespeople were squashed more tightly together. As a result, the place possessed a kind of compressed energy, a tension you could feel immediately—more a submarine than an aircraft carrier. The trading floor at 200 West Street was massive; people were spread out as far as the eye could see. When they interacted, they usually observed the social niceties. Goldman Sachs's London office had different sorts of niceties.

The dress code, for example. Daffey and other partners in the London office loved tossing around the time-honored phrase "Dress British, think Yiddish"—the latter a nod to the firm's Jewish roots, the former an accurate description of sartorial styles at 120 Fleet Street. Suits were big at Goldman London. Everyone wore them, and everyone seemed to have a lot of them. The big hitters got theirs custom-made on Savile Row (at close to £5,000 a pop); the lesser hitters (like me) got them either from Asia or from an Italian tailor, Gianni, who came through town once a month. Typical dress for a Goldman London guy was a bespoke suit and a tieless dress shirt (Turnbull & Asser, Thomas Pink, or Charles Tyrwhitt) with the top two buttons open, so at least a little bit of chest hair was showing.

Patterns were big. People wore checked, striped, and windowpane suits. Colors were big. Neckties, when worn, made a strong statement: green and purple were popular. Basically, anything went, as long as it was stylish. In the much less fashion-forward New York office, you couldn't get away with most of this stuff, especially wearing a suit with no tie. "Casual Friday" in New York meant khakis and a polo shirt. In London, it meant coming in to the office in whatever you'd worn to the club the night before. A couple times I saw people come straight to the office, sleepless, from having been out all night: women in low-cut dresses, guys in jeans and ripped T-shirts. London made its own rules.

The various desks there were organized by nationality. There was an Italian group, a French group, a German group, and a Scandinavian group—not to mention several UK-focused groups. As a result, the trading floor was like a microcosm of Europe itself: each area had its own distinctive sensibility. Between them, language difficulties, cross-border arguments, and frequent misunderstandings, often expressed at high volume, played out constantly.

A managing director who had encouraged my first attempts at writing market commentary was my "friendly" in London. He took me out for breakfast at a private club in the basement of the Lutyens restaurant, across the street from the Goldman offices, to give me the lay of the land. Over omelets, he looked through my schedule and prepped me for each meeting, giving me some insight into who the tough characters were, who would be most supportive. This was extremely helpful. I knew all the names; I had done my homework; but he had worked alongside all of them, sometimes butted heads with them.

He gave me some more background about the position I was being considered for. He confirmed that it was a senior role, and that at least two MDs, including Corey, had been considered for it. But my South African background was in my favor, he said; management saw it as potentially helping me bond with overseas clients. And because they weren't exactly sure what the total business opportunity was, they thought it might be too risky to bring an MD over. They saw my level (VP) and experience as ideal, he told me.

He also warned me a bit about moving to a new office. He had done it three times: from New York to Tokyo to Hong Kong to London. "You've got to think this through," he said. "There are pros and cons. Every time you go to a new office, you're starting from the beginning in terms of new people. You have to impress them; you can't rely on your reputation." He wasn't trying to discourage me; he had no agenda. He was very close with Corey—to some extent, I think he was taking it upon himself to look after me a bit while I was there.

I asked him if I should try to squeeze the firm a bit, to make them realize how much of a sacrifice this was for me. Maybe I could get some kind of financial guarantee from them?

"They're not going to do that," he said. "At best, they'll give you an expat package." I had heard something about this before, but wasn't exactly sure what it was. He explained that the expat package was a salary supplement to compensate for the United Kingdom's higher income taxes and the brutal exchange rate. But it was strictly discretionary on management's part, and given only in rare instances. I knew how management was thinking: they didn't need to give me anything; they'd already be giving me a great opportunity by moving me to London. The benefit for me was potentially to get on the partner track. They were saying, "Here's a whole world of business. Go get it."

And I believed the business was there. I felt more and more excited about the opportunity. From the moment I arrived, I saw that the priorities there were so misaligned that there were major efficiencies to be created and much new business to find. At the time, Goldman Sachs in Europe was focused almost exclusively on structured products. Goldman would never have admitted this to clients, but internally they felt that salespeople should be going after only big, high-margin business—elephant trades. The sales force was ignoring day-to-day, flow business—what Goldman Europe called "low-margin business." At times, they were turning clients away. I saw a wide-open field. All I had to do was go there and start selling plain-vanilla options, swaps, and derivatives to clients whom Goldman Europe seldom called on, and this new business would very quickly add up to what I estimated to be north of $20 million above and beyond the business we were already doing there.

The people I met with over my two-day speed-dating round, mostly the head honchos in sales and trading, were also a cross-section: English, Dutch, Swiss, Belgian. Each twenty- to thirty-minute meeting had a yin-yang to it: I had to convince each manager why I was right for the position, but he or she had to convince me why it was a good opportunity. What remained unsaid was that, as a newcomer, I represented a certain threat to the status quo. It was interesting to see how various people reacted to this. One Dutch MD told me, in his heavily accented English, "This is not a very good opportunity at all. I really don't think there's much business to do here." And then there were people who said, "This is a great opportunity. We don't spend much time on this business." After I got back to New York, one of the people I'd met with sent me an e-mail that read, "Dude, when are you coming over? We have a whole world to conquer together."

And then there was Georgette. A number of people I talked to before

I left had cautioned me to "tread carefully." In the middle of my first day in London, I walked up to her desk and said, "Hey, Georgette, how's it going?" She was looking at her Bloomberg screen and typing something.

"Oh, hey," she said, without turning her head. Zero eye contact.

"I just wanted to update you on some of these meetings I've been having," I said, and mentioned a few of the people I'd talked to. She still didn't look at me. "Is now okay for you?" I asked.

"You know, now is not great," she said. "Just keep me posted afterward on how it all went."

There was something off-putting and vaguely intimidating about her refusal to make eye contact. *I've flown all the way over here from New York*, I thought. *If I do this job, we're going to be working together rather closely. Plus, I've known you for nine years. Couldn't you spare fifteen minutes to have a cup of coffee with me?* But meeting her on her turf was apparently very different from meeting her on mine.

In the middle of the second day, the woman who was coordinating my schedule told me that I was now slotted in for a final meeting with Michael Daffey. This was very good news. The message was that I had done very well, that most people had signed off on me. Daffey was to be the final arbiter.

Meeting with Daffey in London was a very different thing from seeing him in New York at Soho House with a killer buzz under his belt. He was now the global head of Equity Sales, and the head of Securities Sales in London, meaning he managed both FICC and Equities. He had thousands of people ultimately reporting to him. He was now an official Very Important Partner, and a hard guy to see. You had to go through three levels of security, not to mention a strict English lady sitting guard at the desk outside his door, just to get in his office.

At the appointed time, the English lady escorted me into Daffey's impressively big and elegant office. The first thing that caught my eye, besides Daffey smiling and extending his hand, was a large framed lithograph on the wall, a single word in big black type on its white background. It read: PEOPLE. It was the old Daffey. I breathed a sigh of relief. "Dude, great to see you," he said. The assistant closed the door, and

Daffey gave me his undivided attention. "So why do you want to do this job?" he asked.

I told him the truth: that even before I came over, I'd seen it as a potentially exciting opportunity, and that my meetings had all confirmed that idea. I said I thought I was the right guy to do the job, that I knew the business inside and out, and that I really wanted him to give me the chance to make it work.

He was nodding, looking positive. Then, to his credit, he asked me the right question: "What are your concerns about moving over?" he said. "Any issues?"

I spoke my heart, telling him openly and fully of my worries about my family. He and I had known each other a long time, and even though he was now the top guy, I trusted him more than anyone else. But since he was the boss, I also wanted him to know that I'd be making a big sacrifice by transferring to London.

At the same time, I wanted to tell him that I genuinely did relish the idea of working for him again. I reminisced back to when we'd first met, in 2002. "I've always considered you to be one of the highest-integrity people around here," I said. "It would be a special thing for me to work for you again and do you proud."

Daffey looked serious. "Buddy, you've always been working for me," he said. Then, as I took that in, he smiled. "Dude, you're done."

In the outside world, "you're done" does not have good connotations. On Wall Street, however, it does. It means the trade is done; we're in business. What Daffey was telling me was that the job was mine. "In fact," he said, "I'm going to walk back with you to the trading floor."

This was a big deal. Daffey did not go onto the trading floor very often. As we walked in, suddenly the floor went quiet. The seas kind of parted a little bit—and this was hundreds of people. Daffey was talking with me, joking with me. It was the most powerful kind of endorsement. It said, "Greg's my guy."

———

Despite the glow of acceptance, I still had doubts. Goldman lore says that when the firm taps you on the shoulder to go overseas, you're allowed to say no only once or twice. On the flip side, the lore also says that accepting the assignment catapults you to the next level faster than anything else. Virtually every important leader of the firm has spent time in Asia or in Europe. I was torn.

Yet I also remembered how, when I was first invited to join Goldman Sachs, I waited three weeks before accepting, pissing some people off royally. So I knew that if I was going to accept this offer, I needed to do it quickly.

I landed at JFK, rode back into the city, and phoned my friend and consigliere Phil from the taxi. I gave him the background on the offer and the potential opportunity in it. "Come by," he said.

It was 11:00 on a Sunday night. Phil met me on the corner of Sixty-Second and Park. He was staying at his parents' place that night and didn't want to disturb them, so we stood outside in the brisk November air and talked for forty-five minutes, my bags on the sidewalk next to me.

He pushed very hard for me to take the job. "This is Europe," he said. "You're young. This is going to be a great experience. You have to do this."

When I went into work the next morning, I asked a senior MD on the floor if I could talk with him for ten minutes. He was a busy guy, but when he saw how serious I looked, he said yes. I wanted to talk with him because he was a level below my New York bosses, Mr. Cleanse and Beth, and he knew Daffey well. He knew all the players, and I trusted him. He didn't have a dog in the fight. He was the perfect guy to go to for some analytical, agenda-free advice. We went into a glass-walled conference room. I shut the door, then checked the speakerphone—it's a Goldman habit, whenever you go into one of these rooms for a private meeting, to hit the phone's hang-up button a few times, make sure you hear the dial tone, then hang up again. Triple-check. If there's a videoconference machine in the room, you make triple sure that that's off.

The MD asked me what was up. "I need your advice, man," I said, and told him about the London offer. "Is this a good move?" I asked. "I'm not asking them to move me; *they're* asking *me*. All my friends are here. I don't want to be screwed by not being rewarded adequately for pulling up stakes. Do you think they're going to do right by me?"

He looked at me. "Okay, this is completely off the record," he said. I nodded.

"Greg," he said, "I'm telling you this as a friend—way, way off the record. You should go out immediately and get another job offer, so you can squeeze them and make sure you mark yourself to market correctly. Because this *is* a big move, and a big sacrifice. You're picking up your whole life and moving to another country."

I listened very carefully. What he was saying made a lot of sense, from a practical standpoint. During my tenure at Goldman Sachs, I'd gotten a number of calls from other firms. It had happened in various ways: sometimes a bank would contact me directly (as JPMorgan Chase did once); once in a while, a client would try to get me to move over. The head of trading at one of my clients, who had become a bit fed up with Goldman Sachs and knew the head guy at Morgan Stanley, tried to facilitate a switch for me. Now and then, headhunting firms would get in touch. Sometimes they'd call through the switchboard and say it was "your friend" or "your cousin"; sometimes they'd give a made-up name such as "John Spencer." I'd think to myself, "Who's John Spencer?" Then I'd pick up, and the headhunter would say, "Can you put me on privacy?" And I would know immediately what was going on.

As soon as I pushed the Privacy button, the headhunter would say something like "Hi, it's Bob Simons. I'm a headhunter representing Credit Suisse. This is the position we're looking to fill. I'd like to talk to you about it." Then he'd usually say, "Can I get your cell phone number? I'll call you in the evening or this weekend."

I never followed up. In my whole career, I never once met or interviewed with another firm. I guess, in retrospect, I bled GS blue. I took loyalty very seriously, and didn't want anyone to think otherwise.

On the other hand, almost everyone I knew at Goldman interviewed somewhere else at one time or another. The MD who was counseling me was a very reasonable guy, and he was simply acknowledging the truth: the firm didn't repay loyalty in any way; they would fire anyone at any time. It was increasingly becoming a numbers game. If you'd been there ten years, fifteen years, twenty-five years, the only sure way to guarantee they were valuing you correctly was to mark yourself to market by shopping yourself around the marketplace.

Sometimes I wondered why I was so dedicated. I could easily have told my bosses, "You know what? I went out there, and my fair value is $900,000 instead of $700,000—take it or leave it."

But I never wanted to do that, because, as stupid as it may sound, it wasn't all about the money to me. I wanted to succeed at the best firm on the Street. I didn't want to shop myself around to find more money in a lesser firm. Maybe I should have, for my family's sake if for no one else's. But because I didn't, I almost certainly got paid less than I could have been paid. And sometimes I wondered: was I being loyal to a shadow?

———

I caught up with Corey Stevens later in the morning. He pushed as hard as Phil for me to accept the London job, stressing once again that going to London would put me on the track toward upper management. Then I got word from Beth that Goldman might offer me the expat package, the supplemented salary the MD in London had spoken of. I knew the way these things worked: this was a wink-wink. "Might" meant "definitely."

I called my family.

My sister was very supportive; she thought I should do it. My mother said exactly the same thing. "I really don't want this to derail your coming over to America," I told her. She promised it wouldn't. My brother was encouraging, too. My dad was a bit more hesitant, but only a bit. He asked if I was committed in the long term to staying in America. Of course I was, I told him.

On Wednesday I told Goldman Sachs yes.

———

Though I accepted the job in early October, it wasn't officially announced for almost two months. There were miles of red tape to clear up: London's tax burdens made the IRS look lenient. All sorts of sign-offs were required, up to the global division head and the general counsel of the firm. This dragged on for week after week—and in the meantime I wasn't allowed to tell anyone, colleagues or clients.

Still, everyone knew something was going on. It's just the way the Goldman grapevine works: slow leakage. Management almost seems to prefer it that way. My secret was a semi-open one. In November, I went back to London to speak at Goldman's inaugural Latin America conference in Europe, hosted by the firm at the Chancery Court Hotel. As part of my mandate, I would be responsible for helping European clients get access to Latin American derivative products in addition to U.S. products.

It was a nice surprise—ten years and three months after my summer internship—to see Val Carlotti at the conference. My first days at the firm felt like a lifetime ago. And Val had come a long way from his days grilling summer interns in Open Meetings, teaching us about Goldman culture, and going out to nightclubs with us in the evenings. He was now a partner—he'd made it in 2006—and was president of Goldman Sachs Brazil. He had flown in to London from São Paulo to give the keynote address, welcoming all the investors and talking about our expanded capabilities in Brazil. It was a blast from the past, and he and I chatted and reminisced for a few minutes.

After the conference, I spent another two days in the London office with the people who'd first interviewed me. At this stage, they knew I was coming over, so they were excited—most of them were, anyway; a couple of them may have been pretending. But the paperwork still hadn't gone through, so nothing had been announced. I also stopped by to see Laura Mehta, my old boss from New York who'd lent me her summer house in the North Fork. She was now a bigwig in London, and she was happy I'd accepted the role and was making the trek over. After the whirlwind three-day trip, I decompressed by having a Friday night dinner with my brother at a trendy Asian-fusion place called Hakkasan. He was excited that I'd soon be moving over.

I returned to New York for Thanksgiving. A few days later, my paperwork was finished at last. Beth called the whole group into a conference room and said, a little wryly, "As I'm sure many of you may have heard already, we're sending Greg Smith to London. He's going to build up our U.S. derivatives business there. Please join us in wishing him well. No doubt we'll be speaking to him quite a bit." There was a smattering of applause; you couldn't exactly call it a surprised reaction. Beth was smiling—partly because she was genuinely happy for me; partly, I think, because she was pleased with herself for having made it happen.

I was smiling, too. At last I really knew my life was about to change.

————

My farewell party was held on a Thursday night in early December, at SPiN New York, the subterranean table tennis club on East Twenty-Third Street that had somehow managed, almost entirely through the aura of its owner, Susan Sarandon, to turn Ping-Pong from nerdy into sexy. Models were serving the drinks; a DJ was pumping out the latest tunes.

Goldman Sachs farewell parties, I'd found, tended to be a bit hit or miss, depending on the popularity of the person who was moving on. And at Goldman, popularity was always commensurate with value to the firm. When people who were not well regarded professionally or personally (but mainly professionally) were leaving for the Tokyo office or other employment, few people, and especially few from upper management, showed up. It could be quite embarrassing.

Fortunately, I didn't have to be embarrassed. I was touched by the big turnout: two dozen colleagues from my desk and others. Both my immediate partner bosses, Mr. Cleanse and Beth, were there, as were Connors, who had survived his bachelor party, moved to Boston, become an MD, and was now back in New York; Bobby Schwartz; and two other MDs from the desk. I looked around for Corey in the crowd but wasn't surprised not to see him. When it came to farewell parties, he tended to be a bit too cool for school. It was part of his elusive mystique, and I accepted it. Everyone did. Even if the farewell party was for someone very high profile, he'd be somewhere even higher profile, maybe at a movie premiere with a model on his arm.

The party was loud and long and fun. A lot of alcohol was consumed, and a lot of table tennis was played. Early in the evening, I hit for a while with Connors, who was a reasonably good player, and I got to show off a bit, standing fifteen feet back from the table and returning all his smashes.

Then Corey walked in.

He certainly knew how to make an entrance. Nobody had expected him, but there he was, larger (and cooler) than life. Before he could even make his way over, several people came up to me to say what a big deal it was that he'd come. "Wow, Corey showed up," one of my team members said to me. "That's a pretty big endorsement." Even Mr. Cleanse was impressed—I think because it showed that Corey had more respect for me than for far more senior people whose parties he would never have thought about attending.

Corey clapped me on the back and bumped my chest with his. He was smiling significantly as he shook my hand. He looked unsurprised when a stir ran through the crowd behind him: Corey's legendary half-brother, an NFL Hall of Famer, had entered the room.

Everybody crowded around him, wowed at the appearance of this NFL superstar and major celebrity. But to me, Corey's gesture—asking his brother to come to my party—meant even more than the Legend's showing up. It was a gift to me, and a powerful endorsement. He had done right by me my entire career, and tonight was no different. Mr. Cleanse was a huge football fan, and he had never met the Legend before, even though Cleanse was Corey's boss. And then there was the poignancy of the fact that all those years ago, the Legend had picked my résumé—the guy who spoke Zulu...

A little later I was standing with Corey and his brother, who asked, "Are you excited about going to London?" Cleanse was standing right next to us, eavesdropping.

"Greg is going over there to do an important job," Corey told his brother. "He's going to run U.S. Derivatives."

"That sounds great," the Legend said. "Isn't Daffey over there?"

"Yeah, he is," Corey said.

"I'm sure Daffey will look out for you," Corey's brother said—he had met Daffey a few times over the years. "You'll do great there." Then, giving me a wink and a fist bump, he was off into the night.

Later still, after Corey had left and the party had started to die down, I was standing with Mr. Cleanse, who was still glowing from his encounter with the Legend, not to mention more than a few drinks. "So," I said, "who are the important people in London?"

He looked at me intently. "You're the important person in London," he said.

I smiled. "Thank you."

But he wasn't through. "Let me tell you two things," he said. "One is, I know that Jonno loves you"—he was talking about an Australian MD named Jon Clarke, part of the Aussie Mafia, a big, cool, up-and-coming guy—"He's an important dude. Make sure you stay close to him," Cleanse said. He gave his vodka soda a stir. "Actually, Georgette likes you quite a bit, too."

I was thinking about that one when another MD, closer to my age, walked up. "How do you think I should approach things in London, Jesse?" I asked him.

Jesse, too, had had a few drinks. "I'll tell you how you should approach things," he said. "You should show up wearing a cowboy hat and cowboy boots. You should walk right onto the trading floor, right up to Jonno, and punch him right in the face. Knock him out. Don't say a word to anyone else. Then go sit down at your desk."

CHAPTER 11

The Wild West

I should have taken the advice about wearing the cowboy boots. London really was the Wild West.

There was a lot of open terrain for doing my kind of business in Europe. Whether the Goldman Sachs team wanted to play ball, though, was a different story entirely. As I got ready for my first road show to visit clients in Copenhagen, Paris, Milan, Frankfurt, and Munich, I got a taste of what I was in for. I called my guys in New York, the quants and strats whose job it was to help with client presentations. I needed some materials to present the case for why clients should execute U.S. derivatives business with Goldman Sachs.

"I don't mean to be a dick," one strat said to me. "But we've been told by management to focus only on trades that could yield a possible one-million-dollar profit for the firm. Sorry, man."

Click.

Maybe the guys in New York were just in a grumpy mood, I thought. *Let me try the strategists here.* There were a few friendly Frenchmen who could be helpful.

"Right now we are mostly focused on *beezness zat* have high GCs," the French strat said. "Anything less *eez* not worth our time."

Click.

In my first few weeks in London, I couldn't believe how many times people told me that something was not worth their time. I could understand the CEO of the company or the Queen of England thinking of his or her time in such precious terms, but what struck me was that we were supposed to be in a client-service business. If the client was asking to do business with us—even if it wasn't sexy business with a million-dollar payday—what kind of message were we sending by refusing to do it? After the Abacus settlement, the firm had relationships and reputational damage to repair. So my view was, why not show some of the biggest institutions across Europe and the Middle East that we *were* interested in the sort of old-fashioned, plain-vanilla trades that we had been turning away in order to focus on structured products?

On January 10, 2011, I walked into River Court (120 Fleet Street) for my first day of work in Goldman's London office. I had taken my friend Phil's advice and invested in a navy blue Barbour jacket, a waxed cotton jacket worn by all the expats in the City, as the London equivalent of Wall Street was called.

I had stayed up until 3:00 A.M. the night before writing a market commentary piece. I wanted to announce loud and clear to the European offices that I had arrived. I wanted some early visibility, but I also wanted to get the message across that I was there to help. I was there to build the business, not steal their business. Scratchy-eyed, I got to work at 7:00 A.M., wearing my lucky tie, a bright orange Hermès with little black fish on it.

At 7:30 came the morning call. In New York, this rundown of the day's action items is mostly done over the Hoot; in London, everyone gathers in one of the partners' offices to the side of the trading floor. To go with the low-ceilinged, hot-tempered intensity of the London trading floor, the meeting had a tone of aggressiveness that I hadn't seen in New York. In London, the main question seemed to be: How can we convince clients to do what will make our traders the maximum profit?

My first few weeks were a blur. Because I was building a new business, I had to start to learn the systems, the infrastructure, the problems from scratch. What was the difference in tax regulation in Germany versus France, versus Dubai? I had to be very strategic about how I spent my time. There was so much information, it was like trying to drink out of a fire hydrant. *Focus on the important things*, I thought.

Excruciatingly, I also had to prepare for the FSA Regulations exam. I couldn't believe it—ten and a half years after taking the Series 7, I had to buckle down again and memorize a phonebook of arcane European regulations that I would probably never again encounter after the exam was over. The MDs kept pestering me about it: "When are you going to take this exam?" But they were right: I needed to get it out of the way so I could legally start talking to clients in Europe.

On Sundays and sometimes during the week, I was also hustling to find an apartment. The first ten I saw were—excuse my language—absolute shit. Double the price of what I was paying in New York, and much less nice. But finally I struck gold on flat number eleven: an eight-hundred-square-foot duplex on the top floor of a Victorian house in Belsize Park, the neighborhood just south of Hampstead Heath that had become trendy because Gwyneth Paltrow and Chris Martin (of Coldplay) had moved there.

I loved the place: it had recently been remodeled, and everything was white and modern, with big, bright windows and skylights upstairs. What's more, the landlord and his wife had come up with a genius idea: Why not turn the twelve-foot back wall of the living room into a movie screen? So instead of having a TV in the living room, they installed a high-definition projector. I invited people over for movie nights and to watch rugby, cricket, NFL and Stanford football games. Coming home every day was a pleasure.

During my first week in London, I got an e-mail marked IMPORTANT, and reading, "All Vice Presidents need to report to the seventh-floor auditorium."

The occasion was a mandatory training session that Daffey would be delivering: the topic was the results of Goldman's year-long Business Practices Study, which had just been released in January 2011. This was the Board-level study that the firm had conducted to take a long hard look at the causes of all the reputational damage that Goldman suffered during, and since, the crisis. It was designed to suggest remedies in areas such as: conflict of interest, treatment of clients, structured products, and transparency.

A thousand of us sat in the room waiting for Daffey to begin. I'm sure most people in the auditorium had not known what to expect, but I was actually looking forward to the session. For one, if you could hand select someone to give a pep talk to the troops there were few people who were as charismatic and respected as Daffey. Plus, he was a culture carrier. And two, I believed this was an important study that *needed* to be done. Self-reflection was required and I wanted to see whether this was a genuine exercise.

What followed was supremely deflating. Daffey went through the motions, reading down a long list of proposed reforms. It was a flat performance: no emotion, no inspiring words. No "Come on guys. We have suffered some reputational hits, but let's all take it upon ourselves to set an example and do the right thing. Let's show clients through action how we are changing the way we do business." None of that. Just a long checklist of items read in an almost monotone. I wondered to myself whether Daffey was perhaps himself deflated that the firm had fallen so far that we were now fighting for our lives to repair our reputation. Or if deep down he knew that this was just a PR stunt designed to get the media off our back, and that in itself wasn't great either. I didn't need the Sermon on the Mount or "Mr. Gorbachev, tear down this wall!" but I did want to see some conviction behind what he was lecturing us on. What happened to the Daffey that I traded with through the New York blackout of 2003?

After the session, as he was walking up the aisle, I called out his name.

He turned around. "Hey, buddy—welcome," he said. His mood changed, he was now animated. He shook my hand with a smile. Since an American MD was also standing there, the three of us talked about NCAA basketball for a few minutes. Then Daffey was gone, back to his inner sanctum.

———

My very first week in London, a junior associate, twenty-four or twenty-five years old, was telling me about a piece of business he had just done. I had only met the guy a minute earlier.

"My muppet client didn't put me in comp on the trade we just printed. We made an extra $1.5 million off of him." What he meant was that the client was trusting and hadn't checked the price with any other brokers. So the salesperson had effectively overcharged him. This wasn't some rogue associate who'd gone off the reservation. His boss was sitting right next to him, smiling and nodding along.

Times had changed. When I was an associate, you would have been called into a partner's office and severely reprimanded for this type of callousness. You could have even been fired. It would have been seen as counter to the firm's long-held principle that if you don't have the clients' long-term interests at heart, they won't do business with you for very long.

Muppet was a word that, for me, had once evoked childhood memories of cute puppets such as Kermit the Frog. But the way it was used in the London office had nothing to do with cuteness. Being a muppet meant being an idiot, a fool, manipulated by someone else. Within days of arriving in London, I was shocked at how many times I heard people—both very senior and very junior, refer to their clients as muppets. Where, I wondered, had this adversarial viewpoint come from—the idea of the client as someone much less smart than you, someone you could try to take advantage of?

Over the first few months, I heard clients called that name over and over again. One client was deemed a muppet because he didn't pay the very expensive rates Bloomberg Market Data charged for real-time pricing. So when the client's Goldman salesperson was executing a trade, he would give the client a price that had been good fifteen minutes earlier—in other words, the price the client was seeing on his technologically inferior data stream. The salesperson, of course, was looking at real-time data on his Bloomberg as he executed the trade. The difference between the real-time price and the price the client was seeing was, naturally, highly advantageous to the firm, sometimes adding more than a million dollars to the GC on the trade.

Another client was deemed a muppet because he couldn't quite get the concept that, when buying futures, you had to post a certain amount of margin.

Another client mistakenly gave an order on his options contract with the wrong strike price (the stipulated price at which the client could buy or sell the underlying stock in the future). The client asked the salesperson if Goldman could just adjust the price of the strike and leave the price the client paid for the option the same, so he wouldn't get in trouble with his boss. What the client failed to grasp, because he didn't understand options pricing theory, was that the error was in *his* favor. Sure, said the salesperson. The muppet didn't realize that his price for the derivative should've improved significantly, and that he had overpaid for the structure by about $1 million.

Still another muppet, who "had no fucking clue what he was doing," put on a huge short volatility position right before the crisis and got blown up. The list went on and on.

I was struck by how out in the open this attitude was. It was odd, and was so counter to what I thought the firm once stood for. It was also problematic, because in order for me to build my book of business, I needed to build relationships with clients, not muppets.

The basic streams of revenue I wanted to turn on required a little elbow grease at the beginning, but once we could persuade clients who'd done only elephant trades to use Goldman for options, swaps, and plain-vanilla derivatives—and it wouldn't take much persuading—they could provide us with an ongoing stream of profit. This was found money. Low-hanging fruit. Why the resistance?

The first partner I pitched my bread-and-butter business to was one of the heads of sales in Europe. I said, "I've been meeting with your salespeople, and they're all telling me they think the business I'm here to start up isn't lucrative enough. But the clients I've talked to feel differently. What kind of message are we sending to them if we're turning away their business?"

He pushed back at me pretty hard, with what I had now come to recognize as the Goldman company line, European-style. At least he had a colorful (if hostile) way of expressing it. "We only have a certain number of bullets to use with clients," he told me. "We've got to make sure we keep them for the big elephant trades, the high-margin trades."

I blinked. *Where was he coming from?* I wondered. The last time the elephants had run free was 2008. They weren't doing much running anymore. He was holding on, I guess, to the dream of those $1 million and $2 million structured-product deals that were drying up but that could still be sold to the Simple Client or the Client Who Doesn't Know How to Ask Questions.

The business I was planning would bring in $50,000 in fees here and $50,000 there, and at the end of the year we'd have made the $20 million I had projected going into the job. By telling clients, "We don't do smaller, U.S. derivatives-based business," we were just alienating them—or worse, sending them elsewhere. How did we ever expect them to do their big business with us if we were telling them that their small business wasn't good enough?

———

On February 12, I took (and passed) my FSA exam. At last I could start to do business. And on that same day, I embarked, with my boss and a colleague, on my first trip to visit clients, in Milan. I was excited to see Italy for the first time, but I was also very relieved to have my exam out of the way.

Milan was all I expected, and then some. The boss stayed at the Bulgari, a super-fancy hotel that had only one room left. My colleague and I were at the Park Hyatt, which wasn't much less luxurious. I was in a standard room, but "spectacular" would've been a better description: it was like a room in an elegant Italian villa, with a view of the Duomo right across the way, where Napoleon was crowned king of Italy. That first night, we went out for dinner with one of our biggest Italian clients, enjoying an amazing four-course meal at Antico Ristorante Boeucc, one of the oldest and best restaurants in town. This was the good life.

The next day, we met with five of our clients in Milan: hedge funds, mutual funds, and an insurance company. Each of them managed more than $1 billion. Talking with them made me feel optimistic, because it threw into sharp relief just how unaware our people in Europe were about the kind of business I knew we could build quite easily.

From mid-February through May, I was on the road nearly nonstop. I went to Paris, Frankfurt, Munich, Copenhagen, Zurich, Geneva, and

Milan again. On one trip in April, I flew into Paris on a Thursday night, had a day of meetings on Friday, flew to Hong Kong Sunday night, and did two meetings there (and stopped by the Hong Kong office) on Monday. That evening, I flew to Singapore, had dinner with two Goldman Sachs MDs at the Ritz Carlton buffet, and went to the Marina Bay Sands, an incredible new casino by the water with a futuristic Sky Park, Sky Bar, and infinity pool all on the roof overlooking the entire city-state. On Tuesday, I went to visit five different clients in Singapore. That evening, I flew to Dubai for a conference of Middle Eastern high-net-worth individuals—high-net-worth enough that Lloyd Blankfein also made the trip. The next morning, I flew back to London.

The travel was brutal but exhilarating. It was the corrosive atmosphere in the London office that, slowly but surely, started to wear me down.

My travels taught me many things. Client bases varied widely from region to region, and national characteristics often came into play, in almost stereotypical ways. The German clients, for example, were very polite and extremely risk-averse. In meetings, they would just sit quietly and nod their heads. A quant colleague in London told me that the worst meeting he'd ever had was with a big German client. The quant gave a two-hour presentation on derivatives to a room of twenty people, and they all sat politely and nodded, even smiling at times. At the end, he asked, "Does anyone have any questions or feedback?" Silence. Then the senior client, who'd been sitting at the head of the table, told the quant, "By the way, we don't trade derivatives here."

The French, as you might expect from the Adventures of Fabulous Fab, were very different. Ostentation and braggadocio were the rule: French clients loved talking about how smart they were, how sophisticated and savvy. A case in point was the Soc Gen "campus" (Société Générale, one of the oldest banks in France) I once visited in Paris—it was like a massive monument to financial engineering: a beehive of quants, espresso sippers, and cigarette smokers. The French market was very "overbrokered," as financial terminology has it: when clients had ten different banks calling them to get their business, they would split the business ten ways. Markets would quickly become saturated, with each bank getting a tiny slice of the pie.

I sometimes got in the door with new clients by bringing in senior partners from New York. Our meetings made me feel both hopeful and frustrated: hopeful because the business was there to be done; frustrated because the clients themselves were frustrated. I was hearing the same message again and again from clients in Switzerland, France, Germany: "Goldman Sachs is not customer-friendly. In the good times, you'll compete for the profitable business, but in the crisis, when we needed you, you weren't there for us. And now, when we want to do flow business, you make it very, very hard for us to do it. Don't you think it is profitable enough?" By "flow business," this client meant plain vanilla derivatives such as options, futures, and swaps that they need to trade every day.

One big roadblock Goldman was putting up now was our exhaustive legal process. Even if we wanted to trade something as simple as stock options, we'd say, "You have to fill out this fifty-eight-page document," whereas every other bank would say, "Sign this one-page form." It was much easier for clients simply to go with the other banks.

I took on this particular problem as a major project and, with some help from New York, eventually fixed it. By that summer, I'd turned that fifty-eight-page document into a one-page document, and I started signing up dozens of new clients. All it took to make clients happier to trade with Goldman Sachs was to bring a fresh set of eyes to a corner of the business no one had really looked at in a few years. Some people at the firm were impressed: "Wow, I can't believe ten years have gone by and we never realized this." And others (of course) said, "That's great, but these are not elephant trades; these are singles and doubles rather than home runs." Flat-fee commissions weren't going to make you a stud or a rock star. These were literally the terms many at the firm applied to someone who got an elephant trade to the tape. You'd see it in e-mails. You'd hear it on the trading floor.

"Well done, stud."
"You're a rock star, dude."
"X is crushing it."

"Y is killing it."
"Z is printing big trades. She's a printing machine."

Because of the sovereign debt crisis and resultant turmoil in European markets, investors based there were looking to put their money somewhere relatively more stable. My business area, the United States of America, was where their eyes were turned. I saw that there was a ton of dry powder in Europe, client capital ready to be invested. And the clients who'd been burned by structured products now wanted to invest in transparent, exchange-listed business, business that wasn't going to rock anybody's world, but was going to be steady and solid over the next decade.

But in order to do that business, I had to convince the partners that my London colleagues' mind-sets needed to change. I spent the better part of a year in London shouting that message: "This is important business; it's going to pay the bills. But more than that, it's business we need to do to service our clients."

Now and then I was heard; mostly I wasn't.

After I returned from one particularly long and productive trip, I e-mailed Georgette saying I'd like to discuss some of the meetings I'd had. To my surprise, she came over to my desk and looked me in the face. She wasn't smiling. "I don't typically talk to my employees more than once a month," she said sternly. "The only time I want to hear from you is in the form of a one-line e-mail that states how big the trade was and what the GCs were."

————

My first six months in London flew by very quickly. I had been traveling and working hard but I also got to have some fun. I was lucky to be courtside in Paris to see Rafael Nadal beat Roger Federer for his sixth French Open title, and at Wimbledon to eat strawberries and cream and watch Novak Djokovic win his first. I also got to eat at some good places like Pied à Terre in Bloomsbury, St. John in Farringdon, and The Ivy in London's West End. I was grateful for these experiences and tried to remember to smell the roses as often as possible. Here's a tip, next time you are in London: add a lot of salt and pepper to whatever you order. Trust me, it needs it.

In June 2011, I flew back to New York to talk to a couple of the partners and give them my assessment. They were all eager to hear about London.

"What's the culture there like?" the first of the five partners I met with asked.

I was blunt. I said it was a trading culture where people were, first and foremost, concerned about making money for the firm. This partner had spent a lot of time in London, and he agreed with me.

During my time in New York, I also met with a 2004 partner. Unprompted by anything I said, he asked, "So how bad is the culture over there?" When I gave him my assessment, he smiled a little. "The leaders in London generally aren't client guys like we are in New York," he said. "They're focused on getting clients to do things, not asking clients what they need." He added that Michael Sherwood (aka Woody), the co-CEO of Europe, and Gary Cohn really didn't get along.

As I sat there reporting what I thought was wrong with the culture in London, I was thinking that, nevertheless, the mix of the business was exactly the same in New York. The difference between the two offices, it seemed to me, was mainly in tone. Sure, the callous way people bragged about elephant trades in London was more corrosive and more corrupting of young people at the firm, but in New York, elephant trades were every bit as prized.

When you were on the New York trading floor, in the headquarters, right alongside upper management, you had to keep a poker face and act as though everything was on the up-and-up. In fact, it wasn't. In New York as in London, the Simple Client and the Client Who Doesn't Know How to Ask Questions were being persuaded to trade structured products that were highly lucrative for the firm, without fully understanding what it was costing them. It was just that at 200 West Street, people were more careful about the way they discussed these trades—much more careful. They knew that if they spoke callously or bragged, they'd get into hot water.

From time to time I discussed all this with my partner mentor. To my mind—and to his—infighting was eating away at the culture and morale of Goldman Sachs. When partners were more concerned about protecting their own GCs than attending to clients' needs, it set a terrible example down the whole chain of command, from MDs to VPs to associates to analysts. Were some people at the firm simply making too much money to make ethical decisions?

———

Killing someone, or *shooting* them, in Wall Street parlance, means getting them fired, demoted, or strategically transferred to another office, often far afield. It usually happens when there is conflict between two parties and one of them goes to a superior and says, "This is not working out between us; it's disruptive to our business. Besides, this person is doing things all wrong." By the time this conversation takes place, the air has become so bad that management realizes they have to move one of these people—usually the more vulnerable or expendable one—somewhere else.

The practice has a rich if disreputable tradition in the financial world, and it is executed with varying degrees of shamelessness. Certainly, Hank Paulson and Lloyd Blankfein did their share of maneuvering in getting to where they were. They are tough, ambitious men, and Goldman Sachs is not a charitable foundation. But there was a time at Goldman, and on Wall Street in general, when if people crossed an ethical line in trying to advance, they would be fired, demoted, or reprimanded. The way it works now is, you can push as hard as you want and as far as you want, and as long as you keep your power, no one above you is going to step in. But even in today's rough-and-tumble world, there's a certain point where the maneuvering becomes so unethical that it undermines morale at large, and sets a bad example for junior people. It shows the first-year analyst and the new associate that bad behavior gets rewarded.

Georgette was a past master of corporate assassination. A mentor of mine told me: "For whatever reason, she's decided not to kill you— that's the good news. That said, she's still going to keep throwing roadblocks in your way. She'll try to kind of stunt your progress, not outright shoot you." There was only one guy on the whole floor, he said, who'd ever beaten her at her game. He was the same guy who had e-mailed me after my initial interviews in London and said, "We have a whole world to conquer together." He was two or three years junior to Georgette, and his nickname was Punter. The story went that after he inherited some very big clients from someone else, she moved in on him with one of her classic ploys: the 15 percent tax.

The way it worked was as follows: Anytime a salesperson did a trade with a client, the $1,000 commission—or, more commonly, the $100,000 in fees embedded in the product—would be booked next to the salesperson's name. At the end of the year, management would look at the total next to each person's name to determine his or her bonus. In the meantime, Georgette would have moved 15 percent of the total of each person in her group's commission into her own account, thereby raising her own bonus. She would contact Trade Management very openly saying, "Going forward, please move 15 percent of all Laurent's revenues with X, Y, and Z clients to my account." It was sheer highway robbery. People were incredulous, but everybody was too scared to call her on it.

Everybody except Punter.

When Georgette came after him for her cut of his rich new revenues, he simply said, "No fucking way." Even though she was more senior, he told her to back off. The maneuver worked. It worked because Punter was so well respected for legitimately bringing in the bacon that if Georgette had said, "Well, I'm going to take it anyway," she would have looked bad in front of everyone. So she backed down, and never touched him again.

This was the exception that proved the rule. Apparently Georgette once had the nerve to march into Daffey's office and, in full view of the whole trading floor, behind his glass walls, stamp her foot and shout demands while he sat there meekly. "There was nothing Daffey could do about it," my mentor told me. "They're too scared she'll get up and leave the firm; they do whatever she says."

Taking a cut of underlings' GCs was just one of the special practices I was learning about as I tried to win over my colleagues. There were others. Another manager on the floor, one who was purely and unapologetically bottom-line-focused, was said to have done, just before the crisis, a multipronged, cross-asset structured trade with a large European fund that ended up making the firm $100 million. The rumor was that the manager got paid $12 million that year. The client apparently had a nightmare unwinding the trade over a number of years.

This guy's trademark response to any e-mail that had even a whiff of a client trade was a three-character e-mail back: "GC?" No other words; no question about why the client had done the trade, what the trade was, or anything else about it. Just how much money was made on the trade. Oddly enough, once the talk went beyond trading, he was a fairly nice guy, with a sharp sense of humor.

Yet sometimes the focus on GCs went too far. One week in the late summer of 2011, while the European sovereign debt crisis boiled and Moody's and Standard & Poor's were downgrading the U.S. government's credit rating, five or six MDs on the floor each sent an e-mail to all six-hundred-plus people on the trading floor trumpeting the big successes of each of their teams in printing a lot of GCs in the midst of the crisis. In the e-mails, the MDs broke down the millions of dollars in fees in highly granular fashion—by elephant trades over $1 million; by type of client (leaving out client names, for compliance reasons); by type of trade—and patted everyone (but mainly themselves) on the back for a "job well done." Within two minutes, Daffey sent a "Reply All" response to all six hundred people, saying, "It's way too early for victory laps. The markets are open—get involved."

I remember thinking how bizarre this all was. The European economy was melting down; it felt as though Greece, Spain, Italy, and Portugal were on the verge of collapse; and here we were bragging about how much money we were making off these clients who were either panicked by the collapse or, worse, directly involved and losing millions and millions of dollars. It felt all too reminiscent of the panicked clients during the 2008 crisis.

———

A few months after Daffey's town hall meeting on the Business Practices Study results, the firm held a series of follow-up seminars on the study for much smaller groups of vice presidents and managing directors. The one I attended, for just twenty-five VPs, was led by Brett Silverman, the partner who'd accompanied me to Asia right after the collapse of Bear Stearns in the spring of 2008, the creative genius behind that hilarious prank video for the holiday party. He had been transferred to London about three months before me—in part, some said, to try to repair the company culture there.

I thought it was a pretty good session. Silverman said, "When we survey the clients, there is a clear pattern that emerges. They trust their individual sales reps at Goldman Sachs. But they don't trust Goldman Sachs as an organization. We need to change this perception."

After the session, when almost everyone had left the room, I walked up to Silverman and said that I thought it was great that they were having these sessions for VPs, but that the team leaders, the managing directors, needed to put these ideas into practice by setting the right example. "I don't see this happening," I told him. "Young people won't behave well if they don't see the MDs behaving well. The MDs need to be held accountable."

He looked at me with a blank stare and nodded wordlessly, almost robotically.

―――――――

After the Business Practices Study seminar, I saw many sales leaders in different product groups acting as if they'd paid no attention at all. They'd meet with their teams and say exactly what they'd been saying all along: "How many elephant trades did we do this week? Which region did the most? Which structured products can we focus on to increase high-margin business? Which axes do we need to get off our books?"

The axes bothered me. An axe is a position the firm wants to get rid of or a risky position it wants to shore up. The firm believes, deep down, that one outcome is going to transpire, yet it advises the client to do the opposite, so the firm can then take the other side of the trade and implement its own proprietary bet.

One way to understand this is to think of selling doughnuts. Say you

own a Krispy Kreme doughnut store, and you have too many doughnuts in stock and need to sell them before they go bad. In order to drive
up sales, you could say, "Our doughnuts are now fat-free!" That would
technically be a lie, but it wouldn't get you sent to jail. It might open you
up to legal action, but who really wants to go to court? Suddenly people would be rushing in to buy these delicious Krispy Kreme doughnuts,
convincing themselves that if a brand as reputable as Krispy Kreme is
saying the doughnuts are fat-free, then it must be true. Axes are something like surplus Krispy Kreme doughnuts that Goldman wants to clear
from its inventory, making a compelling, but not always completely accurate, case for clients to buy them.

What struck me when I attended our daily morning meetings in London is how often our view of the world changed. The oscillations in
opinion were far too frequent to make any real sense. The day's worldview was usually based on what the traders had on their books, and
what they were looking to get rid of (sell) or load up on (buy). They
would often dispatch strats or quants to the room to persuade the salespeople to persuade their clients to fill these axes. Double GCs were
sometimes awarded for axe-filling successes. Whatever argument the
strats made could in theory have been the opposite of what we actually
thought—just because we wanted clients to take the opposite side of our
trade.

Abacus was the axe du jour in 2007. The axe du jour when I arrived
in London in 2011 was getting clients to buy or sell options (puts or
calls) on the largest European banks, such as SocGen, BNP Paribas,
UniCredit, Intesa. We must have changed our view on each of these
institutions from positive to negative back to positive ten times. I remember thinking, *How can we be doing this with a straight face? No
thinking client could believe that conditions on the ground could change
that frequently*. It was so obviously misleading and disingenuous.

In the case of the European banks, even more clients than usual got
into these trades, including the traditionally more conservative mutual
funds. Goldman and other banks saw an opportunity to make a lot of
money in this sector because countries such as Greece, Portugal, and
Spain were going through the turmoil of a debt crisis, and the U.S.

politicians were in gridlock over whether to increase the federal borrowing limit and adopt a long-term plan for reducing government debt. As a result, it looked as though Standard & Poor's would downgrade the U.S. credit rating—which would cause even more turmoil. The more tumultuous the situation, the more volatile the options, and the fatter the margins for the bank making the prices. Sure, there is more risk, but there is also far more possibility for huge profits.

Aside from the obvious dishonesty of continually switching our recommendations to clients based on what our traders wanted to do, I was bothered by the European bank-options axe also because of the impact it was having on markets. (Some of these European banking stocks could move more than 5 percent in a day.)

And these weren't abstract assets. These were the national banks of sovereign nations, countries with millions of citizens who were depending on their governments to get their shit together. Jerking around the fates of their banks struck me as highly irresponsible.

What made matters worse, and even murkier, was the fact that a well-known Goldman Sachs strategist had come out with a semisecret report that went to only a select number of clients. The *Wall Street Journal* wrote about it. In his commentary, the strategist painted a particularly dire picture and suggested that European banks might need to raise $1 trillion in capital. He suggested some derivatives plays to capitalize on (or hedge against) this turmoil. During the same time period that a Goldman strategist was predicting the implosion of the European banking system, there were many days that our trading desk wanted to convince clients that today is a day to buy—a bullish story.

It was all too much. We had advised Greece all those years ago how to cover up its debt by trading a derivative. Now that the chickens had come home to roost, we were showing hedge funds how to profit from Greece's chaos; and on the other side of the Chinese wall, our investment bankers were trying to win contracts from the European governments to advise them on how to fix the mess.

This complex and conflicted scenario was deflating for many people on the trading floor, and I had many conversations about it with colleagues. People saw the hypocrisy but nobody did anything about it.

The bonus culture was just too entrenched. The numbers themselves militated against change.

There was a time in Goldman Sachs's history when bonuses were very subjective. At the end of each year, your manager made an assessment based not just on how much business you'd brought in, but also on how good you were for the organization. These two factors combined indicated your true economic value to the firm.

But from 2005 until the present day, the system has become largely mathematical: you were paid a percentage of the amount of revenue next to your name. In some years, it would be 5 percent of that revenue; in better years, it would be 7 percent. So, if you brought in $50 million in revenue in a good year, and you were senior enough (VP level and above) to be tied to this formulaic system, you could, in theory, get paid $3.5 million.

The problem with the new system was that people would now do anything they could—*anything*—to pump up the number next to their name. Traders and salespeople, even very young ones, were learning from the bad example set by leadership. Watching the poisoning of young minds really began to weigh on me.

During my eleven years as one of the captains of Goldman Sachs's recruiting effort at Stanford, I had met thousands of the best and brightest undergraduates who would become the future of the firm. There was always something very special about the recruiting process for me, about bringing new blood into a place that I cared deeply about and believed in. Someone had done it for me, when I knew nothing about finance; they saw some potential in me and looked out for me. And now I, in turn, relished doing it for people I believed in. It was extremely rewarding to be on the giving end of this relationship.

Experienced investment bankers often talk about how young people—especially summer interns and analysts who have just graduated from college—bring a sense of renewal and exuberance to the trading floors when they arrive, conveying a fresh spirit of idealism to the rows and rows of tough Wall Street veterans. I felt this was no longer the case.

Now, first-year associates were seeing their bosses, the MDs and

partners, fighting over GCs. Over time, this corrosive behavior had fil-
tered down through the system. Associates started believing they should
be doing the same thing, because that's what their leaders were doing.
I must have had to referee at least ten disputes between associates who
were trying to increase their share of GCs relative to those of their colleagues. When I was an associate, I wasn't even set up in the system to
receive GCs, because they weren't a focus at the firm yet. Now associates saw GCs as the absolute yardstick for the size of their end-of-year
bonus. A typical associate fight went like this:

> ASSOCIATE 1: "I really think I deserve seventy-five percent of XYZ
>   client's GCs. I've been doing far more work than you, and the
>   client loves me."
> ASSOCIATE 2: "Nah, I'm the client's go-to guy for derivatives. I think
>   it should be seventy-five percent the other way—in my favor.
>   Back off."

Goldman Sachs teamwork had gone out the window. In most of
these situations, I would encourage each person to take 50 percent, and
then ultimately some partner would make the final decision—which was
often driven by which associate the partner liked more. Then the associates would remain bitter toward each other.

Meanwhile, Daffey was in his office, behind three levels of security,
with that "PEOPLE" sign on the wall.

———

Another thing that really weighed on me was that I had stopped wanting
to recruit students to come to the firm. At some point in the twelve
months before I left, I started actively avoiding recruiting. This gave me
a louder internal signal than anything else of just how much things had
deteriorated.

This was no longer the Goldman Sachs that, when I joined, young
people were excited about. The images of Weinberg, Levy, and Whitehead had faded to invisibility. Goldman was still the preeminent bank in
the world, but only because it was the cleverest at what it did (and be-

cause our alleged competition had become so weak). I could no longer, in good conscience, advise young people to come and work here.

———————

At the end of every quarter, Goldman Sachs holds a town hall meeting, an internal business update, where the heads of every region go over the quarter's results and talk about the competitive landscape. At the London office a thousand people, from junior analyst to partner, gather in the seventh-floor auditorium at River Court; all the European offices dial in on videoconference. Several thousand people in all participate. At the end of this meeting, which typically lasts about an hour, there are always about fifteen minutes of softball questions teed up—such as "What are the firm's priorities going forward?" or "What do we think of the competition?"

A few months before I left, the town hall presenters were co-CEOs of Europe Michael "Woody" Sherwood and Richard Gnodde, the South African head of investment banking. Each stood at a lectern at one side of the big stage. As the question period drew to a close, a woman in the audience stood up and asked, "What is the firm doing to address the fact that the culture is dying and our reputation is deteriorating?" Absolute silence followed as the speakers contemplated the question.

Woody and Gnodde were utterly flabbergasted—floored not only that anyone would have the audacity to ask this question, but at the prospect of trying to answer it. The two of them looked alternately at us and at each other for a long half-minute. Finally, Woody said, "Richard, do you want to handle this one?"

The scene felt surreal. Nervous laughter rippled through the auditorium.

Gnodde, a big, friendly looking guy with a determined air, said, "Sure, Woody. I guess I'll take this one." He looked down for a second, then faced the audience. "We just did this sixty-three-page Business Practices Study—" he began. The culture was as strong as ever, he said. Goldman was conducting sessions around the firm to make sure people understood the study's findings and put them into practice. He went on for a minute or two, then smiled at this unbelievably impertinent woman as if he had revealed a simple truth.

But she wasn't satisfied with this scripted answer—she was looking for some real acknowledgment of the problem, some introspection. The woman followed up: "But what *specifically* is management doing to fix this problem that is on so many people's minds?"

Another pause. Then Woody took the ball. He waxed philosophical. "Look," he said. "At Goldman Sachs we're all family people; we all have families, we're all good people. We just have to remember that, and we have to go about our business by making good, ethical decisions, just as we would in our daily lives."

There was a smattering of halfhearted applause, and the meeting was called to a close. Everyone walked out with a deflated feeling.

It was time for me to leave.

I knew in my heart there was something deeply wrong in the way people were behaving, in the way they didn't care about the repercussions, in the way they saw their clients as their adversaries. My human reaction was that it was bad for the future of the firm, a place that I had put a lot of heart and soul into. I knew it was time for me to go—the young people's disaffection had told me, the clients' distrust had told me. But the firm's not really caring about what was going on told me the most. So I began to write. Writing was my way to distill into simple terms exactly what I felt was wrong. I remembered how, more than a decade earlier, Carly Fiorina had advised the new Stanford graduates to keep trying to distill things down until we got them to their true essence, what we truly believed.

On airplanes, in airport lounges, in hotel rooms, and in my flat late at night, I tried to set down in writing many of the things that were poisoning the institution I loved. At first the thoughts were lengthy and convoluted. I went over and over them, tried to boil them down to their core meaning.

For the first two or three months, the goal of the writing was just to help me understand exactly what I was feeling. Then gradually I started thinking about an idea: I could leave quietly, say nothing, and let the system fester. Or I could try to change the system—since I could clearly see that the partners I spoke with weren't going to do anything about it. *If the firm's culture couldn't be changed from within*, I thought, *maybe it could be changed from without*. I decided to try to craft an op-ed or editorial, a piece of writing that might alert people to what was going on in the financial world, that might change some minds. The sentences came...*I believe I have worked here long enough to understand the trajectory of its culture, its people and its identity. And I can honestly say that the environment now is as toxic and destructive as I have ever seen it.*

My essay, or whatever it was, quickly ballooned to three thousand words, then five thousand. I knew I had to get to the essence of what I was trying to say—which was what? That Goldman Sachs and Wall Street had lost sight of their mission: servicing clients. That the culture was rotting, which presented a dire threat to the firm and the industry. When the client no longer trusts the bank, calamity ensues. And that the buck ultimately had to stop with the board of directors and people like Lloyd and Gary and Woody and Gnodde who had turned a blind eye to all that was happening right under their noses, on their watch. They had put the sole pursuit of short-term profits ahead of a reputation that had taken decades to build up, but could be destroyed in an instant. They didn't fully realize that you can't just say that you are different and that you put clients first: you actually have to act this way. And if you don't, the smell of hypocrisy soon starts suffocating your employees and your clients.

I discussed with Lex the idea of my leaving Goldman Sachs. I didn't tell him specifically that I had been working on a piece, but I wanted to know if he thought there would be moral value in my saying something publicly about why I was leaving, what I thought was wrong with the system. Idealistically, I thought I could make a difference. I wanted to know if he agreed.

Lex was one of the only people I trusted enough to keep this locked shut. He didn't drink much. He didn't mix in crowds where he could let it slip. We had such a long history; we'd always stood by each other.

Lex had known over the course of my career how my mind-set had evolved. Over the last year, I'd told him a number of times about my growing disillusionment with the firm.

Lex vigorously urged me, as my friend, not to say anything publicly. "Look," he said, "while there's merit in what you're saying and what you're arguing, you're going up against a behemoth. I worry for your personal safety, and your legal well-being. I worry about the consequences. You have to think about yourself here. It's not worth the risk."

He let me think about that for a moment. It was a Sunday and I was at a restaurant in Smithfield, near the City, trying to talk into my iPhone as discreetly as possible.

Lex went on: "You've got to think of yourself. This might just get ignored, and then you've walked away from a career, you've taken a financial loss by losing your unvested stock." Lex meant that I would lose all my future income: salary, bonus, plus stock in Goldman Sachs that had been promised to me for the next few years as an incentive to stay with the firm.

I pushed back, getting on my high horse. In my mind, I told Lex, the moral benefits outweighed the risks. I felt incredibly strongly about this.

"Great," Lex said. "I'm telling you, this thing is too risky. I wouldn't do it."

That was the end of the conversation. I didn't speak to Lex again until my piece had been published.

———

For the next month, I kept going to work every day, doing my job as I'd always done it, as best I could, and writing and honing my op-ed piece late into the night—and telling no one. By early February, I'd finally whittled the piece, titled "Why I Am Leaving Goldman Sachs," down to 1,500 words. I decided that the place it would have the most impact was the op-ed page of the *New York Times*, but I didn't know anyone there to send it to. The op-ed page listed only a mandatory general e-mail address to which all submissions needed to be sent: oped@nytimes.com. Deciding to entrust my fate to the newspaper gods, and with the feeling of making an irrevocable but completely correct decision, I hit the Send button.

———

There was no response from the *Times* for a month. Radio silence. My piece had disappeared into the ether; but I decided to give it another shot.

Protocol or no protocol, I thought I would have a better chance if I sent the piece to specific people instead of into a vacuum. So I looked up the individual e-mail addresses of the editors. On the night of March 7, 2012, I sent the piece to four of them.

By the next morning, I heard back.

The *New York Times* was interested in running the piece on the op-ed page. I discussed with the editors how strongly I felt that it should be published in the form I had written it—it had taken me five months to whittle my five thousand words down to what I really wanted to say, I believed in it with all my heart, and I wasn't willing to see a chopped-up or sanitized version in print. I was taking too big a risk, and this was my one shot.

Once the *Times* agreed to publish it, I didn't hesitate.

As I continued to work day to day as a derivatives sales trader at Goldman Sachs London, the final editing of my op-ed proceeded under conditions of maximum secrecy. Then an unusual request came from one of the *Times* editors.

"We need to verify with one-hundred-percent certainty that you are who you say you are. We want to send one of our reporters to come and meet you at the Goldman London office to absolutely prove that you are genuine."

"How on earth can that happen?" I said. "I'm happy to give you any evidence you need, but having a *New York Times* reporter show up at the front desk of the Goldman Sachs London headquarters and ask for me is insane."

It was like something out of a spy novel.

"Don't worry. My guy will be discreet."

The *Times* sent over one of its London-based business reporters, Landon Thomas Jr., to make sure I was exactly who I was purporting to be, and that there was no scandal surrounding me, nothing that would blow up in the face of the paper of record. Thomas, who had been covering Goldman Sachs for the *New York Times* for a decade, came to the reception desk at 120 Fleet Street.

We had arranged for him to arrive at 9:30 A.M. on Monday, March 12, and to ask for me at reception. When the receptionist called me, I would come down and meet him in the lobby. We hadn't discussed if he would use his real name, but to my surprise, precisely at 9:30 A.M., the front desk called: "Landon Thomas is here to see you."

"I'll be right down," I said.

I went to the rest room near my desk to quickly splash myself with water. *This is going to be interesting*, I thought. Interesting? Unprecedented. I walked down, cool and calm. I saw a tall guy with a shoulder bag: Landon. I walked right up to him, and we shook hands in the Goldman Sachs lobby. "Nice to meet you," he said with a smile.

"Feel like going to grab a coffee?" he asked.

We walked up Fleet Street, away from St. Paul's Cathedral. I suggested that we walk not to the closest Starbucks to Goldman, but perhaps to one that was two or three stores away. We walked for about ten minutes. Finally we settled on a Starbucks across the road from the Royal Courts of Justice. In London, most coffee shops have a lounge area in the basement, so we got our coffees and headed downstairs, where it was quiet. Once again, it felt like espionage.

Landon could tell that I was sincere, and the vetting turned into regular conversation. I told him up front that it would all be off the record.

He asked me all the questions I would have expected him to ask. First, why did I want to do this?

Because I thought it was the morally right thing to do and I wanted to make a difference, I told him. I would have felt wrong not doing something about it.

Was I disgruntled?

No. I was saddened, though, that a firm I had devoted so much of myself to had lost its way.

Was I about to be fired?

No, I said. In fact, I had built the business 35 percent in my first year in London, had fixed a decade-long legal hurdle, and had increased the numbers of clients we traded actively with by 80 percent. I had been roundly praised in my year-end reviews.

Was I upset about my bonus or not getting promoted?

I told him I had outperformed my peers by 10 percent on my bonus, and yes, I would like to have been promoted. But the average age to move from vice president to managing director was thirty-five or thirty-six, and I was thirty-three. I had been told by multiple partners that a promotion was about two years away for me.

Was I naïve? Thomas asked. Hadn't things always been done this way on Wall Street? Had I been living under a rock?

No, I said. First of all, I told him, let's say this *is* the way things have always been done on Wall Street. Why does that make it okay? Second, things had changed. Over the three years since the crash of 2008, I had seen the bank's fiduciary responsibility erode so far that it was now actively trying to take advantage of clients. This was happening all over Wall Street, but Goldman Sachs was supposed to be a leader. By 2012, I said, the firm had completely lost sight of a long-run mentality in favor of a profit-at-all-costs model. No lessons had been learned from the crisis.

Why didn't I speak to my bosses about this?

I had spoken to nine partners over the last year about culture and ethics at the firm, and while behind closed doors half of them agreed there were problems, I could tell that not one of them would do anything about it. They were simply making too much money.

We chatted for about forty-five minutes and then started walking back.

"How are you feeling about this?" Thomas asked me. "This is really going to happen."

In the crisp late-winter air, with some rare rays of sun making St. Paul's Cathedral all the more beautiful, I told him that I was feeling good about it. Happy, in fact. Optimistic that I could make a difference, however small, in reforming the system. But I told him I did not know how to anticipate what the reaction would be. Neither of us knew.

Landon wished me well. We shook hands, and he headed off in the other direction. I went back up to my desk on the trading floor at 120 Fleet Street.

The op-ed was finally scheduled, for Wednesday, March 14. I edited it up until the very last minute. It was fact-checked thoroughly, and I was proud of what would be published.

On Saturday the tenth, I went in to the office at around 8:00 P.M. to clean out my desk. I'd specifically chosen a Saturday night because I knew there wouldn't be many people around. This was a firm that had been my entire working life, and I didn't want to rush out of there. I wanted to take my time packing up my belongings, reminiscing a little bit about my career. The trading floor was empty; it was just me and a security guard. Most of the lights were off, for energy conservation, as was the air-conditioning. It was hot and stuffy. I sat at my desk, rolled up my sleeves, and took off my watch. I had a few bites of a McDonald's Filet-O-Fish I'd picked up around the corner. Then I started clearing out my belongings. I saw the deal toy for the Turkish communications company and the button Rudy cut off my shirt after my first trade. I thought of my days with Corey and all he'd taught me about the business and how to be a person of integrity. I found the dusty picture book from my summer internship: out of the seventy-five who started at Goldman in that summer of 2000, there were only seven of us left. I packed an old Springbok rugby ball, and the cricket ball I used to toss around the trading floor in New York during the old days with Daffey. It occurred to me again just how much the tone and the culture of the place had changed in the twelve years that began with my first day in the Open Meeting.

For the next four hours, I sat, alone and utterly calm, in the midst of the eerily quiet floor—no traders shouting, no phone lines ringing—carefully listing everything I needed to do to make my departure at midday on Tuesday as quick and unobtrusive as possible. I was planning to fly back to New York, to begin the next chapter of my life, whatever it might be. When I walked out the door, I wanted the break to be as clean as possible. I wanted my desk empty of personal effects. I wanted to leave the office with no *i* undotted, no *t* uncrossed.

Finally, a little after midnight, early on Sunday morning, I logged out of my computer, took my backpack and a small box that contained a decade's worth of memories, and left. Goldman would later tell me they had surveillance video of me walking out the front lobby with my box and backpack. They thought I had larceny in my heart, when all I had was freedom.

Afterword

I landed in New York at JFK International close to midnight on the day the op-ed was published. My picture had been all over the place, and I wasn't sure if people would recognize me, so—perhaps stupidly—I wore a makeshift disguise: a dark brown straw fedora and an unshaven beard. I headed straight for Phil's place on Seventy-Ninth Street and Third Avenue. Phil had arranged a blow-up mattress for me to sleep on, and said I should come straight over when I landed.

I had not known what to expect that day, and hadn't spent a lot of time planning for it. The argument I was making in the piece was one I believed in strongly, and I thought publishing it was the right thing to do. I would deal with the reaction when it came. And once it did come, I was overwhelmed with both how broad it was and how many thousands of messages I started receiving from the general public: from rural Texas to Russia, to India, to China. I also heard from dozens of former colleagues and clients.

The messages had one theme: support. People liked the idea of trying to reform a system that had lost its way. They liked the idea of speaking truth to power. They liked the idea of taking a risk to do what you think is right, even at personal cost. I was touched by the outpouring of encouragement I received. But once the media barrage came, I am glad that my first instinct was not to respond. My brother, and my best friends, Lex and Dan, shared my instinct on this front. Here's why:

The op-ed had taken me almost five months to write, and it captured exactly what I wanted to say. It distilled my argument down to its essence. I had thought it out fully. Anything I could have said that day would have distracted from letting the op-ed speak for itself. I was proud and excited that, in some small way, I was contributing to a debate on irresponsible behavior and conflicts of interest in the financial industry, a debate I believed was vital for the public to have. With all the media attention, it was extremely comforting to be able to go straight to a good friend after I had landed in New York.

As I got out of the cab and started gathering my suitcases, Phil's doorman walked outside to help me. Suddenly his face lit up, and he gave me the biggest, most welcoming smile I could have ever imagined.

"You're Greg Smith, aren't you?" the doorman asked excitedly. I was shocked that he would recognize me. I had been on a plane from London most of the day and hadn't realized the full extent of the news coverage.

"Welcome to New York," he said to me warmly when I first arrived. "I just want you to know that you have a lot of support here. Normal people like me are behind you—we thank you for speaking up for us." I was touched and humbled by what he had said. I took a moment to think about the poignancy of it as I waited for the elevator to arrive in Phil's pre-war building. I then got in—excited to see my friend.

Kelvin, the doorman, was a young African American guy in his early twenties who wanted to break into finance someday. He was working at Phil's building to pay for his education in the evenings and to support his family. The guy loved finance. He was optimistic and idealistic about it. He was fascinated with stock markets—what made them go up and down, how to value companies, how to understand balance sheets.

Over the three weeks that I slept on the blow-up mattress at Phil's place, I chatted with Kelvin every day as I came in and out of the building. We talked about which finance textbooks he should be reading, which were the best market periodicals, what he could do to give himself an edge to get into the financial industry.

Kelvin reminded me of why I'd gone into the industry in the first place. And why anyone should decide to do anything: because they are passionate about it. I hope he breaks into finance. I hope it doesn't let him down. Because it needs people like Kelvin.

When it comes to the financial industry, there is a major fallacy that exists: that Wall Street deals only with elite, rich people who deserve to lose their money, and that Mom and Pop are not directly affected by the antics and conflicted practices in the industry. This couldn't be farther from the truth.

Even when Wall Street CEOs are hauled in front of Congress—as Lloyd Blankfein was amid the SEC fraud charges against Goldman Sachs, and as Jamie Dimon was after JPMorgan Chase lost $6 billion on bad trades—they try to make this argument. "We are all big boys." "We are all sophisticated institutional investors who know exactly what we are doing." But stop and think about this for a second. Whose money is being played with anyway?

Look at *just* the recent scandals: Who gets affected when a county in Alabama trades a structured derivative with JPMorgan that goes sour, and brings the county closer to bankruptcy? Who gets impacted when a government such as Greece or Italy trades derivatives with Goldman Sachs or JPMorgan to cover up its debt and kick its problems down the road? Who ultimately loses when Morgan Stanley misprices the Facebook IPO and mutual funds lose billions of dollars of retirement and 401(k) savings? Mom and Pop, that's who.

Whose lives are affected when a sovereign entity such as Libya loses a billion dollars of its own people's money betting on derivatives? Who loses when Barclays and other major banks rig the London Interbank Offered Rate (LIBOR), the interest rate that underpins trillions of dollars in student loans and mortgages? Whose savings evaporate when JPMorgan brokers sell underperforming mutual funds to their clients to generate more fees?

The list goes on and on and on. All this ultimately affects the citizens, teachers, pensioners, and retirees whose destinies are tied to these organizations that are managing their money. Mom and Pop are more affected by the bad behavior on Wall Street than anyone else—it is *their* money on the line.

But how does Wall Street make so much money, anyway? Surely

there are times when they must lose? Don't count on it. Think about this:

There are certain quarters when a Wall Street bank makes money every single day of that quarter. Yes: ninety days in a row. One hundred percent of the time, it generates a profit. Bank of America recently pulled off this amazing feat. That is like batting a thousand. A perfect record. How is this even possible?

Two words: *asymmetric information.* The playing field is not even. The bank can see what every client in the marketplace is doing and therefore knows more than everyone else. If the casino could always see your cards, and sometimes even decided what cards to give you, would you expect it ever to lose?

Here's how it happens: Because Wall Street is facilitating business for the smartest hedge funds, mutual funds, pension funds, sovereign wealth funds, and corporations in the world, it knows who is on every side of a trade. It can effectively see everyone's cards. Therefore, it can bet smarter with its own money.

Worse, if Wall Street can persuade you to trade a custom-made structured derivative that serves the firm's needs, it is as if your cards have been predetermined. Certainly not much scope for the casino to lose in this scenario.

Now consider where the gambling takes place. In a real casino, it is on a casino floor with cameras all over the place. Even if you don't like Las Vegas gambling, it *is* regulated.

On Wall Street, the gambling can be moved to a darkened room where nothing is recorded, observed, or tracked. With opaque over-the-counter derivatives, there *are* no cameras. In this darkened, smoke-filled room, there is maximum temptation to try to exploit clients and conflicts of interest. And this temptation and lack of transparency are what led to the global financial crisis in 2008.

Finally, think about the dealer. Your salesperson or trader might seem objective—like a friendly casino dealer who jokes around and is on your side—but there are times when he or she might be trying to steer you toward the thing that makes the casino the most money. If you were playing blackjack and you had 19, would you ever expect the dealer to tell you to hit? Sometimes, on Wall Street, they urge you to take another card.

Ironically, real casinos may actually be better regulated than Wall Street banks. The SEC and the U.S. Commodity Futures Trading Commission (CFTC) were not able to stop what led up to the crisis, and are still struggling to put appropriate measures in place to limit the conflicts I've described. With all these advantages, how can Wall Street ever lose? Even real casinos don't make money every single day of the quarter.

As proof of this information advantage: Why do Goldman Sachs and JPMorgan Chase mutual funds—housed in their respective asset-management divisions on the other side of the Chinese wall—underperform their peers, as measured by Morningstar? Why do some hotshot traders from banks such as Goldman Sachs, Morgan Stanley, and JPMorgan go out on their own, start their own hedge funds, and flounder? Because they no longer have the advantage of being able to see everyone's cards. No more asymmetric information, no more batting a thousand, when you are out on your own without unfair advantage.

The reforms Wall Street is pushing back the hardest against are in the areas it knows are the most profitable: opaque derivatives and proprietary trading. But these also happen to be the areas that are most dangerous to the stability of the financial system. The Wall Street lobby has already spent more than $300 million trying to kill measures to regulate derivatives (so that they are brought into the light of day and become transparent on exchanges), and to eliminate proprietary trading so banks can no longer bet against their customers using their information advantage as prescribed by the Volcker Rule. Wall Street hates transparency and will fight as hard as possible to prevent it from coming.

I am a capitalist. I am all for people getting rich and for businesses making as much money as possible. It is the fuel that keeps our economy growing and wealth should be an aspiration to motivate entrepreneurs everywhere. But I want it to be done fairly. I just don't believe that capitalism is embedded with some kind of assumption that ethical boundaries should be pushed as far as possible, and that deceiving your customers is necessary to generate maximum returns.

I believe in a business model that is long-term-oriented, where there is an intrinsic fiduciary responsibility to do right by your clients so they will keep coming back to you. Not only is it the right thing to do, but it is also better for business. You will make just as much money—but you will make it more slowly and steadily and transparently. This should be good for shareholders, too, who like a predictable revenue stream and a steadier book of business. Today's take-the-money-and-run model is just not responsible, or sustainable.

How can it be that four years after the crisis nothing has been done to fix any of this? Don't we live in the greatest democracy in the world? People should be outraged that there is no political will to fix a problem that hurts everyone, enriches a super minority that has learned to rig the game, and could threaten the world with another calamity in a few years' time.

People know that there is something deeply wrong with the system, but very few can put their finger on what the problem is. After the crash in 1929, the U.S. Senate conducted the Pecora Hearings, to investigate the causes of the crash. This inquiry led to real reforms that held banks accountable and eliminated the abusive practices that had caused the stock market crash. This was followed by decades of calm in the financial system. If I achieve one thing with this book, I hope it will be to empower some people with enough understanding to call their congressman, congresswoman, or senator and ask this question: Why don't you have the guts to do the same thing?

Author's Note

Everything I discuss in this book is as I remember it from my twelve-year career at Goldman Sachs. My goal was to use my career and experiences at Goldman Sachs to tell a story about a system and an industry that has become rife with conflicts of interest that encourage—and sometimes require—individuals to push ethical boundaries and compromise their integrity in order to succeed.

Because my goal was to bring light to the system—and not to individuals—I have changed names or descriptors for some people.

The stories I tell are from memory, and I have tried to reconstruct the dialogue as closely and accurately as possible to retain the spirit of how they originally occurred. Any errors in fact, of omission or commission, are my responsibility alone.

My main hesitation in publishing the op-ed was not the argument I was making—which I believed in strongly—but rather the moral question of writing a broad statement about an organization, and an industry, that has thousands and thousands of honest people who are going in to work every day, doing their jobs, working hard for their families. Many of these people have been tremendously kind to me over the years, both inside and outside of work.

But after dozens of conversations with colleagues over the twelve months before I left, I saw how many shared my disappointment in a system that more and more asks for morally dubious decision making. Sometimes, when you see people doing things, and they are getting away with it, and they are making money, the human brain tells you that it must be okay. But sometimes it isn't.

This helped clarify my decision. *If I write the op-ed, and it contributes in some small way to a more ethical system, then all those people will hopefully be better off in the long run.* My goal for the op-ed, and for this book, is a constructive, not a destructive, one: to try to improve a system by bringing transparency and accountability to it.

Acknowledgments

First of all, I would like to thank Grand Central, for giving me the opportunity to write this book. My publisher, Jamie Raab, was a class act: knowledgeable and thoughtful from our first meeting, and consistent throughout. I am grateful to the whole team at Grand Central (in particular Kallie Shimek and Meredith Haggerty) for all their hard work and expertise.

I have never written a book before—and I have not worked with editors—but I have to think that John Brodie must be one of the best in the business. Equal parts kindness, wit, knowledge, and perceptiveness, I have appreciated his thoughtful guidance, and his capacity and willingness to listen to me from day one. Throughout the process, I felt lucky to have him by my side.

I would like to thank the following people for all their help and integrity: Jonathan Leibner, Paul Fedorko, Jen Rohrer, Tess Dmitrovsky, Sammy Bina, Fred Newman, Sheryl Galler, and Mark Levine.

I would also like to thank James Kaplan for his wisdom and invaluable help during this process.

I am so grateful to have been with my brother, Mark (in person), and my best friends, Lex Bayer and Dan Lipkin (on Skype), just minutes after the op-ed was published. None of them knew it was coming but it was so comforting to have them with me, and to have their advice and friendship, which I value so highly.

My close group of friends rallied to my side and supported me without question immediately: Jackie, Phil, Adam, Amitav, Ariel, Shimrit, Michael, Alexandra, Dov, Gavin, Sean, Jody, Sentheel, Brian, Ralph,

Rowan, Hayley, Kevin, Alon, Gopal, John, and Kris. Thank you for being some of the most decent people and best friends a guy could ask for.

I have a very special family whom I rely on and love very much. Thank you to my aunt Pat; my brother, Mark, who teaches me so much; my best mate Carly, who is such an inspiration for me; my dad, for showing bravery in taking his pharmacy exam and moving to America; and my mom, for all she has done for me in my life.

Thank you also to Mr. Elliot Wolf, Mr. Digby Ricci, Jim Montoya, and Jon Reider.

A Glossary of Trader-Speak

Agent: The person or entity who executes a trade on behalf of the client on an exchange, without committing the bank's own capital to facilitate the trade. Also see: PRINCIPAL.

Analyst: A recent college graduate; the most junior title on Wall Street.

Asset management: The professional management of securities such as stocks, bonds, commodities, and derivatives in order to meet specified investment goals for the benefit of investors such as pension funds, endowments, sovereign wealth funds, and individuals.

Associate: Typically an MBA graduate or an analyst who has been at the firm for three or more years. "Associate" is the second most junior title on Wall Street.

Attribution: The sum total of gross credits (GCs) that sits next to a salesperson's name—i.e., how much bacon he or she brought home from client business. Also see: GC (GROSS CREDIT).

Axe: Wall Street–speak for the stock or other product a firm tries to get rid of by persuading clients to invest in it: because it is not seen as having a lot of potential profit for the firm.

Bid-offer spread: The difference between the lowest price someone is willing to sell at (the offer) and the highest price someone is willing to buy for (the bid). The market maker is often able to capture part of this spread as profit.

Bigs: Slang for the original big S&P 500 futures contracts that trade in the open-outcry pits of the Chicago Mercantile Exchange. Bigs were surpassed in popularity by the E-mini futures contracts, which are one-fifth the notional size and which trade electronically almost twenty-four hours a day.

Bip: Wall Street slang for basis point, a unit equal to one-hundredth of a percentage point. If an asset moved 1 percent, you might say it moved 100 bips.

Blocking and tackling: The day-to-day basic tasks of servicing clients on a sales and trading floor: picking up the lines, taking orders, stamping tickets, executing trades, confirming prices with clients.

Bloomberg Terminal: A computer system that is the industry standard news and market data service that people on Wall Street use to get real-time information and to communicate with one another and with clients. Bloomberg L.P. is the company founded by the mayor of New York, Michael Bloomberg.

Bloomie: Slang for a message you may send to a client using the messaging feature on your Bloomberg Terminal. Communicating via Bloomies and Bloomie chat rooms or instant messages has become ubiquitous in the industry—even more common than speaking on the phone.

Blown up: Description used for a trader who goes out of business or loses a significant amount of money because of a poorly timed trade.

Buck: Wall Street slang for $1 million. "That hedge fund just traded five hundred bucks of silver futures without blinking." "His loft in Tribeca cost eight bucks."

Call option: A type of derivative that gives the purchaser the right to buy an underlying security at a stipulated price in the future.

CDO (collateralized debt obligation): A type of security that played a significant role in inflating the real estate bubble, the subsequent 2008 crash, and the downfall of Bear Stearns, Lehman, Merrill Lynch, Wachovia, and Washington Mutual. CDOs package mortgages together and serve to connect investor capital with the U.S. housing market. Significant fees accrue to the investment bank and everyone along the mortgage supply chain.

CDS (credit-default swap): An opaque derivative that serves as a type of insurance policy an investor can buy to protect against the default or bankruptcy of a company, a mortgage, or even a sovereign nation. The seller collects a premium from the buyer for the insurance, but agrees to deliver a certain payoff to the buyer if default does occur. AIG ultimately took a $170 billion taxpayer bailout partly because of overexposure to CDS protection it had sold on the real estate market.

Cheap as chips, mate!: The way a British colleague would tell you that something was bargain-basement dirt cheap.

Chinese wall: An information barrier that separates people on the public side of the business (sales and trading, asset management, research) from people on the private side who have access to material information that has not been made public yet (investment banking, corporate finance, mergers and acquisitions); designed to limit conflicts of interest within investment banks.

Commercial killer: Someone who is particularly adept at bringing in business; usually the quickest way to rise up in the company.

Commission: An agreed-upon fee a customer pays for transactions with the firm (e.g., 2 cents per share, 50 cents per futures contract).

Culture carrier: Someone who is particularly good at retaining and spreading the culture, values, and tradition of the firm to those around him or her.

Custy: Wall Street slang for "customer" or "client."

Derivative: A catch-all term for options, swaps, futures, exotics, and structured products. In general, a derivative derives its value from some underlying security such as a stock, bond, commodity, or index.

D/K: The short form for "don't know"; used when a client claims not to recognize a trade or its details and tries to stick you with it. It is used on Wall Street also to denote any form of rejection, as in: "Ouch, Rick got brutally d/k'ed when he tried to ask that girl out."

Don't be a dick for a tick: Said to a client who is haggling over pennies, or a tick, i.e., the smallest increment by which a security can change.

Don't get sore, buy some more: Said to get clients to keep trading even if their order is moving against them and they are losing money.

Dressin' British, thinkin' Yiddish: A nod to the tailored suits in London, and the founders of the firm.

Elephant trade: A trade that brings in more than $1 million to the firm in one hit.

E-mini: The most liquid and most popular futures contract in the world, trading hundreds of billions of dollars per day. It is the first instrument of choice for hedge funds because of its supreme liquidity and the fact that it trades electronically for almost twenty-four hours a day.

ETF (exchange-traded fund): An investment fund that acts like a stock and is designed to mimic the performance of indexes (e.g., the S&P 500) or a commodity, such as gold, which would otherwise be difficult for a retail investor to get exposure to.

Exchange-traded: Listed on an exchange with a public market that is transparent. Also see: OTC (OVER THE COUNTER).

Exotic: A type of dancer. Also: a type of derivative that is far more complex than a plain-vanilla derivative and requires sophisticated models to value it accurately. A very profitable, high-margin product for Wall Street. Also see: STRUCTURED PRODUCT, OPAQUE.

Fast market: Originally a stock exchange term to indicate extreme volatility, but now an excuse used by busy traders with too many balls in the air to help someone: "I'm in a fast market here. Back the fuck off." Also see: SHIT SHOW.

Fast money: Typically, hedge funds that trade a lot and move in and out of positions very frequently.

Fat-finger: To make a trading error by hitting the wrong button or too many buttons because of clumsy fingers. If you add three extra zeros to the size of your order, for example, it can have a huge multibillion-dollar adverse impact on the market.

Fill or kill: A trade order instruction a client gives a broker that means "execute it immediately and completely, or not at all" (i.e., cancel it).

Futures contract: A derivatives contract between buyer and seller where price and quantity are agreed upon today, but delivery and payment occur in the future. The term originated with farmers who were trying to hedge their crops against droughts, rains, and uncertainty of demand.

G: Wall Street slang for $1,000. Usage: "Randy's bull market trip to the Bahamas set him back eight Gs."

GC (gross credit): The term used for how much revenue each salesperson is bringing into the firm from each client. Also see: ATTRIBUTION.

Handle: A term to describe the general level where a security is trading. If Google were trading at $634, you would say it was trading with a 6 handle. Or, applied to civilian life, "Jim put on so much weight, he is now trading with a 3 handle" (i.e., more than 300 pounds).

Hedge fund: An investment fund that can undertake a wide range of strategies, including using leverage and derivatives, both going long (buying) and getting short (selling, without actually owning the asset). Because hedge funds are not highly regulated, they are only open to very large investors, such as pension funds, university endowments, and high-net-worth individuals.

High-net-worth individuals: A polite term for people who are mega-rich or loaded.

Hit a bid: To sell something at the price the market maker is willing to pay for it (i.e., the bid price).

Hit the tape: Complete the trade; or the announcement of some news. It originates from the ticker tape that was used to transmit stock price information from 1870. Wall Streeters use this term all the time: "My new kid hit the tape" (i.e., we had a new baby). "Ben and Kelly are dating? When did that hit the tape?"

Hoot: A little intercom on everyone's desk that is used to make announcements to the whole trading floor.

Hundo, hunge: Wall Street slang for $100. Usage: "My Hermès tie cost me two hundo." "Dinner at Per Se? Eight hundo, minimum."

I see: Corporate-speak for "Go fuck yourself," as in: "Um, Peter, we're going to need you to go ahead and come in to the office on Saturday." "I see."

Illiquid: Very difficult to trade because of lack of buyers and sellers. Trading in and out of illiquid securities can have an outsize impact on the market.

Investment banking business: The private side of the investment bank that helps corporations, governments, and individuals raise capital by underwriting the issuance of securities; and also gives companies advice on merging with or acquiring other companies. Also see: IPO

IPO (initial public offering): A stock market launch where shares of stock in a company are sold to the general public for the first time, on a securities exchange. Through this process, a private company transforms into a public company.

Leverage: A tool for multiplying one's gains or losses by either borrowing money or trading derivatives. Leading into the financial crisis, the banks were leveraged thirty to one—i.e., they were borrowing and betting thirty dollars for every one dollar they actually had.

Levered money: A term for hedge funds, who often use leverage to multiply their possible returns.

Lift an offer: To buy something for the price at which the market maker is willing to sell it (i.e., the offer price).

Liquid: Very easy to trade, with limited impact (lots of buyers and sellers available in the marketplace).

Make a market: To show a client a principal risk price—both a buy and a sell price—on a security it is looking to trade. The firm risks its own capital but stands to make a spread or commission on the trade. Also see: BID-OFFER SPREAD, PRINCIPAL.

Managing director: Second most senior rank; usually, but not always, a team leader who makes more than $1 million a year.

Mark to market: An accounting term generally interpreted to mean to value your positions accurately, or "square up," at the end of each trading day instead of waiting until the end of the month.

Market color: Commentary offered to clients on the themes being seen in the marketplace; advice given to clients on how to implement these themes by trading securities.

Muppet: A furry, cute puppet. Also: British slang for "idiot."

Mutual fund: A regulated and professionally managed collective investment scheme that pools money from many investors, including the general public, to purchase securities such as stocks and bonds.

Noted: Corporate-speak for "Blow me," as in: "Oh, hey, Peter, we're going to need you to go ahead and be more diligent submitting those TPS reports." "Noted."

Notional value: The total value of a leveraged position's assets. Commonly used in the options, futures, and derivatives markets because a very small amount of invested money can control a large position (and have a large consequence for the trader).

On the hop: Wall Street term for "immediately," as in: "I need you to pick up that client on the hop. He has a trade to execute."

On the wire: Wall Street terminology for "immediately over the phone" or in real time. When a client asks for a price, sometimes the salesperson has to consult with his trader and then call the client back. Really demanding clients stay on the phone to receive their price and then make a decision "on the wire."

Opaque: Not transparent; sometimes hard to understand or to value correctly. Typically used in reference to complicated derivative products. Also see: EXOTIC, OTC (OVER THE COUNTER), STRUCTURED PRODUCT.

Open outcry: The old-school method of trading on exchanges such as the Chicago Mercantile Exchange, where people stand in a pit and shout orders back and forth and use hand signals to communicate amid the chaos. In the past decade, most securities have transitioned from open outcry to electronically traded. Also see: E-MINI.

Option: A type of derivative that gives the purchaser the right to buy or sell an underlying security at a stipulated price in the future. Also see: CALL OPTION, PUT OPTION.

OTC (over the counter): An off-exchange derivatives trade negotiated directly between buyer and seller that is not transparent to the outside world. The bank will typically make part of the bid-offer spread as a fee for the trade. Also see: EXOTIC, STRUCTURED PRODUCT.

Partner: The most senior rank at the firm; this person typically makes in the millions of dollars per year.

PATC (per annum total compensation): An employee's total pay for the year, including salary and bonus.

Pension fund: A fund designed to provide retirement income. Both private and public pension funds exist. They are the largest category of investor in the world, representing trillions of dollars in assets.

Pit: The place on the exchange where all the traders stand and yell back and forth at one another, using hand signals to indicate buy versus sell, and quantity. Also see: OPEN OUTCRY.

Plain-vanilla: Your favorite flavor of ice cream. Also: describes straightforward derivatives investments, such as put or call options or futures; usually very transparent and listed on an exchange. The opposite of: EXOTIC, STRUCTURED PRODUCT. Also see: CALL OPTION, PUT OPTION, FUTURES CONTRACT.

Portfolio manager: The person within an asset management firm who has the final say, or "ultimate trigger pulling ability," on which securities to invest in. A PM employs researchers to help inform his or her decisions.

Pre-IPO partner: A Goldman Sachs partner from before the firm went public in 1999. Could be worth in the tens or hundreds of millions of dollars. One certainty: almost always has a tan—even in the winter.

Principal: The person or entity who takes the other side of a client's trade—i.e., commits the firm's own capital to facilitate the trade. Also see: AGENT.

Proprietary trading: Engaging, as an investment bank, in trading securities for one's own account with one's own money to make a profit much like a hedge fund. This is opposed to facilitating trading for one's customers. The Volcker Rule in the Dodd-Frank Act seeks to outlaw proprietary trading because of the role it played in the lead-up to the financial crisis in 2008 and because of the inherent conflict of interest with client trading.

Put option: A type of derivative that gives the purchaser the right to sell an underlying security at a stipulated price in the future.

Quant: Within the sales and trading business, the person who does a lot of the mathematical heavy lifting: pricing derivatives, analyzing risk for the traders, building complex structured products for the sales force to pitch to clients. Many quants have PhDs in areas such as physics, mathematics, and electrical engineering, and leave their field of study for the allure and higher salaries of Wall Street. Some quants go out on their own, build their own models, and start hedge funds.

Real money: Institutions such as mutual funds and pension funds, which have longer-term investment horizons than hedge funds and use little or no leverage (i.e., only real money).

Research analyst: The person who works within the research division of an investment bank and whose primary role is to research a number of stocks in a particular sector using fundamental analysis, then write research reports designed to tell clients whether the recommendation is buy, sell, or hold.

Rip someone's face off: To rip off someone (a client) without his knowing it. Corollary: The art of the client ripping you off without your knowing it.

Run over: Screwed on the outcome of a trade. Similar to rip someone's face off or blown up, but far less egregious. Typically when you get "run over," you live to fight another day. Traders at investment banks complain that a client has "run them over" when that client splits its order up among multiple banks: a term called "spraying the Street."

Sales and trading business: Within an investment bank, the business that focuses on buying and selling equity, bond, currency, commodity, and derivatives securities on behalf of clients such as hedge funds, mutual funds, pension funds, insurance companies, and sovereign wealth funds. The bank will serve as both an agent and a principal, ready to commit its own capital to facilitate client trades when necessary. The three roles in the sales and trading business are sales trader, trader, and quant. Also see: MAKE A MARKET.

Salesperson: Often used synonymously with sales trader.

Sales trader: Within the sales and trading business, the job of the sales trader (often used interchangeably with salesperson) is to speak to the client about the market, give it ideas, and try to win its business. The sales trader then works with the trader to execute the client's order.

Series 7: The six-hour mind-numbing exam that every new college graduate has to pass before he or she can legally talk to clients and execute trades.

Shit show: Wall Street slang for a complete fucking nightmare; chaos. Usage: "The market's tanking, every client phone line is ringing, there are trade tickets all over the place. This is a shit show."

Short squeeze: What occurs when a lot of people are short a security and suddenly everyone starts buying. A short squeeze can cause a lot of pain and trading losses.

Smart money: Slang for hedge funds or other savvy investors.

Sovereign wealth fund: A government-owned investment fund that invests in stocks, bonds, commodities, real estate, private equity, and hedge funds.

Stick: Wall Street slang for $1 million. Usage: "To everyone's surprise, Billy got paid three sticks last year."

Strat: See: QUANT.

Structured product: A prepackaged investment strategy offered by a bank to its clients—usually embedded with derivatives such as options, futures, and swaps—designed to achieve a specific investment thesis that cannot be easily replicated with plain-vanilla products. When your bank calls you with a structured product, the following thought should enter your head: "Run for the exits. Now."

Swap: A type of OTC derivative in which counterparties exchange cash flows of one party's financial instrument for those of the other party's financial instrument; a swap can be made on any asset class. Also see: CDS (CREDIT-DEFAULT SWAP).

Take a view: To express an opinion on the markets by executing a trade that will profit if you are right.

Talking your book: Wall Street slang for spinning everything you say publicly to help your own trading positions. If you were long gold futures, and you went on TV and said gold was due for a big rally, you would be "talking your book."

Tick: A small arachnid that sucks your blood while you sleep at night. Also: on Wall Street, a tick is the smallest possible increment by which a security can change.

Trader: Within the sales and trading business, the person who makes markets and executes trades to facilitate the client's business. The trader works closely with the sales trader, who speaks directly to the client.

Vice president/executive director: A position typically achieved after seven or eight years at the firm or in the industry; it is a midlevel title.

Working your order: In motion, executing a client's trade. Often used as slang on trading floors to signify that you are looking out for someone, as in "Don't worry, dude. I'm working your order. You will be happy with your bonus."

Yard: Wall Street slang for $1 billion. Usage: "Right after the blackout, the portfolio manager was so panicked that he sold 2 yards (i.e., $2 billion worth) of equity market exposure."

You're done/you're filled: Your trade has been executed; your price will follow shortly.

Index

Welch, Jack, 166, 190–91
Wendy's, 49
Whitehead, John, 4, 61, 111–12,
    136
Who's the Boss (TV show), 7
"Why I Am Leaving Goldman
    Sachs" (op-ed), 238–43,
    245–46, 251–52
Wicked Clients, 161
Willingham, Tyrone, 56

Wise Clients, 160–61, 165
Wolf, Robert, 158
"working your orders," 265

yards, 265
"you're done/you're filled," 265

Zahn, Paula, 42
Zulu language, 64

About the Author

GREG SMITH resigned in the spring of 2012 as the head of Goldman Sachs's U.S. Equity Derivatives business in Europe, the Middle East, and Africa. Born and raised in Johannesburg, South Africa, Smith graduated from Stanford University before going to work for the firm full time in 2001. He spent his first ten years in the New York headquarters before moving to London in 2011. He currently lives in New York City.